BERNARD SHAW
& the Art of Destroying Ideals

*The University
of Wisconsin
Press
Madison
Milwaukee and
London 1969*

BERNARD SHAW
& the Art of Destroying Ideals

The Early Plays

Charles A. Carpenter

Published by
The University of Wisconsin Press
Box 1379, Madison, Wisconsin 53701
The University of Wisconsin Press, Ltd.
27–29 Whitfield Street, London, W. 1
Copyright © 1969 by the Regents of
The University of Wisconsin
All rights reserved
Printed in the United States of America by
NAPCO, Inc., Milwaukee, Wisconsin
Standard Book Number 299–05300–8
Library of Congress Catalog Card Number 69–17323

To my own maternal genius, Randi

Preface

Throughout this study I have abbreviated the titles of four works which are cited frequently:

CL, I   Shaw's *Collected Letters, 1874–1897*, ed. Dan H. Laurence (New York, 1965).

HMC   Archibald Henderson's last authorized biography, *George Bernard Shaw: Man of the Century* (New York, 1956).

MCE   Shaw's *Major Critical Essays* (London, 1932), the standard Constable edition of *The Quintessence of Ibsenism*, *The Sanity of Art*, and *The Perfect Wagnerite*.

OTN   Shaw's *Our Theatres in the Nineties*, 3 vols. (London, 1932), the standard Constable edition of the 1895–98 *Saturday Review* drama critiques.

To avoid occasionally misleading complications arising from Shaw's revisions of the *Plays Pleasant and Unpleasant* and *Three Plays for Puritans* for the standard Constable editions of 1931, I have quoted from the editions which were standard in 1900. Moreover, I have used the American printings, which eliminate the slight vagaries in spelling that Shaw adopted to improve the appearance of the printed page (the contractions without apostrophes, for example). These are the printings of Herbert S. Stone & Co., Chicago and New York, 1898 and 1900. I have, however, checked quoted passages against the London editions of the same years as well as against the Constable editions of 1931. When quoting, I have italicized Shaw's stage directions only when they must be distinguished from accompanying dialogue.

In its embryonic stages, this study profited greatly from the sophisticated counsel of Anthony Caputi of Cornell University. For further valuable criticisms, I am indebted to Robert M. Adams, University of California at Los Angeles; Dan H. Laurence, New York University; John Gaywood Linn, Queen's College of the City University of New York; Ronald E. Martin, University of Delaware; Frederick P. W. McDowell, University of Iowa; Martin Meisel, Columbia University; Arthur Mizener, Cornell University; and Charles H. Shattuck, University of Illinois.

My earliest labors on this book were supported by a generous grant from the Samuel S. Fels Fund, and one stage of revision was facilitated by a University of Delaware Summer Faculty Fellowship. I am grateful to both organizations.

I wish to thank the following publishers for permission to reprint material in the text:

The President and Fellows of Harvard College and the Harvard College Library, for a quotation from a letter in Henry James, *Complete Plays*, ed. Leon Edel.

The University of Minnesota Press, for a quotation from Bertolt Brecht, *The Good Woman of Setzuan*, originally published in *Parables for the Theatre: Two Plays by Bertolt Brecht*, ed. Eric Bentley. © Copyright 1947, 1948 by Eric Bentley.

George Braziller, Inc., for a quotation from *The Green*

Crow by Sean O'Casey; reprinted with the permission of the publisher. Copyright © 1956 by Sean O'Casey.

Oxford University Press, for a quotation from C. S. Lewis, *English Literature in the Sixteenth Century*.

Simon & Schuster, Inc., for a quotation from Bertrand Russell, "George Bernard Shaw," *Virginia Quarterly Review*, XXVII (1951), 1–7.

Binghamton, New York   CHARLES A. CARPENTER
February 1969

Contents

BERNARD SHAW
& the Art of Destroying Ideals

Chapter 1

Artistic Means to
Ethical Ends

The extravagant vigor, efficiency, and purposefulness that stamped Bernard Shaw throughout his inordinately long and prolific career—qualities that fix him securely in the very tradition he scorned—compelled him during the twenty-five years he spent in Victorian England to become, by general repute, "the astonishingly ubiquitous G.B.S." He proclaimed in 1889: "My business is to incarnate the Zeitgeist" (*CL*, I, 222); and no other earnest Victorian moved so resolutely and conspicuously like the Zeitgeist itself.

From the start, Shaw's progress upward and outward was inexorable. He came to London in 1876, just short of twenty, fleeing a mind-deadening job as cashier in a Dublin land agency, but also vaguely reaching out for the kind of total self-fulfillment that would leave him "thoroughly used up" before he was finally "tossed on the scrap heap." By 1883 he had already composed five long novels, contributed to several study groups and debating societies, and infiltrated most of the avant-garde intellectual and social circles in the London area. The later eighties brought an even greater burgeoning of activities. He discovered the Fabian Society in 1884 and began his frenetic career as socialist committeeman and orator. Later that year, William Archer helped him get established as a reviewer, and he was soon greatly in demand as a critic of all the arts. In 1885 he relinquished his hallowed virginity and from then on dedicated countless hours to philandering with every variety of New Woman. Meanwhile, he wrote the equivalent of a book on the theories of Karl Marx, kept up a massive correspondence (at the rate of five or six letters per day), and toyed in his notebooks with dramatic dialogues. From 1890 to 1897 Shaw all but reached his goal of being "used up." His love affairs—and near escapes from others—tediously multiplied. The Fabians, with Shaw serving as their chief propagandist, extended their sophisticated tactic of permeation to national politics, and Shaw himself became borough councillor for the St. Pancras vestry. Moreover, week after week he met deadlines for long, rigorous criticisms of music and drama, and on the side wrote *The Quintessence of Ibsenism*, *The Sanity of Art*, the seven *Plays Pleasant and Unpleasant*, and *The Devil's Disciple*. It was not until 1898 that Shaw more or less settled down, and then only under the pressure of a serious leg infection. Charlotte Payne-Townshend snagged him in his defenseless condition and took over much of his busywork; he quit his post as dramatic critic for the *Saturday Review*; and for a year after his marriage he limited himself to one book, *The Perfect Wagnerite*, and two plays, *Caesar and Cleopatra* and *Captain Brassbound's Conversion*. With the end of the century, his era of relentless ubiquity came to a close.

The ten substantial plays that Shaw found time to write during this era constitute a distinct period in his evolution as a dramatic artist. Shortly after finishing *Captain Brassbound's Conversion*, he told the actress Ellen Terry: "And now no more plays—at least no more practicable ones. None at all, indeed, for some time to come: it is time to do something more in Shaw-philosophy, in politics and sociology. Your author, dear Ellen, must be more than a common dramatist."[2] This proved prophetic. Between 1899 and 1903 Shaw completed only the brief Elizabethan parody, *The Admirable Bashville*, which he wrote in a single week. Then, putting "all his intellectual goods in the shop window," he published the immense philosophical, political, and sociological drama *Man and Superman*—obviously an uncommon and impracticable play for the watery theatre of Pinero, Jones, and their followers. In itself, the purely actionless and argumentative dream sequence of the play represents a turning point in Shaw's artistic progress. He once remarked (referring as usual to himself): "all the great artists who have lived long enough have had a juvenile phase, a middle phase, and a Third Manner."[3] He singled out *Man and Superman* as the first play of his middle phase.[4]

Still, a turning point, however unmistakable, does not guarantee that a distinct, unified period has preceded it. More crucial is the fact that Shaw's early plays have in common certain characteristics and tendencies that the later plays do not. Many critics acknowledge this singularity, while differing in the ways they define it. Shaw called his nineteenth-century plays "juvenile" works; most textbook commentaries prefer the term "Ibsenite." They note undeniable similarities between these plays and Ibsen's naturalistic dramas, the kind Shaw had briskly defended against middle-brow excoriation in *The Quintessence of Ibsenism*. On the other hand, an eminently knowledgeable student of Victorian drama, Martin Meisel, finds the theatrical effects, techniques, and conventions of the early plays—if not their subject matter and ideas—much less closely linked to the vilified mode of Ibsen than to a few widely popular dramatic genres of the eighties and nineties. These genres can be traced back to the French "well-made-play" factories of Scribe, Sardou, and Augier. A number of drama historians, among them Allardyce Nicoll and Eric

Bentley, have argued that Shaw actually owes a great debt to the school of "Sardoodledom," despite his blatant loathing for it.[5]

All of these views, however, put too much stress on the relatively peripheral matter of sources and influences. Fortunately, Meisel also looks at Shaw's plays as artistic achievements possessing their own peculiar methods and effects. Detecting the same three stages that Shaw pointed out, he concludes that the first stage features the more emotional types of drama, the second increasingly discursive types, and the third "symbolic-analogic" types (*Shaw and the Nineteenth-Century Theater*, p. 443). These classifications seem valid. Among the early plays are the romantic *Arms and the Man*, the sentimental *Candida*, the celebrative *Caesar and Cleopatra*, the farcical *Philanderer* and *You Never Can Tell*, and the melodramatic *Mrs. Warren's Profession*, *Devil's Disciple*, and *Captain Brassbound's Conversion*. The middle period includes a "discussion," a "disquisitory play," a "debate," and a "sermon"; and the late period embraces all the "political extravaganzas," the "farfetched fables," and the "true histories that never happened." These stages reflect the definite progression in Shaw's career from stringently realistic problem plays at the very beginning to freely conceived, sometimes fantastic vehicles for ideas at the end.[6]

Though no doubt valid and useful to the literary critic, such formal distinctions nevertheless exude a certain irrelevance. If Meisel's subject were almost any other notable artist, his strictly aesthetic criteria would seem appropriate enough. But his subject is the intense rhetorician and journalistic "battering ram," Bernard Shaw. Everyone conversant with Shaw recognizes that he was first of all—if not finally—a vitalist and reformer. His "own devouring malady," as he said, was "a passion of pure political *Weltverbesserungswahn* (worldbettermentcraze)."[7] Meisel

thus suggests a sounder approach to Shaw when he says
that the development of his drama might be measured by
his progress from plays that attack the orthodoxies of the
past to plays that give shape to the orthodoxies of the future
(p. 446). For Shaw's bent was dominantly ethical.[8]

From this ethical standpoint, his early drama is marked
by its consistent adherence to the aim of destroying ideals.
A few months before the notion of becoming a playwright
struck him, Shaw said that the time was ripe "for the emergence of an extremely unpleasant and unpalatable author,
one who would tackle the large number of shams, repres-
sions, sentimentalities, insincerities and ideals of which the
English were so proud."[9] He took the first step toward his
own belated emergence by composing part of *Widowers'
Houses* in the winter of 1884.[10] On the brink of his public
debut as a playwright six years later, Shaw announced to
an ally: "I have opened fire from the depths of my inner-
most soul against [the] confounded ideals of Truth, Duty,
Self-Sacrifice, Virtue, Reason and so on" (*CL*, I, 254). By
1898, he had completed seven plays, all of which had proved
unpleasant and unpalatable to the average Englishman. He
accounted for their reception by explaining that they embody a "general onslaught on idealism" (Pref., *Pleasant
Plays*, p. xviii).

Shaw never wholly abandoned this attack, though it
became secondary to him in the twentieth century. Some
time after 1900, he claimed that a dramatist who "found a
flaw in the conventional morality and corrected it . . .
[was] fulfilling a duty of the most indescribable sacred-
ness."[11] As late as 1944, he insisted that the most important
works of art are those "which, as instruments of evolution,
dare to criticize public opinion and existing institutions."[12]
All of Shaw's plays—more than fifty, composed over a
stretch of sixty-five years—involve to some perceptible
degree an assault on social, moral, and philosophic "senti-

mentalities." Such hallmarks as characters who voice ideal points of view, situations that show ideals punctured by facts, and arguments that reduce ideals to absurdity occur in *The Doctor's Dilemma* (1906) and *The Millionairess* (1935) as well as in the early plays. But they occur less frequently and less centrally; Shaw's emphasis lies elsewhere. In his middle period he is largely preoccupied with defining urgent problems and testing a wide range of proposed solutions; in his late period, with depicting his own "petty tentatives" for a better world. None of his major twentieth-century plays derives its main thrust, its *dynamis*, from his ideal-destroying aim; the aim survives, but only in subordinate or indirect form. *Major Barbara* (1905), for example, includes an "incarnation of morality," Lady Britomart, and her moral offspring Stephen, who can do nothing except judge the difference between right and wrong. But the play is organized to tangle with a sinewy ethical problem: roughly, "What price salvation?" The guide to conduct that Lady Britomart and her son offer—always do what every good Englishman recognizes as the "right" thing—hardly gets serious attention, even from its two advocates. Other plays sometimes secure the disturbing effects of an assault on ideals without encouraging them directly. In *Getting Married* (1908), for example, the radical revisions of English marital law which are seriously pondered by a bishop, a beadle, and a visionary (among others) may strike a conventional person as impossibly shocking or ludicrous alternatives to the ideals he was weaned on. Such incidental effects, however, are much less significant than the varieties of "torment" that Shaw deliberately evokes through the concerted iconoclastic strategies of his early plays. These strategies are best viewed within the context of his total rationale for creating a unique, sophisticated, and viable art of destroying ideals.

SHAW'S ETHICAL AIMS

Shaw's 1891 volume, *The Quintessence of Ibsenism*, contains the core of his ethical ideas. Despite its subject (and its value as an analysis of Ibsen), the book is still an uncamouflaged piece of Shavian propaganda. In a preface, Shaw speaks of it as "the living word of a man delivering a message to his own time" (*MCE*, p. 5). In the text, he even scolds Ibsen for deviating from the straight Shaw line.[13] Not that he ignored the actual import of Ibsen's plays; rather, he looked for—and found—the "ism" that tallied with his own. By using this tactic, Shaw was following one of his basic convictions. In 1905 his newly authorized biographer, Archibald Henderson, told him that he was determined to write a "just" as well as accurate book. Shaw replied:

> Be as accurate as you can; but as to being just, who are you that you should be just? That is mere American childishness. Write boldly according to your bent: say what you WANT to say and not what you think you ought to say or what is right or just or any such arid nonsense. You are not God Almighty; and nobody will expect justice from you or any other superhuman attribute. This affected, manufactured, artificial conscience of morality and justice and so on is of no use for the making of works of art: for that you must have the real conscience that gives a man courage to fulfil his will by saying what he likes. (*HMC*, p. xxv)

The thesis of *The Quintessence of Ibsenism*, and the main root of Shaw's ethical convictions, is that man must follow "not the abstract law but the living will" (*MCE*, p. 122). He must cast off the "artificial conscience" imposed upon him by his misguided belief in the validity of moral codes and social institutions, and must replace it with a "real conscience" that springs from his own aspirations. Both the negative and positive sides of this dictum are fundamental elements in Shaw's thought from *My Dear Dorothea* (1878) to *Everybody's Political What's What?* (1944).[14] Let us first consider the negative, or destructive, side.

Shaw's overriding purpose in life was to promote "world-betterment": the gradual movement of society and man to higher and higher forms of organization. In the *Quintessence*, he argues that the forces striving for evolution are continually obstructed by "abstract law," variously referred to as "institutions," "ideals of goodness," or simply "duty." He explains how the conflict inevitably occurs within society: "social progress takes effect through the replacement of old institutions by new ones; and since every institution involves the recognition of the duty of conforming to it, progress must involve the repudiation of an established duty at every step" (*MCE*, p. 17). But in the *Quintessence* as a whole Shaw calls for much more than the destruction of outmoded institutions and codes. He finally wants to eliminate the very basis of man's tendency to cherish ideals: the assumption, normally unquestioned, that people ought to direct their lives by some set of ethical absolutes. In his opinion, "abstract law" in the broadest sense is the major deterrent to evolution. Shaw also rejects the common expectation that ideal formulas for the arrangement of society and the conduct of its members will be developed some day. He anticipates that at any conceivable level of advancement (except perhaps within the "vortex of pure thought" envisioned at the end of *Back to Methuselah*), men will still have grounds for dissatisfaction and will recognize that further improvement of their lot is possible. To Shaw the only formula is that there is no formula (p. 125); there is no such thing as a real ideal.

The positive, constructive side of his ethical convictions is grounded in "the living will." He defines the will not mainly as a restraining faculty (our "will power"), but rather as man's passionate desire to do what he wants to do. As such, it becomes the immediate stimulant of all forms of evolution. To Shaw, as to Schopenhauer, the human will reflects a cosmic *Wille zu Leben*, a force as real as gravity, even though it can be discerned through its effects alone.[15] Shaw's universal will to live, however, is also a will to propagate selectively (Doña Ana's Life Force) and to improve the conditions of life (Don Juan's).[16] According to this meliorist view, human volition is the specific agent of a cosmic drive for world-betterment. When neither inhibited nor misled by ideals, Shaw says, the will acts as "our old friend the soul or spirit of man," hopefully doing the work of a power analogous to the Holy Spirit (*MCE*, p. 20 n.). But it also operates collectively, within an ever-growing "social organism" (p. 25). There it serves as the final measure of the validity of institutions, since none will be workable in the long run which are not constructed to fulfil man's will (p. 20). In sum, the gradual fulfillment of individual wills actually constitutes the growth of the social organism, and thus makes possible the physical, mental, and spiritual evolution of man himself.

But man cannot fulfil his will simply by following its promptings blindly. As Shaw's spokesman, Don Juan, points out, it needs a brain to steer it to its goal. Shaw is convinced that the mind has the capacity to direct the will at once successfully and economically. In the *Quintessence* he remarks: "Only the other day our highest boast was that we were reasonable human beings. Today we laugh at that conceit, and see ourselves as wilful creatures. [But] ability to reason accurately is as desirable as ever; for by accurate reasoning only can we calculate our actions so as to do what we intend to do: that is, to fulfil our will" (*MCE*, p. 22). Even in Shaw's basically irrationalist conception, the intellect has an indispensable evolutionary function and must therefore be developed as fully as possible. The will to

live better demands a change in life as it is, or gives birth
to the image of a better life; the intellect ponders the why
and the wherefore. As Shaw once explained it, reason does
not determine the destination, but it searches for the short-
est way. [17] The highly intellectual "philosophic man," according to Don Juan, is a man who "seeks in contemplation
to discover the inner will of the world, in invention to discover the means of fulfilling that will, and in action to do
that will by the so-discovered means."

To carry on its work effectively, the mind must first of
all free itself from illusory ideals. Many times in the *Quintessence,* Shaw declares that man must repudiate duty,
which restricts the mind and thereby obstructs the fulfillment of the will (*MCE,* p. 40); he must regard ideals as
"only swaddling clothes which man has outgrown, and
which insufferably impede his movements" (p. 31). At
best, he should attain a state of "vigilant openmindedness"
(p. 123). But the intellect requires more than mere freedom
from the pressures of abstract law. It also requires materials
with which to formulate the higher modes of life that the
will hints at and campaigns for. These materials are ideas.
To Shaw, ideas are the stepping-stones of progress, since
by means of them man visualizes the paths that his will
may follow. Not only are they the materials that the mind
creates, then deliberately works with as the hand works
with tools; they also have lives of their own, independent
of man, and thus "wills" of their own. As a result, ideas
have peculiar powers of intruding themselves into the mind
and implanting themselves there, with or without man's
conscious consent.[18] Shaw defends his whole approach to
Ibsen's plays by insisting that "the existence of a discover-
able and perfectly definite thesis in a poet's work by no
means depends on the completeness of his own intellectual
consciousness of it" (p. 12). He even explains away the
heretic atmosphere of Darwinian fatalism in the plays by

maintaining that Ibsen's "prophetic belief in the spontaneous growth of the will" made him a Shavian meliorist despite his nod to the theory of natural selection (p. 53). Shaw's view of ideas as both usable materials and wilful entities is remarkably appropriate to his evolutionary doctrine.

At the risk of oversimplifying, then, we can say that this doctrine consists of three basic elements. The human will, man's link with a cosmic force, channels the evolutionary impulse; the intellect, a distinctively human faculty, looks for the most efficient way to fulfil the will; and ideas, man-made articles which yet exist apart from man, are the alternative paths that the intellect considers in its search. These elements are the fundamental ingredients of Shaw's ethical aims, the directives for human conduct which he believes will enable himself and others to contribute markedly to world-betterment. Each element has its corresponding aim. First, Shaw attempts to eliminate the main obstruction that the will encounters, man's sense of duty to established moral and social codes. Second, he tries to strengthen and refine the human brain so that it will become as efficient an instrument of the will as possible. And third, he seeks to supply men's minds with ideas which might prove useful in the process of evolution. In short, he consistently aims to destroy ideals, to cultivate the intellect, and to implant ideas.

SHAVIAN DRAMATIC METHOD

The first of these aims, the ground-clearing phase of Shaw's evolutionary program, was quite naturally the dominant one during the early period of his playwriting career. A well-known essay he added to the 1913 edition of *The Quintessence of Ibsenism*, "The Technical Novelty in Ibsen's Plays," describes his own dramatic methods at some length.[19] Without assuming critical infallibility on his part (though we are surely safe in applying his discussion of "the theatre since Ibsen" to early Shavian drama), we will profit from knowing what Shaw himself said about the "terrible art" of destroying ideals. Seen against a background of conventional turn-of-the-century opinion, the essay actually provides an illuminating analysis of the purposes, strategies, and structural principles of his first ten plays.

The great majority of the playgoing public that Shaw had in mind when he issued the expanded *Quintessence* would have assumed that a play should be designed primarily to give the audience pleasure. Among the leading dramatic critics in London between 1890 and 1915, for instance, all but Shaw were solidly in accord on this point.[20] More crucial to this view than we can now scarcely conceive was the attendant maxim that drama should uphold, defend, and at best enhance society's revered ideals. Above all, they were not to be subjected to indignities—much less genuinely shaken.[21] What Shaw regarded as silly and often treacherous delusions about Womanliness and Manliness, Marriage and the Family, Goodness in morals, Propriety in business, Justice in the state, and Heroism in war were generally considered the very foundation-stones of society, the removal of which would cause anarchy. Even members of truly avant-garde socialist and theatrical circles, men who certainly shared some of Shaw's doubts about the validity of such absolutes, drew the line at a serious attack on them.[22]

Shaw's 1913 essay takes direct issue with this widespread opposition. "In the theatre of Ibsen," he declares, "we are not flattered spectators killing an idle hour with an ingenious and amusing entertainment: we are 'guilty creatures sitting at a play.' " The journeyman playwright's methods of pleasing the audience are "no more applicable than at a murder trial." Though Ibsen and his followers necessarily make some use of the pleasureful techniques of "the orator, the preacher, the pleader, and the rhapsodist," their plays are engineered for "recrimination, disillusion, and penetration through ideals to the truth." To accomplish this, the evolutionary dramatist chooses subject matter that is realistic and immediately relevant, thus "making the spectators themselves the persons of the drama, and the incidents of their own lives its incidents" (*MCE*, p. 146). He manipulates this subject matter so that his plays are capable of causing "grievous mortification," of "hurting us cruelly" if we happen to harbor assailable ideals. In short, he practices a "terrible art of sharpshooting at the audience, trapping them, fencing with them, aiming always at the sorest spot in their consciences" (p. 145).[23]

This general strategy has two main varieties. One is to present idealists in conflict with each other and with anti-idealists. In the new plays, Shaw says, the drama arises not through "vulgar attachments, rapacities, generosities, resentments, ambitions, misunderstandings, oddities and so forth as to which no moral question is raised," but rather through "a conflict of unsettled ideals" (*MCE*, p. 139). In this conflict, it is the ideals themselves that fight for survival—ideals that exist in spectators' as well as characters' minds. Accordingly, as Shaw puts it elsewhere, the author's indignation and disapproval embodied in the play pass over the characters on the stage and hit the audience.[24] Shaw's *Pleasant Plays* feature this method. In *Candida*, for instance, the conflict of ideals takes place between Morell, a moral and religious idealist, and Eugene, a poetic and romantic one. Candida herself is both the focal point of the conflict and the chief ideal-destroying agent.

The second variety of sharpshooting strategy is closely related but differs in emphasis. "Never mislead an audience" was once a theatrical bylaw, Shaw states; "but the new school will trick the spectator into forming a meanly false judgment, and then convict him of it in the next act"

(*MCE*, p. 145). The spectator forms such a judgment if he holds certain preconceptions and automatically applies them to the case. These preconceptions are evoked in the play for the express purpose of shattering them: that is, for the sake of pressuring playgoers into realizing that their assumed ideals may be invalid, ridiculous, or even repugnant. Most often, the dramatist will trap the audience into mistaking a hero for a villain. In the post-Ibsen drama, Shaw says, "the conflict is not between clear right and wrong: the villain is as conscientious as the hero, if not more so: in fact, the question which makes the play interesting . . . is which is the villain and which the hero. Or, to put it another way, there are no villains and no heroes" (p. 139). A "villain" exists as such only in the minds of misguided spectators who have relied upon conventional standards to form their moral judgments, and these judgments are shown to be "meanly false." This method is predominant in the *Unpleasant Plays*, notably in *Mrs. Warren's Profession*. Shaw first compels all but the most advanced thinkers in the audience to blame Mrs. Warren for having become a prostitute, then "convicts" them of a judgment that turns out to be rooted in a typically British set of moral and economic ideals.

The purpose of early Shavian drama, then, has little to do with pleasing the audience. The total effect that Shaw usually intends is something closer to torment than pleasure, although it will depend upon the individual spectator's attitude toward the ideals under attack.[25] Whatever ideals the spectator believes in, consciously or not, may become Shaw's targets. As a "specialist in immoral and heretical plays" (his own boast[26]), he is finally out to get "abstract law" itself.

The basis for the structural organization of most of Shaw's first ten plays is thus didactic rather than mimetic. In this respect, also, his dramaturgy diverges sharply from canons of playmaking then standard, for Shaw was violating the long-ascendant ideal of drama as an "imitation of an action." The quasi-Aristotelian doctrine that the plot, or system of actions, in any play should be its "soul"—at once the determinant of its structure and the essential source of its effect—had almost universal support from critics and dramatists of the day. Among them were the many advocates of the Scribean well-made play, men who habitually and unthinkingly regarded the construction of a tight, logical plot as the playwright's first task.[27] But even the London critic Shaw respected most, A. B. Walkley, was a doctrinaire Aristotelian who maintained that Aristotle's definition of a play was "absolutely valid for all drama in all time," and proclaimed that Shaw, by ignoring it, "cheerfully let the quintessential drama go hang."[28]

Countering this opinion in "The Technical Novelty in Ibsen's Plays," Shaw explains his own brand of structural organization. He begins by comparing the well-made-play structure with the kind found in Ibsen's *A Doll's House* (and very conspicuously in *Candida*): "Formerly you had . . . an exposition in the first act, a situation in the second, and unravelling in the third. Now you have exposition, situation, and discussion; and the discussion is the test of the playwright" (*MCE*, p. 135). This extension of the old dramatic form, he continues, "conquered Europe and founded a new school of dramatic art." Since then, moreover, "the discussion has expanded far beyond the limits of the last ten minutes of an otherwise 'well made' play. . . . We now have plays, including some of my own, which begin with discussion and end with action, and others in which the discussion interpenetrates the action from beginning to end."[29] In such plays, the system of actions "consists of a case to be argued" (pp. 138–39). The structure of this drama, in other words, is not the mimetic one described in Aristotle's *Poetics*; it is the didactic one described (with no reference to drama) in his *Rhetoric*. Shaw

himself terms it "forensic" and notes that it "is new only on
the modern stage. It has been used by preachers and orators
ever since speech was invented" (p. 146).

All of Shaw's early plays are to some extent arguments
or demonstrations. The plot of each constitutes "a case to
be argued," always a case against ideals. Late in the period,
the ethical focus in his dramatic and nondramatic work
shifts slightly away from destroying ideals and toward
refining and toughening men's minds. The brain-teasing
element of discussion—more accurately, impassioned debate
over problematic issues—becomes very nearly central in
Caesar and Cleopatra (1898). That play, with its deliberate
warping of historical tradition, its oratorical hero, and its
frequent (one-sided) debates on the issue of justice, is the
most highly developed forensic drama of the period. All,
however, are partly geared to provoke intense thought, and
all concur with the Shavian dictum, extravagantly but aptly
worded in the *Quintessence*, that "an interesting play cannot in the nature of things mean anything but a play in
which problems of conduct and character of personal
importance to the audience are raised and suggestively
discussed" (*MCE*, p. 137).

By creating a forensic drama geared to assault highly
revered Victorian sentiments, Shaw was flouting not only
the moral and social Establishment but also the reigning
powers of English theatre. This fact posed a serious compli-
cation, one that confronted him in different ways throughout his early period. He could not contribute significantly
to his present ethical goal by writing plays that would
rarely reach the stage before the very ideals he was attacking had gone out of fashion. In short, he had to win a foothold in the theatre. To do so, he devised certain expedients
calculated to make his radically unconventional plays more
tolerable to conventional people. One that had the fringe
benefit of actually bolstering his "sharpshooting" strategies

was the tactic of adapting currently popular forms of drama to his own purposes.[30] All of his first ten plays are strategic remoldings of dramatic genres that were comfortably familiar to playgoers of the nineties: the problem play, romantic drama, domestic drama, farcical comedy, melodrama, and the history play. Martin Meisel's *Shaw and the Nineteenth-Century Theater* discusses the various interrelationships in detail, but does not stress the connection between this tactic and Shaw's ideal-destroying aim. The kinds of drama that were West-End favorites carried their own set of expectations with them, so that spectators would anticipate certain types of characters, certain lines of action, a certain atmosphere, and so forth. Inevitably, some of these expectations were accredited ideals: the greatest act of heroism is self-sacrifice; the family is a natural and sacred institution; capitalism is the best economic system. Shaw's targets were thus readily at hand when he used (and abused) a popular genre. *Arms and the Man*, for example, arouses the expectations of one type of romantic drama, military melodrama, then debunks its normally assumed illusions about the military hero. In Shaw's eyes, the discrepancy between the "stage world" of deluded spectators and the "real world" was, "in a sense, the subject of the play."[31] By making a virtue out of a necessity, Shaw may very well have increased the potency of his onslaught on idealism. As might be expected, however, he did not succeed in captivating many idealist theatre managers or drama critics.[32]

By now it may seem that Shaw was almost never positive or constructive until he had outgrown his "juvenile" phase in drama. He attacks people's beliefs; he manhandles dramatic forms. He is like John Tanner in *Man and Superman* boasting to Ann Whitefield that since the birth of moral passion in him he has become ten times more destructive than he was before: "The moral passion has taken my destructiveness in hand and directed it to moral ends. I have become a reformer, and, like all reformers, an iconoclast. I no longer break cucumber frames and burn gorse bushes: I shatter creeds and demolish idols." One may be tempted to reply, with Ann, "Destruction can only destroy."

But Tanner's retort is corrective: "Yes. That is why it is so useful. Construction cumbers the ground with institutions made by busybodies. Destruction clears it and gives us breathing space and liberty." Logically considered, the process of shattering creeds and demolishing idols is the necessary preliminary to the more constructive stages of Shaw's total evolutionary program. Furthermore, in the nineties Shaw believed that society would improve largely of its own accord if idealized institutions that obstructed it were removed. Thus he sought "breathing space and liberty" for the social organism.[33] This is not to say, however, that the early plays amount to little more than social, moral, and economic bulldozers. Every negative idea has a positive side, and Shaw was indirectly recommending something every time he was directly undercutting something else. His anticapitalistic plays—*Mrs. Warren's Profession,* for instance—are also pro-socialistic, though they breathe not a word about socialism. His antiromantic plays—*Arms and the Man, Candida,* and *You Never Can Tell*—subtly "affirm the worth of the real." And his antiheroic plays are almost more positive than negative: in *Caesar and Cleopatra* and *Captain Brassbound's Conversion,* especially, the strikingly Shavian images of male and female heroism are projected with great force.

The positive side of Shaw's artistry is just as evident as that of his ethical strategies. His early artistic achievement involves both the modernization of certain "classic" forms of drama and the creation of original forms. However interesting his first ten plays may be as antitypes of currently popular genres, they are still examples in their own right of other genres. *Arms and the Man* no longer arouses the expectations of military melodrama, its expired ancestor, and the fact that it ever did is at best a secondary matter. Enough spectators still cherish some of the romantic ideals it attacks to justify calling it a critical comedy, as I will call it, but its enduring effects put it clearly in the class of those romantic comedies which have evoked harmless laughter and uncomplicated sympathy since Shakespeare's time. Shaw's *Pleasant Plays*, while remaining undeniably modern in cast, all have strong traditional generic ties of this sort.[34] The case of his *Unpleasant Plays* and *Three Plays for Puritans* is quite different. Deeply imbued with Shaw's more specialized concerns, anticapitalistic and prohumanistic respectively, they reveal less important affinities with classic types of drama. Because of their thorough injections of Shavian doctrine, these plays embody innovations in form to the extent that both groups deserve recognition as new dramatic genres. For reasons to appear subsequently, I have labeled the first group "propaganda plays" and the second "humanizations of heroic types of drama."

Chapter 2

Bertolt Brecht's The Good Woman of Setzuan:
"SHEN TE. . . . *I'm not at all sure that I'm good.*
I'd like to be good of course, but how am I to pay my
rent? Well, I'll confess it to you: I sell myself in
order to live, and even so I can't get along. There are
many others who have to do the same. I'm ready to do
anything; but who isn't? I'd be happy to honor my
father and my mother and speak the truth. It would be nice
not to covet my neighbor's house. It would be pleasant
to attach myself to one man and be faithful to him. I too
should like not to exploit anyone, not to rob the helpless.
But how? . . . How can I be good when everything
is so expensive?
    THE SECOND GOD. *We can't do anything about that. We*
mustn't meddle with economics!"[1]

Propaganda Plays

Until the nineteenth century, Shaw wrote in 1895, great dramatists were never social reformers. Likely candidates such as Aristophanes, Jonson, and Molière knew all the burning issues of their times and reflected them in their plays; "but their theme finally was not this social question or that social question, this reform or that reform, but humanity as a whole." They avoided making social questions necessary to the conflict in their plays because, first of all, they realized that a drama with an essentially economic or legal problem for the motive cannot outlive the solution of that problem. But every dramatist, past or present, realizes that. What made the difference in the past was that such problems were "too sectional, too topical, too temporal to move a man to the mighty effort which is needed to produce great poetry." Since the industrial revolution, however, the growth of population in the cities and the wide publicity given to the plight of the working class have brought about "a steady intensification in the hold of social questions on the larger poetic imagination." We therefore see the greatest modern dramatist, Ibsen, turning from dramatic poems on the grandest scale (e.g. *Emperor and Galilean*) "to comparatively prosaic topical plays on the most obviously transitory social questions, finding in their immense magnitude under modern conditions the stimulus which, a hundred years ago, or four thousand, he would only have received from the eternal strife of man with his own spirit." These problems will continue to attract the great dramatist, since "the highest genius . . . is always intensely utilitarian." Until governments abandon their reverence for outmoded institutions which prevent urgent social problems from being solved soon after they arise, the highest genius will persist in doing "public work" by treating the theatre as a "platform for propaganda."[2]

This statement of Shaw's is partly a rationale for his own activities before 1895. His "public work" in the theatre commenced with outright propaganda in dramatic form: three plays designed to force specific social problems into the light in order to encourage satisfactory solutions. His objective is the "utilitarian" one of improving society through the destruction of impeding economic and sociological ideals. In this group of plays, Shaw appropriately works within the outlines of the problem play form, usually designated at the time (not often justifiably) by the term "realistic play." *Widowers' Houses*, an "original didactic realistic play" first conceived in 1884 but not completed until 1892, has tenuous connections with the pseudorealistic well-made plays of Sardou and Augier. *The Philanderer*, a "topical comedy" written in 1893, capitalizes upon the craze for scandalous Ibsenite topics which had begun to appear in the problem plays of Jones and Pinero, but it also contains what Shaw calls "that fantastic atmosphere of moral irresponsibility" found in contemporary farcical comedy (*OTN*, II, 121). If *Mrs. Warren's Profession* (1893–94) had reached the stage in the nineties, it would have reminded playgoers of a series of plays, from *La Dame aux Camélias* by Dumas *fils* to Pinero's *The Second Mrs. Tanqueray*, in which the heroine is a fallen woman. Shaw's label for it—simply "a play"—hints that he thought of it as a *drame bourgeois*. Shaw refers to these three works as his "realistic plays," but he also describes them as "dramatic pictures of middle class society from the point of view of a Socialist who regards the basis of that society as thoroughly rotten economically and morally. . . . All three plays [are] criticisms of a special phase, the capitalist phase, of modern social organization" (*CL*, I, 632). That is, they are "propagandist dramas" (Pref., *Pleasant Plays*, p. vii). To convey this fact and to differentiate them from the typical problem play, I will call them "propaganda plays."

There is a danger in adopting this kind of term, however: Shaw is never a socialist more than he is a Shavian. Like Bertolt Brecht after him, he never quite prostituted himself to the party line. Adhering to his formula that there is no formula, Shaw regarded political, economic, moral, and philosophical "solutions" from the perspective of his own intuitive beliefs, assimilating whatever matched them and modifying whatever came close. In his terms, he followed his own will. One consequence was that his earliest plays emerged less from standard socialist doctrine than from his own still-developing conceptions of the will, ideals, and social evolution. The precise ethical purposes of these plays will remain obscure until they are set against this background. The same is true of their artistic strategies— highly specialized techniques that defy comprehension except when seen in the light of Shaw's current ideas about the methods of reforming society. In short, his propaganda plays must be viewed in relation to his peculiar brand of propaganda.

THE WILL, IDEALS, AND SOCIAL EVOLUTION

About five years before Shaw completed *Widowers' Houses* in 1892, his well-established belief in the primacy of will and his habitual contempt for ideals converged with a new awareness that the best way to promote the evolution of society was to eliminate existing economic and social codes. As a result, he not only redoubled his usual efforts to negate these codes; he also recognized that drama could be fashioned into a useful weapon in that broadly based campaign. He had become convinced that social evolution meant nothing like the Marxian revolt of the masses he had envisioned a few years before, but rather the gradual and spontaneous growth of the social organism through the fulfillment of man's collective will. The titan of this subtle evolutionary force was the ideal-destroyer, since ideals obstruct the will. Its methods were those of the London Fabian Society, in the late eighteen-eighties a tiny splinter group of intellectual socialists who, with Shaw as their main theorist, heretically favored constitutional measures and a gradualist approach to social reform. The chief method was that of "permeation." The ideal-destroyer infiltrated a domain where ideals were upheld and sought acceptance by working, contributing funds, or even entertaining. He then systematically chipped away at the vulnerable ideals, using arguments backed by facts and ridicule tempered with amiability. The Fabians permeated capitalist associations, political parties, and newspapers in this manner. Shaw himself, noting his special talents, decided to permeate another stronghold of capitalist ideals, the English theatre.

The specific ideas underlying this decision do not emerge in Shaw's available writings until 1888, but their conceptual roots exist in most of his earlier fiction and prose. They can be traced in his first long essay, *My Dear Dorothea: A Practical System of Moral Education for Females Embodied in a Letter to a Young Person of That Sex*.[3] Written when Shaw was twenty-one, this exercise in witty polemic reveals an already distinctive focus on will, thought, and ideals, though not on social evolution. Shaw instructs the imaginary Dorothea that her "Individuality"—the manifestation of her unique will—is her most valuable possession. "Let your rule of conduct always be to do whatever is best for yourself," he recommends. In fact, "be as selfish as you can." Shaw cautions, however, that genuine selfishness must involve careful thought: "When you make up your mind to be very selfish, you must be quite sure that you know how to be so." You do not learn how by asking a supposed authority for a code of behavior (Shaw has accused the girl of "idolatry" toward her relatives); you find out "by thinking, without asking anybody." Soon, with the growth of your self-respect, "you will be too proud to act badly." Dorothea should also collect ideas wherever she can, Shaw counsels. "If you are told that any book is not fit for you to read, get it and read it when nobody is looking." Stories are preferable to textbooks, he adds; "They teach you more, and are much pleasanter to read." He concludes: "Remember constantly this rule: the more you think for yourself, the more marked will your Individuality be."

Symptomatically, the emphasis in *My Dear Dorothea* falls upon thought more than upon will or ideas. (Sounding much like Charteris in *The Philanderer*, Shaw professes "the rational interest of an experimental philosopher" in his addressee.) Shaw passed through a rationalist phase which lasted until about 1881 before he unreservedly subordinated the intellect to the will. The word "rational" occurs again and again in his first two novels, *Immaturity* (written in 1879) and *The Irrational Knot* (1880); and the hero of the second is tainted by the kind of systematic Rationalism that Shaw later scorned. But in his third novel, *Love Among the Artists* (1881), personal volition plays a central role. The domineering will of Shaw's first "artist man," a vehement composer partly modelled on Beethoven, leads him to endure poverty and to forgo renown for the sake of complete artistic self-expression. The story also includes such anti-idealistic characters as a girl who deserts her parents to become an actress and a lady who orders her husband not to accompany her on a concert tour because he would distract her. The novel purposely "exalts the wilful characters to the utter disparagement of the reasonable ones."[4]

Shaw acknowledged that *Love Among the Artists* "marks a *volte face* on my part. I had before kept within intellectual bounds: here I let myself go and guessed my way by instinct."[5] His reversal can probably be attributed to his reflections on the subject he knew best at the time: music. For example, he had learned that Beethoven first stunned critics by boldly expressing emotions which no previous composer had considered appropriate for musical rendering.[6] And he himself had been momentarily repelled at the apparent incongruity of Wagner's unprepared major ninths in *Tannhäuser*.[7] It finally dawned upon Shaw, as he recorded later, that he vastly preferred the "licentious musical anarchists"—especially Bach, Mozart, Beethoven, and Wagner—to the fashionable composers who adhered to "rational" standards.[8] The fulfillment of musical genius, perhaps of all genius, seemed to spring from the artist's unscrupulous, intuitive wilfulness.

By 1881, then, Shaw's basic convictions about will and intellect had been rearranged in the order they retained until his death. He now conceived of the intellect as the servant of the will, not its peer—a necessary preliminary to his subsequent extension of the will beyond human bounds. His novel of 1882, *Cashel Byron's Profession*, treads water in his development, but *An Unsocial Socialist* (1883) and the first two acts of *Widowers' Houses* (1884–85) obviously follow his pivotal reading of Marx. Long after the first volume of *Das Kapital* afflicted him in the winter of 1882–83, Shaw called his exposure to Marx a turning point

in his career. "Marx was a revelation. . . . He opened my
eyes to the facts of history and civilisation, gave me an
entirely fresh conception of the universe, provided me with
a purpose and a mission in life."[9] At the time, this mission
was not at all typically Shavian, as *An Unsocial Socialist*
betrays; it was an open, angry assault on laissez-faire capitalism. Shaw commented at a Fabian conference in 1892:
"If any delegate thinks that the Fabian Society was wise
from the hour of its birth, let him forthwith renounce that
error. . . . In 1883 we were content with nothing less than
the prompt 'reconstruction of society in accordance with
the highest moral possibilities.' " He added that the Society's
1886 Tract, "What Socialism Is," merely restated the Com-
munist Manifesto.[10]

The new world view that Shaw discovered in Marx was
not the organistic meliorism of his maturity as a theorist.
Das Kapital did not finally supply him with a metaphysic,
a pattern of history, or even with an economic system.
What he does seem to have taken from it was the idea that
society possesses its own indomitable will, manifested in the
aspiration of the masses toward better things. Marx's social
organism, however, is an odd one, moving toward its pre-
destined flowering in the spontaneous Darwinian manner,
yet somehow dependent upon a carefully nurtured revolt
for its ultimate success. In 1884, having failed to resolve
this apparent contradiction, Shaw described it in a socialist
journal as if the joke were on his own ignorance (the article
is signed "G.B.S. Larking"). He then waited for someone
to refute him, but no one did.[11] A year later, he was alerted
to further weaknesses in *Das Kapital* when a professional
economist (and early Ibsenite), Philip Wicksteed, amusingly lacerated a defense of Marxian economics that he had
written.[12] This type of shock treatment gradually cured
Shaw's Marxist monomania. He and his fellow Fabians
joined a study group conducted by Wicksteed; taught

themselves history, economics, sociology, and political theory; and in the process, Shaw says, "found that we were of one mind as to the advisability of setting to work by the ordinary political methods and having done with Anarchism and vague exhortations to Emancipate the Workers." The Fabians soon became "the recognized bullies and swashbucklers of advanced economics."[13]

In 1888, Shaw stated his newly developed ideas about social evolution in two long speeches that became parts of the durable volume, *Fabian Essays in Socialism*.[14] The first stresses the need to explode illusions about the capitalist system so that the collective will of the exploited masses may be liberated; the second predicts the kind of evolution that the unobstructed will should bring about. The Fabian essayists as a group speak of social evolution as an advance which is inherent in the nature of man and society.[15] In a chapter on the ethical basis of Socialism, Sydney Olivier (quoting Hegel) states the principal Fabian axiom: it is "subjective volition, passion . . . that sets men in activity: men will not interest themselves for anything unless they find their individuality gratified by its attainment" (p. 105). This is Shaw's starting point as well. His first essay contends that man, being primarily wilful, has the capacity to transform society in the long run if he can purge himself of capitalist ideals. A kind of passive conspiracy operates among those who profit from capitalism at the expense of others: however compassionate they may be as individuals, they can hardly avoid believing in the eternal validity of precepts that give them an advantage in a competitive world. These profiteers are the very men who hold the margin of power to pass laws and determine binding social commandments. Thus it is clear why an idealized but wholly "rigged" system exists which contains such ominous ingredients as the postulate that everyone must be willing to sell himself, body and soul, to make a living (the main theme of *Mrs. Warren's Profession*). It is also clear how the ill effects of capitalism can be obliterated. Men whose natural will to live better has been repressed by apparently valid codes must realize that "the source of our social misery is no eternal well-spring of confusion and evil, but only an artificial system susceptible of almost infinite modification and readjustment—nay, of practical demolition and substitution at the will of Man" (p. 27).

The greatest illusions that stand in the way of social evolution, to Shaw, are those which ignore or preclude the activity of the will altogether. One of the most important is rationalism.[16] The rationalist believes that a logical economic or moral code is necessarily a workable one, despite evidence to the contrary. He counters objections to the code by logical arguments and insists that the protesters should be satisfied. Shaw's point of view—embodied in *The Philanderer*, which features a rationalist hero-villain—is that man is wilful rather than rational, so that reasons satisfy him only if they support the promptings of his will. In any event, logic cannot be used to justify suffering: too often Reason is rationalization in disguise. Two other leading obstructions to social evolution, Shaw declares, are pessimism and optimism. The pessimist assumes that the will to improve society is hopelessly gratuitous, since the makeup of the world is beyond man's power to change. He may take the position, for example, that the survival of the fittest is an immutable law of nature duly reflected in society, even though fitness may imply nothing more than the ability to make money or the luck to have inherited it. The main characters in *Widowers' Houses* act on this assumption. Underlying the play is Shaw's conviction "that there is no cruelty and selfishness outside Man himself; and that his own active benevolence can combat and vanquish both." But no less damaging than pessimism is optimism— "the folly of believing anything for no better reason than that it is pleasant to believe it." Optimists tend to shift the burden of active benevolence from man to a supernatural ideal: either the Christian image of God, a kindly father-figure "overruling all evil appearances for good; and making poverty here the earnest of a great blessedness and reward hereafter," or the Marxist concept of History, a self-pro-pelled mechanism driving society, through a relentless class struggle, toward a final Elysium on earth. (In the "pleasant play," *Candida*, the Christian Socialist Morell is a deluded optimist of the best sort.) Until recently, Shaw concludes, the stifling forces of rationalism, pessimism, and optimism generally held sway. But, providentially, the Fabian meli-orist stepped in with "the discovery that though the evil is enormously worse than we knew, yet it is not eternal—not even very long lived, if we only bestir ourselves to make an end of it" (*Fabian Essays in Socialism*, pp. 27–29).

In his second essay, Shaw explains that a vital component of the meliorist stand is "the inevitability of gradualness."[17] After describing the advantage of a change to Socialism, he warns: "The benefits of such a change as this are so obvious to all except the existing private proprietors and their parasites, that it is very necessary to insist on the im-possibility of effecting it suddenly. . . . The necessity for cautious and gradual change must be obvious to everyone" (*Fabian Essays in Socialism*, pp. 182–83). The social organ-ism will grow only at its own pace, and only if it is aided by careful thought. As Shaw responded to altering circum-stances through the eighteen-nineties, he placed increasing emphasis upon the constructive side of securing the evolu-tion of society: the use of thought to discover practical means of fulfilling the will. (Caesar and Lady Cicely in his last two early plays are impressive thinkers of this type.) Around 1890, however, he usually assigned thought the specific role of finding ways to destroy ideals efficiently. The seed of evolution lies within society itself, he said with his fellow Fabians; this seed will grow and flower if the obstructing ideals are removed. The problem to think about, first and foremost, is how to uproot ideals that nearly everyone accepts.

The Fabians solved this problem to their own satisfaction by working out the eminently gradualistic strategy of permeation. In practicing it, they not only infiltrated groups sharing their general aims; they tried to "educate, agitate, organize" everywhere. And they did not seek power or recognition; they sought effect. One of Shaw's Fabian colleagues said in 1895: "We should continue our policy of inoculation—of giving to each class, to each person, coming under our influence, the exact dose of collectivism that they were prepared to assimilate."[18] Following his intention, stated in 1893, to "go uncompromisingly for Permeation" (CL, I, 377), Shaw extended this policy to the English theatre. (A letter to Harley Granville-Barker equates the terms "higher drama," "Propagandist Repertory," and "Permeation."[19]) The immediate products of Shaw's decision were three plays that use the techniques of permeation to attack economic and sociological illusions fostered by capitalists and opposed by Fabian Socialists.

THE *UNPLEASANT PLAYS* AND
FABIAN PERMEATION

Widowers' Houses

The standpoint taken in *Widowers' Houses* is "impartially Socialistic," Shaw said in 1893. "It is a propagandist play—a didactic play—a play with a purpose. . . . It deals with a burning social question, and is deliberately intended to induce people to vote on the Progressive side at the next County Council election in London."[20] The immediate issue of the play is the housing of the poor. One of Shaw's objectives was to convey a distressingly accurate idea of the sordid, degrading tenement life that was the common lot of industrial laborers at the time. To do so, he drew upon his own rent-collecting experiences as well as upon records of official investigations called "bluebooks," one of which becomes a key prop in Act III.[21] More important for the dramatic effect of the piece, he used his precise knowledge of the machinery of a capitalist economy to expose how the rental situation that fostered such miserable living conditions was exploited for profit, actively or passively, by a surprisingly wide range of capitalists, from petty cohorts in municipal jobbery to aristocratic inheritors of land.

The cast of characters in the play is a virtual cross section of such profiteers. On the lowest social level is the rent collector Lickcheese, a shabby "human terrier" who has kept his family alive by wringing money out of destitute tenants and ignoring most of their demands for repairs. The person who has compelled him to do his job so conscientiously, his employer Sartorius (a widower—thus the play's biblical title), has climbed from rags to riches (specifically to a frock coat with silk linings and a white hat—thus his name) by purchasing ramshackle houses, renting them by the room, half-room, or quarter-room to the poor, and administering them ruthlessly. Higher on the social scale are two passive exploiters, the well-connected young doctor, Harry Trench, and a titled Englishwoman of inherited wealth, Lady Roxdale. Trench's modest independent income derives entirely from interest on a mortgage he holds on Sartorius's property. Shaw incriminates him by unrealistically postulating that Trench has no idea of the nature of that property, then by having Sartorius enlighten him and rub salt in his wounds: "It is because of the risks I run through the poverty of my tenants that you exact interest from me at the monstrous and exorbitant rate of seven per cent, forcing me to exact the uttermost farthing in my turn from the tenants." Lady Roxdale, a member of the idle rich class, owns the land on which Sartorius's "slum shop" operates. She does not actually appear on stage, but her presence hovers over it and influences the action, especially since her aristocratic social and economic points of view are repeatedly voiced by Trench's confidant, William de Burgh Cokane. The other significant character is Sartorius's daughter Blanche. At first she seems free of complicity; she neither owns nor manages property, and (again unrealistically) she has never learned that her father lives off the poor. It becomes obvious during an argument with Sartorius, however, that she too must be considered a thoroughgoing profiteer. Like Vivie in *Mrs. Warren's Profession*, Blanche has not only escaped a grim youth of deprivation because of her devoted father's business acumen, but also stands to inherit all of his accumulated profits. Shaw makes it clear that her involvement, though even more innocent than Trench's, is finally as deep as anyone's.

This systematic picture of widespread profiteering is effective enough as a realistic exposé of one momentous type of corruption encouraged in capitalist society (indeed, sanctioned: even Sartorius has never stepped outside the letter of the law). But Shaw's main point of attack lies elsewhere. Ultimately, his broad target is the prevalent assumption that capitalism is the best of all possible economic systems; and in *Widowers' Houses* he focuses on a highly significant outgrowth of this assumption, the illusion that poverty and its consequences are inevitable. Underlying all the play's examples of deliberate and innocent exploitation of the poor is the unquestioned belief that the poor as a class will always exist. Harry Trench, for instance, is full of medical-student sympathy for the destitute, but it never occurs to him that society might be reshaped to render his sympathy unnecessary. Before he finds out that he is subsisting on tainted money, he remarks that his blood used to boil when repulsive conditions arising from poverty were brought to his attention. What disturbed him primarily, however, was that "such things couldn't be prevented." After Sartorius enlightens him, he tacitly agrees that "every man who has a heart must wish that a better state of things was practicable. But unhappily it is not." Presumably like all people, the slum mortgagee and landlord are "powerless to alter the state of society." The enervating pessimism of this attitude is exactly what the play is calculated to help erase.[22]

None of the characters in *Widowers' Houses* either ridicules or preaches against this attitude, and none even hints at the melioristic alternative offered in Fabian Socialism. Shaw's strategy throughout is the indirect, behind-the-scenes strategy of permeation.[23] The positive applications of this strategy cluster where we would expect them to: in the part of the play written after 1890 (Shaw revised the 1884–85 part, but not substantially). The early acts do not violate the rules of permeation, so to speak; but they carry them out only in the negative sense of avoiding overt doctrinal inculcation. By the end of the second act, both Trench and Sartorius have been absolved of any exclusive guilt for a crime that Shaw privately attributes to the "ideal" system of laissez-faire capitalism. The spectator has been led to feel that if anyone deserves the blame, it must be the entire society that condones such an ideal. The Shaw of 1884, clamoring for revolution in a fortnight, would most probably have steeped his third act in sermons, instructive parables, and displays of incriminating evidence. This is how he fills a large part of *An Unsocial Socialist* (1883), which also aims to convey a generalized sense of guilt. But as a meliorist in 1892, he works toward the same result by a subtler method. He dramatizes the unpleasant effects of the precept that poverty is inevitable, and induces the spectator to associate unpleasant sensations with it.

Shaw's chief means to this end lies in his strategic handling of the hero, Harry Trench. At first he makes Trench a mildly attractive character. His comfortable manners and genial spontaneity contrast so favorably with the affectation of his "constitutionally ridiculous" friend Cokane that he gains a considerable following despite lapses of self-possession. After he erroneously concludes that Sartorius is a vile oppressor of the downtrodden masses, his attractiveness heightens—a crescendo before the dying fall. Shaw has prepared for this crescendo by leading the audience to form the same harsh opinion of Sartorius and by keeping it ignorant of Trench's modicum of guilt. Now he capitalizes upon Victorian sentiment by having Trench nobly refuse to accept slum profits as a dowry for his marriage to Blanche. When Shaw pits the indignant "stage Socialist" against Sartorius in the eagerly anticipated showdown scene, moreover, he shifts the irritating apostle of tact, Cokane, over to the villain's side and has him bleat for sweet reasonableness precisely when the audience wants mayhem.[24]

During Trench's illuminating clash with Sartorius, Shaw manipulates the young man's changing moods so that the spectators' sympathies first become strained, and then drift away. The landlord's defense of his policies toward his tenants is strong enough to remove Trench from his pedestal as champion of the oppressed, although when the deposed hero learns that he is just as much of a profiteer as Sartorius, his dazed acknowledgment of the fact makes him an irresistibly pathetic figure for a moment. (He is transformed into a "living picture of disillusion.") But when he begins to "take his disenchantment philosophically," as Shaw accurately puts it, he gradually surrenders even the appeal of pathos. No one in the audience wants him to resign himself to his guilt. From the standpoint of the dramatic effect that Shaw intends, he does so only because Sartorius and Cokane remind him of the consoling theorem that exploitation of the poor is a permanent fixture of the best of all possible economic systems.

In the following act (four months later), Trench unmistakably reveals the deteriorating influence of this pessimistic delusion. His apparent loss of Blanche's love, indirectly caused by his initial revulsion at the thought of living on tainted money (Blanche never really cares whether it is tainted or not), does not account for his dominant new attitude, which Shaw describes as "coarsened and sullen." What does account for it is his new point of view toward business, a logical consequence of his resignation to capitalist guilt. He now looks at things "simply as a question of so much money." To be sure, this contracted perspective brings with it a fact-facing liberation from the moral hypocrisy that the other men display, but its narrowness and cynicism alienate the audience's sympathies once and for all. In contrast to the buoyant, *négligé* personality of Act I and the impetuous stage Socialist of Act II, Trench seems markedly less good-humored and considerate after his conversion, to say the least. The playgoer regrets the change—and consciously or not, associates his discomfort with the underlying reason for that change.

Shaw's tactics follow the lines he later details in the 1913 *Quintessence of Ibsenism*. By making Trench attractive, he misleads the audience into sharing the hero's righteous indignation toward Sartorius. Then, through revelations of fact emerging in brief, heated debates between the deluded and the authoritative characters, he "convicts" Trench and the audience of their "meanly false judgment." For the disconcerted spectator, the play suddenly contains no villains and no heroes—only a grimly realistic situation which has led the former hero to adopt a grimly pessimistic

attitude. Both the situation and the attitude stand out all too
sharply as commonplaces of thoroughgoing capitalism, and
both strike the audience as intensely unpleasant.

The last moments of the play unite three elements which
give this effect a resounding finale. First, the personal conflicts between Trench, Sartorius, and his daughter are
resolved in a manner typical of comedy. Trench is reconciled with Blanche after she learns to her delight that
he will no longer permit sentimental notions about tainted
money to delay their wedding or lower their standard of
living. He also agrees to go along with Sartorius's plan to
improve the slum properties in spite of the financial risk
involved. The principals and their business associates,
Lickcheese and Cokane, troop amiably off the stage, arm
in arm, toward the feast and marriage which culminate
many plays in the comic mode.

Second, however, the concluding reconciliation is also
patently dramatized as a union of conspirators. Lickcheese, fired by Sartorius in the second act, has become
prosperous by illegally obtaining secret information about
business developments and profiting from it. Having recently learned that several of his former employer's tene-
ments may be bought by the city and torn down to clear
the way for a new highway—and sensing further profit—
he goes to Sartorius and suggests that now is the time to
make improvements so that the buildings will bring a
higher price if the city does buy them. The practical landlord likes the idea and asks Trench for his backing. Trench,
looking upon the situation as "simply a matter of so much
money," at first calculates the risk and refuses to take it,
but Sartorius shows him that his interest can be drastically
cut if he does not agree to go along with the deal. Lickcheese would even prefer to have him seal the bond by
marrying Blanche; and, baldly stated, this is what Trench
agrees to do in the comic resolution of the play. Further-

more, a significant degree of the comic "catharsis" derives from the fulfillment of Blanche's desires. When we recognize that these desires consist of an "erotic ferocity" toward Trench and a "ladylike" inclination to escape the "disgrace of harbouring such wretches" as the poor, we see very clearly that the play's resolution, at least to an audience of the nineties, would yield much more unpleasantness than gratification. Even today, the total effect of ugliness is apparent to the discerning spectator, and the amiable concord represented on stage only intensifies this impression.

The third element that contributes to this unpleasant effect is the one which Shaw considered of primary importance: he puts the blame squarely on society as a whole. Trench chooses between alternatives over which he has no real control; and since the limitations which confront him are those of the capitalist system, he chooses the only reasonable alternative. Rejecting the proposed deal would simply lower his own income and finish him with Blanche. Lickcheese and Sartorius would be inconvenienced a trifle, but they would carry out their plan in any event. Moreover, their scheme, while designed to reap profit from an impending misfortune which will leave many of the poor homeless, neither heightens that misfortune nor replaces another course of action which might alleviate it. The mere existence of an indigent working class accounts for the restricted range of alternatives available to both Trench and Sartorius. Thus it is capitalist-oriented society, especially its pessimistic dictum that poverty is inevitable, which commits the cardinal sin of the play.

Widowers' Houses therefore evokes a punitive or corrective response which is thrown into strong relief by the comedic resolution. Consistent with his purposes in the *Unpleasant Plays*, Shaw directs this response away from the characters and toward contemporary society. More precisely, he aims at the middle ground where the two share a reprehensible attitude: pessimism regarding the obvious blight of poverty. The spectator, compelled by an urge to censure and yet unable to blame a villain, is driven to seek an object of condemnation among the achievements and assumptions of capitalism. Or at any rate he is fashioned into a receptive vehicle for socialist ideas—roughly, those leading to a welfare state—which are blocked by the pessimism of Trench and Sartorius. In short, the spectator is goaded into searching for the solution to a problem, and that solution awaits him in the *Fabian Tracts*.

The Philanderer

Shaw's second play propagandizes the audience in a similar way. But in *The Philanderer* he is after bigger game: the capitalist institution of marriage and the "rational" attitude toward it. Shaw did not have to handle the subjects of *Widowers' Houses* with much dramatic ingenuity to make them seem highly unpleasant; poverty and pessimism are repelling enough in themselves. Such was hardly the case when he dealt with the lofty Victorian ideals of Marriage and Reason. The belief that people who love each other should commit themselves to the eternal bond of marriage was perhaps the most widely accepted Victorian sentiment; and an automatic preference for intellect over will, reason over passion, logical "truth" over wishful thinking, was so common that Shaw himself had had to exorcise it from his own mentality. With targets of this dimension, he needed an ideal-destroying strategy that was subtle and sustained. Accordingly, he focused sharply on the conflict between two central characters, fashioned one into a brilliant but jarring rationalist, and shrewdly combined elements of farce and melodrama to achieve a final effect of enigmatic torment.

Like its predecessor, *The Philanderer* contains a galaxy of characters linked by their opinions and circumstances to the main theme. On one side are those who have thoroughly conventional views of marriage, courting, and philandering. A prime example is the drama critic Cuthbertson, who has formed his convictions from idealistic plays rather than from life, and who therefore exhibits nothing but stock responses to love alliances—despite his own incongruous marital experience (his wife heretically proved incompatible). On the opposite side are the characters who hold "advanced," "Ibsenist," or "rational" views. These range from the absurd young apostle of unwomanliness, Sylvia Craven (called "Craven" at her insistence), to the genuine New Woman with a "thoroughbred heart" and an ingrained wariness about the power of love, Grace Tranfield. The total scheme also includes one person who moves freely in both camps, though she decidedly belongs in the first: the voluptuous opportunist Julia Craven. Julia pretends to maintain attitudes toward marriage prescribed by the avant-garde (and joins the Ibsen Club), but only for the sake of inducing the man she loves, "the famous Ibsenist philosopher" Leonard Charteris, to become an orthodox husband.

Compared to *Widowers' Houses*, however, *The Philanderer* makes little didactic use of this thematic cross section of characters. The earlier play employs the device to hammer the point, through a series of revealing disclosures, that everyone with a sufficient income is most likely a profiteer in poverty. No analogous strategy exists in *The Philanderer*. Its secondary characters have two main functions: to supply a near-farcical atmosphere as "jam for the propaganda pill" and to serve as comic counterparts, reflectors, or simply confidants of the major conformist, Julia, and the major Ibsenist, Charteris. Shaw's ideal-destroying strategy centers almost exclusively on the conflict between these two key figures.

The conflict has already erupted before the play begins. The freethinking Charteris (approximating Shaw's experience during his apprentice affair with Jenny Patterson) has finally yielded to Julia's aggressive advances, but not until he has made her agree that they will part immediately if either merely asks to be released. Specifically, he has argued that present marriage laws are a trap for both partners, so that a noncommittal friendship—involving equally noncommittal lovemaking—would be the less perilous and less dishonorable relationship.[25] Charteris is sophisticated and detached enough to make the best of this arrangement, but Julia is not. When he becomes attracted to another woman and claims his right to halt the affair, Julia is unable to suppress her passion for him, refuses to comply, and pursues him tempestuously from then on. At the beginning of the play, therefore, she draws our amused derision as a jealous termagant. Charteris alternates bantering wit, logical persuasion, and plain muscle to fight her off, easily winning the audience's favor in the process. At the end of the play, however, Julia pathetically smothers her frustration by agreeing to marry an infatuated fool who promises to be good to her; and as the curtain falls, she communicates "the presence of a keen sorrow." Charteris, who has remained indifferent to her passion throughout, is the only person incapable of sympathizing with her. He mocks her lightly but pitilessly—a final, striking display of his characteristic attitude. He thus loses the audience's favor, and in accord with the play's general strategy, thereby completes a cycle of effect from attraction to repulsion.

The broad ideal Shaw attacks in *The Philanderer* is capitalist society's postulate, derived from its economic system and enforced by its laws, that marriage should be a tie that binds for life. Charteris tries to reason with Julia by reminding her that she once regarded marriage as "a degrading bargain, by which a woman sold herself to a man for the social status of a wife and the right to be supported and pensioned in old age out of his income." The play merits the term "unpleasant," Shaw asserts, because he has shown "the grotesque relations between men and women which have arisen under marriage laws which represent to some of us a political necessity . . . , to some a divine ordinance, to some a romantic ideal, . . . and to some that worst of blundering abominations, an institution which society has outgrown but not modified, and which 'advanced' individuals are therefore forced to evade" (Pref., *Unpleasant Plays*, p. xxx). Again, Shaw attempts to undermine a capitalist institution by awakening the spectator's desire to have it modified, presumably along Fabian lines. Also similar to *Widowers' Houses*, Shaw's more basic target is an attitude toward society that prevents its improvement. Charteris grasps the realities of current social "abominations" with admirable perception, but like Sartorius, he acts on assumptions that bolster the corrupt status quo. Sartorius and his convert, Trench, are pessimists; Charteris is a rationalist. He reacts to social defects by relishing the knowledge he can gain from them as a man of reason and an experimental philosopher. Most of the nondated, lasting unpleasant effects of the play spring not from the originally scandalous air of cynicism about the English ideal of marriage, but rather from the manifestations of this rigid rationalistic attitude.

It manifests itself in a negative sense every time Charteris shows that he cannot tolerate, or even comprehend, Julia's inability to subordinate her passion to the liberated views that she allegedly upholds. She becomes little more than an object of mockery to him when she spurns the implacable syllogisms he presents in support of his "Ibsenist" demands.[26] Despite his reliance upon logic, however, his demands are essentially unreasonable. He tells Julia inexorably: "I now assert the right I reserved—the right of breaking with you when I please. Advanced views, Julia, involve advanced duties: you cannot be an advanced woman when you want to bring a man to your feet, and a conventional woman when you want to hold him there against his will. Advanced people form charming friendships: conventional people marry. . . . You chose friendship instead of marriage. Now do your duty, and accept your notice." The very terms of Charteris's declaration give him away. Although he has certainly caught Julia in a logical bind, a direct consequence of her hypocritical opportunism, he is still commanding her to do her duty according to a rational code. To Shaw, the quintessence of genuine Ibsenism is that there is no formula, no code (no "charter"); and Charteris has erected one on the groundwork of Ibsenist thought. Moreover, he is committing Julia's sin by using his code opportunistically, since he knows well that Julia is far from an advanced woman. He is able to live up to the code himself in this case because Julia has never succeeded in "snaring" him in the way Blanche snares Trench or Ann snares Tanner. But, as Julia's erotically dynamic outbreaks of desire intimate, nature has strategically made her the slave of a passion for Charteris.[27] For whatever reason she once professed advanced views, she cannot help violating them. Shaw implies that the power which ultimately causes this impasse, though it by no means renders Julia a more desirable partner for Charteris—or a more attractive character in the spectator's eyes—cannot be ignored in any reasonable outlook on society.[28] Charteris, by consistently failing to look beyond the blinders of his rational code and sense the presence of the irresistible (and irrational) force that motivates Julia, is forced to incur the silent condemnation of the audience. On nearly all other counts, the audience is greatly pleased by the witty philanderer and amusingly irritated, if not revolted, by his antagonist.

Near the end of the play, Julia calls Charteris a "vivisector." It is an apt label, for he manifests his rationalistic attitude most overtly in this role. When Julia informs him of her engagement to Dr. Paramore, a vivisector in the literal sense, Charteris gloats: "Our vivisecting friend has made a successful experiment at last." Julia retorts: "It is you who are the vivisector—a far crueller, more wanton vivisector than he." Charteris can offer only a flimsy defense: "Yes; but then I learn so much more from my experiments than he does! And the victims learn as much as I do." A moment later he cancels out the redeeming part of his statement by noting that Julia has not really learned anything after all. At the same time he expresses his point of view spontaneously and sincerely: "Oh, what I have learnt from you!—from *you*, who could learn nothing from me! I made a fool of you; and you brought me wisdom: I broke your heart; and you brought me joy: I made you curse your womanhood; and you revealed my manhood to me [i.e., his free spirit]. Blessings forever and ever on my Julia's name! (*With genuine emotion, he takes her hand to kiss it.*)" This is an extraordinary effusion, and not simply because of the startling intellectual point of view that it displays. Addressing the victim of his experiment in philandering, a hopelessly overmatched virago whom he later likens to a "fine animal" (and who has earlier complained that everyone treats her like a Persian cat), Charteris offers her his personal justification for having made her suffer, and offers it with such intense conviction—and with such obliviousness to Julia's feelings—that he blesses her "with genuine emotion" for granting him the joy of added wisdom at the cost of her broken heart. This is philosophical passion with a vengeance. From the standpoint of strategy, it dramatically reveals that the rationalist Charteris is a thoroughgoing vivisector as well as a philosopher.

The play secures its cumulative impact of unpleasantness by progressing from the attractions of the gay philosopher to the revulsions of the pitiless vivisector. The hero gradually becomes the villain—or more accurately, his appeal in either capacity gradually diminishes. The concluding moment of the play crystallizes this depleted image. Julia, her frenzy of resentment at Charteris's gleeful mockery exhausted, tolerates his show of good will (which actually celebrates his own escape) and mutters:

> You are right. I am a worthless woman.
> CHARTERIS (*triumphant, and gaily remonstrating*). Oh, why?
> JULIA. Because I am not brave enough to kill you.
> GRACE (*taking her in her arms as she sinks, almost fainting, away from him*). Oh, no. Never make a hero of a philanderer. (*Charteris, amused and untouched, shakes his head laughingly. The rest look at Julia with concern, and even a little awe, feeling for the first time the presence of a keen sorrow.*)

In *Widowers' Houses* the final propagandistic effect arises when the superficial comic resolution of the play intensifies a punitive response which is deliberately left unsatisfied. The spectator's impulse to condemn is thereby directed toward the economic facts presented, and his sense of hostility is affixed to an anti-Fabian attitude. In *The Philanderer* the case is somewhat different. Here, the propagandistic strategy revolves about a single character, the philanderer himself, to a much greater extent. The play as a whole is not precisely a more comic play, but it yields more laughter per scene because of Charteris's sophisticated wit and his main avocation. The ending once again evokes a punitive response, but intensifies it by resolving only the minor conflicts and by sharpening the central one between Charteris and Julia. Shaw does this because he has made the hero a much greater source of interest and pleasure than Harry Trench. Although the playgoer generally favors Trench and comes to regret the loss of his endearing qualities, this partiality is not nearly so binding as it is in regard to

Charteris. Shaw therefore uses different tactics to render the once-irresistible philanderer deplorable.

From the standpoint of dramatic form, these tactics include a gradual movement from effects which are closely allied to farce toward their serious counterparts, effects closely allied to melodrama. Manifesting the same qualities of perception, cleverness, and lack of sympathy, Charteris first defends himself, then offends Julia. He continues to wield his rapier of rationalistic wit throughout, even when he no longer needs it for parrying. The characteristics that grant him distinction, in fact, emerge most often in situations which show Julia beaten by his cleverness. The nature of the situation determines whether these characteristics produce ludicrous or pathetic effects. Charteris thus accumulates appeal when Julia is viewed as the comic butt of farce, and he forfeits it when she becomes the persecuted damsel of melodrama. At the curtain, everyone on stage except Charteris senses pathos in her plight; he sees only ludicrousness.

It does not follow, however, that the audience expels its measure of punitive desire by gnashing its teeth at Charteris. For the spectator, Charteris does not become deplorable rather than irresistible: on the contrary, he becomes both at the same time. His distinctive qualities obviously smack of great potential value and have yielded keen intellectual pleasure during the play. They remain too attractive, even in Julia's sorrow, to permit unqualified repudiation. Indeed, they are finally enigmatic: Charteris's personality itself poses an unsolved problem. By concluding on an enigmatic note, Shaw again torments the spectator as he did in *Widowers' Houses*. Again the spectator is compelled to grope for, define, and possibly answer the questions which the unpleasant outcome of the play imposes upon him. Again the problem lies in the actual conditions of contemporary society and in an attitude which obstructs their melioration. And, again, publications issued by the Fabian Society await with the remedies spelled out.[29]

Mrs. Warren's Profession

As examples of propaganda by dramatic permeation, Shaw's first two plays are apprentice works compared to his third, *Mrs. Warren's Profession*. *Widowers' Houses* fails to gather much impetus until the 1890 and 1892 parts of the play. *The Philanderer* suffers from its intermittent exploitation of a short-lived fad: in Shaw's words, "unless there has been plenty of chatter . . . about Ibsen, 'the new woman' &c, the play, which is highly topical on these points, won't do" (*CL*, I, 486). Moreover, these two plays betray Shaw's tendency to spread the "jam" for his "propaganda pill" somewhat too thickly when he relies heavily upon unpleasant effects. *Widowers' Houses* contains frivolous patter and theatrical gesturing that apparently escaped Shaw's critical eye when he revised the original edition.[30] The vestiges of "mechanical farce" and "realistic filth" in *The Philanderer* embarrassed him, despite their pertinence to his design (*CL*, I, 644). Of course, *Mrs. Warren's Profession* is not totally free of such stagey, galvanic elements. When Vivie greets Praed with a powerful handshake and he massages his fingers, or when she suddenly pulls the barrel of Frank Gardner's rifle around to her breast, it is all too evident that Shaw is again resorting to the surefire effects of rudimentary farce and melodrama.[31] Nevertheless, the play still achieves a degree of dramatic impact which far exceeds that of its predecessors. Nothing else in the Shavian canon matches it in raw anticapitalist power. Shaw reflected in 1897: "When I wrote that, I *had* some nerve" (*CL*, I, 770).

The three propaganda plays are labeled "Unpleasant,"

according to their preface, because "their dramatic power is used to force the spectator to face unpleasant facts" (p. xxix). Shaw elaborated upon this statement in 1902, when J. T. Grein, who had instituted Shaw's public career as a dramatist by daringly staging *Widowers' Houses* at the Independent Theatre, expressed strong objections to *Mrs. Warren's Profession* after a Stage Society performance.[32] Shaw subsequently issued a lengthy *Author's Apology*, part of which illuminates his propagandistic intentions:

> [Mr. Grein] complains that Mrs. Warren is not wicked enough, and names several romancers who would have clothed her black soul with all the terrors of tragedy. I have no doubt they would; but if you please, my dear Grein, that is just what I did not want to do. Nothing would please our sanctimonious British public more than to throw the whole guilt of Mrs. Warren's profession on Mrs. Warren herself. Now, the whole aim of my play is to throw that guilt on the British public itself. . . . The notion that prostitution is created by the wickedness of Mrs. Warren is as silly as the notion . . . that drunkenness is created by the wickedness of the publican. Mrs. Warren is not a whit a worse woman than the reputable daughter who cannot endure her. Her indifference to the ultimate social consequences of her means of making money, and her discovery of that means by the ordinary method of taking the line of least resistance to getting it, are too common in English society to call for any special remark. Her vitality, her thrift, her energy, her outspokenness, her wise care of her daughter, and the managing capacity which has enabled her and her sister to climb from the fried fish shop down by the mint to the establishments of which she boasts, are all high English social virtues. Her defense of herself . . . is not only bold and specious, but valid and unanswerable. But it is no defense at all of the vice which she organizes. It is no defense of an immoral life to say that the alternative offered by society collectively to poor women is a miserable life, starved, overworked, fetid, ailing, ugly. Though it is quite natural and *right* for Mrs. Warren to choose what is, according to her lights, the least immoral

alternative, it is none the less infamous of society to offer
such alternatives. For the alternatives offered are not morality and immorality, but two sorts of immorality.[33]

The same kind of choice operates as a structural principle in
Widowers' Houses and *The Philanderer*. In all three plays,
the attacks are directed against the spectators themselves
as responsible citizens of capitalist society.

Mrs. Warren's Profession, however, is designed to reach
a much wider range of spectators than its forerunners. The
obvious fact that prostitution is a more sensational subject
than slum landlordism or Ibsenist philandering needs to be
stressed, not merely chalked off as self-evident. Shaw was
not above dangling the bait of an apparent aphrodisiac in
front of people whose collective will he considered the
prime instrument of social evolution. Gloating over critics
who were baffled by the play, Shaw proclaimed: "Can I be
expected to refrain from laughing at the spectacle of a number of respectable gentlemen lamenting because a playwright lures them to the theater by a promise to excite their
senses in a very special and sensational manner, and then,
having successfully trapped them in exceptional numbers,
proceeds to ignore their senses and ruthlessly improve their
minds?"[34] A letter of 1895 states that the play's "cold
bloodedly appalling" subject matter is treated in such a way
as to make the audience "thoroughly uncomfortable" (*CL*,
I, 566). Given spectators trapped by their attraction toward
forbidden sex, the play pursues its effect of torment partly
by exploiting their repugnance toward prostitution. That is,
it postulates rather than attacks an accepted moral judgment.
Shaw told a parliamentary committee investigating stage
censorship in 1909 that *Mrs. Warren's Profession* is "perhaps the most moral of the three [unpleasant plays] in the
sense that it appeals to ordinary morality. It does not require
a change of morality for its acceptance."[35] Shaw designed
the play to produce "a very strong and very painful impres-

sion of evil," and he capitalized upon the abhorrent as well as the enticing qualities of his subject (*Apology*, p. 39).

Nevertheless, prostitution is his real subject only in the sense that it is a glaring symptom of a pervading disease. The "unpleasant facts" that Shaw wants spectators to face are not facts about the profession itself or about the people who organize it. Shaw focuses his dramatic attacks on ideals that mask realities—in this case, the particular mode of conduct fostered by the capitalist ethic. In the terms of the play, it is Vivie's "Gospel of Getting On" and the "Crofts philosophy of life"; in other Shavian terms, it is the idealized worship of Mammon which accepts proprietary respectability as its goal and reward. Shaw is convinced that the reality of capitalist aspiration, when unmasked, will appear irrevocably immoral to the common man. That is why he lures a large audience and "appeals to ordinary morality." Prostitution represents for him an ultimate example, as well as a patently shocking one, of the "White Slave Traffic" on all levels: the bartering of human lives and destinies that the capitalist ethic condones.

Mrs. Warren's Profession therefore casts a backward glance at the employer-employee relations of a brothel-keeper and her female assistants, then a forward one at an energetic young accountant and her male assistants. It relates that in her youth Mrs. Warren sold herself to men as the sole outlet to a life of reasonable comfort; and it presents Frank Gardner, in his youth, trying to sell himself to Vivie (consciously using his good looks as bait, in fact) because his only way to security is to become a paid husband. To Shaw, the difference is one of degree, not of kind; capitalist prostitution is involved in all such relations. By blending the repugnance spectators associate with Mrs. Warren's profession into the sympathy or apathy they feel toward the forms of prostitution which enjoy good reputations, he attempts to blacken the capitalist ethic itself.

Shaw's preface to the *Unpleasant Plays* makes it clear that his subject is prostitution in the universal sense of selling oneself to make a living or buying those who must. In *Mrs. Warren's Profession*, Shaw claims,

> I have gone straight at the fact that, as Mrs. Warren puts it, "the only way for a woman to provide for herself decently is for her to be good to some man that can afford to be good to her." . . . I believe that any society which desires to found itself on a high standard of integrity of character in its units should organize itself in such a fashion as to make it possible too for all men and all women to maintain themselves in reasonable comfort by their industry without selling their affections and their convictions. At present we not only condemn women as a sex to attach themselves to "breadwinners," licitly or illicitly, on pain of heavy privation and disadvantage; but we have great prostitute classes of men: for instance, dramatists and journalists, to whom I myself belong, not to mention the legions of lawyers, doctors, clergymen, and platform politicians who are daily using their highest faculties to belie their real sentiments. (pp. xxx-xxxi)

In his economic writings, early and late, Shaw pinpoints the moral dilemma of capitalism by using the graphic metaphor of the White Slave Traffic. The proletarian, he declares in a Fabian essay, "has nothing to sell—except himself." Lacking commodities and the means of producing them, he unavoidably treats himself as a commodity, and in effect, "sells himself openly into bondage" at a price set by supply and demand in the "traffic of men." From the business point of view, the transaction differs little from the ordinary market exchange. The human commodity himself, however, "renounces not only the fruit of his labor, but also his right to think for himself and to direct his industry as he pleases." Thus "the economic change is merely formal: the moral change is enormous." Shaw's essay is in part an attempt to convey the "latent horror" of this everyday transaction (*Fabian Essays in Socialism*, pp. 11–12, 18).

In *The Intelligent Woman's Guide to Socialism and Capitalism*, Shaw poses the same dilemma by means of an example so relevant to Mrs. Warren's situation that his comments amount to an analysis of her role. Discussing the moral implications of the proletarian woman's lot in the labor market, he asserts:

> It is easy to ask a woman to be virtuous; but it is not reasonable if the penalty of virtue be starvation, and the reward of vice immediate relief. If you offer a pretty girl twopence halfpenny an hour in a match factory, with a chance of contracting necrosis of the jawbone from phosphorus poisoning on the one hand, and on the other a jolly and pampered time under the protection of a wealthy bachelor, which was what the Victorian employers did and what employers still do all over the world when they are not stopped by resolutely socialistic laws, you are loading the dice in favor of the devil so monstrously as not only to make it certain that he will win, but raising the question whether the girl does not owe it to her own self-respect and desire for wider knowledge and experience, more cultivated society, and greater grace and elegance of life, to sell herself to a gentleman for pleasure rather than to an employer for profit.
>
> . . . .
>
> In short, Capitalism acts on women as a continual bribe to enter into sex relations for money, whether in or out of marriage; and against this bribe there stands nothing beyond the traditional respectability which Capitalism ruthlessly destroys by poverty, except religion and the inborn sense of honor which has its citadel in the soul and can hold out (sometimes) against all circumstances. (pp. 199, 201)

Putting his point in capsule form, Shaw says: "If a woman accepts Capitalist morality, and does what pays her best, she will take . . . the wages of sin rather than the wages of sweated labor" (p. 200).

Three of the four essential elements in Mrs. Warren's character and background are highlighted here. First, circumstances caused by poverty induced her when she was young to choose the reward of vice rather than the penalty of virtue. She convinces her daughter that she owed this choice to her own self-respect; and Shaw's *Apology* describes the choice she made as "natural and *right*." Second, she unquestionably lacks the "inborn sense of honor" which might have compelled her to resist the pressure of circumstances, or which would at least have steered her away from prostitution once this pressure disappeared. Frank Gardner divines immediately that she is an "old wretch," "ever so rowdy"—or, as he airily puts the crucial distinction, "a good sort but a bad lot." Vivie, on the other hand, overreacts to her mother's self-justification and gets sickeningly sentimental about her for a while, a phase that is halted with a jolt when she learns that her mother has moved up in the business, not out of it.

Third and most important, Mrs. Warren "accepts Capitalist morality, and does what pays her best." Shaw says in a program note to the play: "Mrs. Warren's profession is a vested interest; and when a woman of bold character and commercial ability applies to herself the commercial principles that are ruthlessly applied to her in the labour market, the result is Kitty Warren. . . . You will hear her justify herself completely on those principles."[36] Within the bounds of capitalist morality, to recall Shaw's *Apology* again, she demonstrates many of the "high English social virtues." She is an efficient manager, treats her girls well, and raises her daughter with care and passable wisdom. However misdirected her capacities may be, Mrs. Warren employs them in full accord with English standards. Furthermore, the goal that she admires her sister for having attained and expects Vivie to pursue is the ultimate personal ideal of the capitalistic ethic: proprietary, churchgoing respectability.

Yet Mrs. Warren herself has been satisfied to forgo respectability despite her accumulated wealth, and this incongruous fact points to a fourth characteristic that Shaw gives her. She has passed up the chance to adopt an idle and irreproachable life because she is a woman of immense vitality. In Shaw's idiom, she is a creature of such volition that she rejects the confines of her most cherished ideal, while never doubting that ideal for a moment. Her equally vital daughter Vivie at last perceives that she is her "mother's daughter," since she also likes to work and make more money than she needs; but she repudiates the corrupting ideal of worthless respectability that her mother wants her to accept. When she bids her mother goodbye once and for all in the final scene, she offers as her only valid reason the key statement: "You are a conventional woman at heart." This stands in violent contrast to her conclusion halfway through the play that her mother is "stronger than all England." Vivie is right the second time: Mrs. Warren is exactly as weak as the capitalist ethic can make her.

Mrs. Warren, therefore, is an example of extreme "wilfulness" vitiated by an ideal. Shaw dramatizes her in a way that produces a strong impression of waste. Along with the feelings of repugnance which the play evokes almost without artistic effort, this impression of corrupted or misapplied vitality ranks high among the effects that Shaw uses for his dramatic propaganda. It is typical of him to compel thought by stirring emotions; in his unpleasant plays, these emotions are appropriately unpleasant. It is also typical of him to give his audience the materials for a clear understanding of the problem it is emotionally provoked to consider; thus Mrs. Warren's ideal and its various outgrowths—her own circumstances, Crofts' proposition to Vivie, Frank's pursuit of a keeper and his pastor-father's encouragement—are lucidly set forth.

The strategy in this play, however, leads Shaw to do

something which he rigorously avoids in *Widowers' Houses* and *The Philanderer*. In order to intensify the impression of waste stemming from Mrs. Warren and her false aspirations, he directs Vivie's similarly vital impulses in the meliorist path momentarily. Like Trench in *Widowers' Houses*, Vivie learns that her own secure situation in life is solely the product of tainted money. Like Trench again, she says to the informant, Crofts: "I believe I am just as bad as you." Crofts assures her that the world is like that; bad or good, it is simply the state of affairs—the same argument that had transformed Trench into a "coarsened and sullen" spokesman of the business point of view.[37] But Vivie is not "morally beggared" in the manner of Trench; she turns on Crofts and declares:

> When I think of the society that tolerates you, and the laws that protect you—when I think of how helpless nine out of ten young girls would be in the hands of you and my mother —the unmentionable woman and her capitalist bully—
>
> CROFTS *(livid)*. Damn you!
>
> VIVIE. You need not. I feel among the damned already.
> (Act III)

Later, she again voices the meliorist impulse that lies behind this show of indignation toward her society. When she tells Praed that Mrs. Warren is not simply an unmarried mother, he cautions her against breaking the proprieties by saying more, and she asserts: "I am sure that if I had the courage I should spend the rest of my life in telling it to everybody —in stamping and branding it into them until they felt their share in its shame and horror as I feel mine." Unlike Shaw (whose intention the above words surely imply), Vivie suppresses impulses of this sort, partly because she can make a decent living within the existing structure of capitalist society, but also because she has become tainted by the pessimistic outlook toward social improvement that infects Trench. Near the end of the play she acknowledges rather

morosely that "life is what it is" and that she is "prepared
to take it as it is." Then she encloses herself in an accounting
office "for the rest of [her] life."

Vivie's final actions convey an almost palpable sense of
wasted vitality. After her dismissals of Praed, Frank, and
Mrs. Warren, all justified moves that fully resolve the
audience's expectations, her vigorous plunge into actuarial
calculations leaves a marked residue of frustration. Two
feelings are evoked: admiration for her energy and distaste
at its specific application. The resulting dissatisfaction spurs
the audience to reflect that Vivie's choice of profession, like
her mother's, derives sheerly from typical capitalist "circumstances." In the last act Mrs. Warren says: "I must have
work and excitement, or I should go melancholy mad. And
what else is there for me to do? The life suits me: I'm fit
for it and not for anything else." Vivie replies: "I am like
you: I must have work, and must make more money than
I spend. But my work is not your work, and my way not
your way." She says nothing here about being fit for only
one kind of work, but she has already stressed that fact
during her memorable talk with Praed in the opening moments of the play. There we have learned that the process
of winning honors in mathematics at Cambridge University
has made Vivie an "ignorant barbarian" in all other subjects,
and that she sought the distinction only because her mother
offered her fifty pounds to win it. Clearly, circumstances
based on capitalist morality—doing what pays best—have
inflicted her profession upon her. She has taken money from
a brothel-keeper to prostitute herself to "nothing but mathematics." Luckily, the life suits her.

Shaw's chief dramatic method in his three propaganda
plays is that of "convicting the audience of a meanly false
judgment." The most sophisticated and forceful example
of its use occurs in the first two acts of *Mrs. Warren's
Profession* (a four-act play), where almost every single ac-

tion, speech, and word contributes to this goal. After Mrs. Warren has vindicated herself at the end of Act II, the artistic conditioning of effects proceeds on a new foundation; thus her overthrow of Vivie, which is simultaneously an indictment of the audience, occupies a pivotal spot in the play. Shaw's techniques up to this turning point merit detailed analysis.

Act I of the play misleads the audience into expecting a conventional revolt of the daughter scene in which, for obvious reasons, the daughter emerges victorious. We learn at once that Vivie has not lived with her mother most of her life and has never heard her father mentioned. She meets Praed, a devotee of the arts (and a convenient expository device) who knows Mrs. Warren well enough to predict her feelings and report them to Vivie. The "prompt, strong, confident, self-possessed" young woman, after a handshake that bristles with these qualities, acquaints Praed with her desire to work as a mathematician, and to his dismay, with her aversion to doing "all that makes womanhood beautiful." Praed remarks that she is as far from Mrs. Warren's ideal as she is from his own. Vivie then explains that she has definite plans to join an accounting firm and that she anticipates a "battle royal" with her mother on the issue. Praed has hinted that her mother is an authoritative sort of woman, but he has said nothing about her claims to such authority. Vivie, whose faint suspicions about these claims are awakened (in turn stimulating the audience's), resolves to win the battle at any price. To prevent her from hitting harder than necessary in her ignorance, Praed decides to tell her all he knows about her mother. But just then Mrs. Warren arrives, and the scene is abruptly set for the impending clash between mother and daughter.

In the Shavian manner, the forces have been distinctively and sharply aligned against each other. After Vivie exposes her antiromantic masculinity to Praed and the audience, she supplies the appropriate choral comment herself: "Now you know the sort of perfectly splendid modern young lady I am." Shaw describes her in a letter as the heroine "in whom I have sought to put on the stage for the first time (as far as I know) the highly educated, capable, independent young woman of the governing class as we know her today, working, smoking, preferring the society of men to that of women simply because men talk about the questions that interest her and not about servants & babies, making no pretence of caring much about art or romance, respectable through sheer usefulness & strength, and playing the part of the charming woman only as the amusement of her life, not as its serious occupation" (*CL*, I, 566–67). Mrs. Kitty Warren, her prospective opponent, has been introduced so far only by the title of the play, by Praed's hints, and by Vivie's expressions of doubt about her. These suggestions strongly imply, however, that she will turn out to be more than a mother-figure, to say the least. When she is seen to be accompanied by Sir George Crofts, a callous-looking man-about-town whom she calls one of her oldest friends, the implication becomes a certainty.

Mrs. Warren's initial actions bolster the probability that her daughter will soon rebel. She greets Vivie by saying idly, "Put your hat on, dear: you'll get sunburnt." Praed takes her aside and warns her that Vivie should be treated with more respect since she is now a grown woman. Genuinely amazed, Mrs. Warren replies: "Respect! Treat my own daughter with respect! What next, pray!" The presence of Crofts, moreover, tentatively confirms whatever suspicions about her mother that Vivie might have passed on to the spectator. He is unmistakably flashy and brutish: "a tall, powerfully-built man of about 50, fashionably dressed in the style of a young man. . . . Clean-shaven, bull-dog jaws, large flat ears, and thick neck." (Frank Gardner later nails him down amusingly: "Sort of chap

that would take a prize at a dog show, ain't he?") Crofts
incites more suspicion when he shows an immediate interest
in Vivie's good looks, an interest which later heightens to
a "carnal gleam" even though Vivie—almost thirty years
younger—shows that she is instinctively repelled by him.
The fact that such a man is Mrs. Warren's crony suggests
an ominous answer to the question, What *is* her mother?

The remainder of Act I ostensibly settles this question
and raises another: Who is Vivie's father? First Crofts, then
Samuel Gardner, pastor-father of the *jeune premier*, make
it obvious that she has been at least a promiscuous woman.
Sir George asks Praed if he knows who Vivie's father is;
Praed replies that he has never had anything to do with
"that side" of Kitty's life. In a clanking turn of plot, Gardner begins to develop the horrifying suspicion that he is
himself the father of the girl his son wants to marry. While
the spectator weighs the implications of these hints, another
development prepares him further for the drama of Vivie's
revolt. He is easily led to expect that she will smoke out the
truth of her mother's past and use it as a weapon in the
battle: at the curtain she is seen overhearing Gardner con-
fusedly address Kitty as "Miss Vavasour."[38]

Moreover, before this moment an anticipatory revolt
occurs. During a brief encounter between Gardner, a *man*
with a past, and his "agreeably disrespectful" son Frank,
the son triumphs over his hopelessly assertive father in a
flourish of levity and self-assurance. This conflict is partly
the reverse of the one the audience expects between Vivie
and Mrs. Warren. Frank is demonstrably "good-for-nothing"; Vivie exudes purpose and parades her useful quali-
fications. Gardner exhorts his son to work his way into a
profession "and live on it and not upon me"—precisely
what Vivie plans to do in opposition to her mother's wishes.
Frank has already learned the crucial facts about his father's
past, whereas we await the shock of Vivie's discovery.

Other elements in the two parent-child relationships, however, are conspicuously parallel. Like Mrs. Warren, Gardner
invokes the conventional authority of parenthood and shows
a primary concern for his son's social position; Frank, in
response, takes Vivie's stand and declares: "I don't care a
rap about that." Most strikingly, Frank overpowers his
father by reminding him of his scandalous past; and we
learn in seconds that his past coincides with Mrs. Warren's.
Thus Shaw deceptively confirms the picture of future
possibilities which has formed in the spectator's mind.

The second act culminates in the mother-daughter battle.
Until a few minutes before Vivie and her mother are left
alone, every event in the act stirs antagonism against Mrs.
Warren. Concurrently, the audience is encouraged to ap-
prove of those qualities in Vivie which make her well-
equipped as an agent of her mother's downfall (though their
blatant unwomanliness hardly permits unqualified favor).
Frank pairs off with Mrs. Warren, flirts with her, and
finally tempts an indulgent kiss. The two radiate what
Frank later calls the "freemasonry" that exists among "thoroughly immoral people." Then, despite Frank's chuckled
warning that "your little girl is jolly well able to take care
of herself," Mrs. Warren abruptly reverts to her irritating
role as overprotective mother. Twice she voices concern for
Vivie, who has not yet returned from a walk with Praed
in the dark. Frank declares his intention to propose to Vivie,
and Mrs. Warren blandly assumes that her own word—at
first an approval—will certainly be final. Then, galling the
spectator in a different way, she rejects the proposal not
because Frank is good-for-nothing or thoroughly immoral,
but simply because he has no money and no prospect of
earning it. In a romantically oriented theatre, her unflinch-
ingly practical rationale would chafe the audience: "Your
love's a pretty cheap commodity [note the term]. . . . If you
have no means of keeping a wife, that settles it: you can't

have Vivie." The confident levity of Frank's retort would attract at least scattered applause: "Mrs. Warren: I cannot give my Vivie up even for your sake. . . . I shall lose no time in placing my case before her."

Accompanying this series of events which mildly incriminates Mrs. Warren is another sequence which makes her downright repulsive in the eyes of those spectators who have fallen into the trap of believing that Frank is Vivie's half-brother. Between the end of the first act and the beginning of the second, Crofts has evidently heard Gardner admit that he might very well have fathered Vivie. (Actually not even Shaw could answer this academic question, much less the former prostitute, Kitty Warren.[39]) The two men come onstage together, and they are both shocked to hear Mrs. Warren first favor the idea of Frank's marrying her daughter. Frank brings up the possibility and his father remonstrates: "Once for all, it's out of the question. Mrs. Warren will tell you that it's not to be thought of." Crofts adds: "Of course not." To the completely deceived and not radically freethinking spectator, Mrs. Warren's reply is almost that of an insensitive monster: she says, "Well, Sam, I don't know. If the girl wants to get married, no good can come of keeping her unmarried." This vein continues to an appalling climax:

> REV. S. *(astounded)*. But married to *him*!—your daughter to my son! Only think: it's impossible.
> CROFTS. Of course it's impossible. Don't be a fool, Kitty.
> MRS. WARREN *(nettled)*. Why not? Isn't my daughter good enough for your son?
> REV. S. But surely, my dear Mrs. Warren, you know the reason—
> MRS. WARREN *(defiantly)*. I know no reasons. If you know any, you can tell them to the lad, or to the girl, or to your congregation, if you like.

The gradual incrimination of Mrs. Warren attains its height soon after she withdraws her consent and Frank vows to propose at once. During a moment alone with him, Vivie roundly denounces her mother. Unlike the audience, of course, she is not yet sure that her mother has been a promiscuous woman, so that the only grounds she has for denouncing her are the dubious ones of youthful rebellion and the vague ones of natural dislike. The audience is highly gratified, therefore, when she articulates a position that nearly everyone can affirm. With intense contempt, she asserts: "If I thought that *I* was like that—that I was going to be a waster, shifting along from one meal to another with no purpose, and no character, and no grit in me, I'd open an artery and bleed to death without one moment's hesitation." This vitalist point of view plays a major role in Vivie's attitude toward Mrs. Warren throughout the play. Later it will cause her to admire her mother; here, both Vivie and the audience misapply it. Her declaration is the climax of a long series of effects artfully calculated to plant a meanly false judgment in the spectator's mind, the judgment that Mrs. Warren is a shameless waster. Along with Vivie, he is soon convicted of it.

A significant skirmish pitting Mrs. Warren against her apparent ally, Crofts, intervenes between the false judgment and the conviction. It demonstrates, to the audience's partial relief, that she is not really an insensitive monster—indeed, that in spite of her way of life and her stress on the pounds-and-shillings value of Vivie's suitors, her instincts as a mother are still stronger than her habits as a manager of prostitutes. Crofts follows the lead intimated by her rejection of Frank on financial grounds, and "with a carnal gleam in his eye and a loose grin," makes a straight money proposition for Vivie's hand. But Mrs. Warren responds with a consummate rebuke: "Faugh! So it's come to that with you, George, like all the other worn out old creatures." Her forceful comparison strikes the audience as a saving grace.

The remaining business before Vivie meets her mother head on reactivates two impressions which have dwindled since Act I: the strong impression that Vivie will rebel and win, and the less distinct one that her argument will focus on her mother's shaky grounds for claiming parental authority. Gardner and his son engage in a second anticipatory conflict, again with Frank emerging unscratched and banteringly victorious. Mrs. Warren, whose refusal to act as procuress for her own daughter has already reemphasized her mother role, fusses over Vivie with an "affectation of maternal patronage even more forced than usual." After the men leave, these two expectations are at first fulfilled in the normal pattern of a *scène à faire*.[40] As Vivie sums up this part of the battle to her mother: "You attacked me with the conventional authority of a mother: I defended myself with the conventional superiority of a respectable woman." Her defense (or rather her counterattack) springs directly from the point of view she expressed to Frank: that of living purposefully. Mrs. Warren informs her that since she will not be going back to college, they will be seeing a great deal of each other. Vivie replies: "Do you think my way of life would suit you? I doubt it." Her mother's response, a series of ultra-maternal clichés, sets her up for the kill. Mrs. Warren huffs: "Your way of life, indeed! What next? . . . Your way of life will be what I please, so it will. . . . Do you know who you're speaking to, Miss?" Vivie snaps back: "No. Who are you? What are you?"

> MRS. WARREN (*piteously*). Oh, my darling, how can you be so hard on me? Have I no rights over you as your mother?
> VIVIE. *Are* you my mother?

Vivie proceeds to spell out the issue which, from all appearances, will remain the principal one:

> MRS. WARREN (*appalled*). Am I your mother! Oh, Vivie!
> VIVIE. Then where are our relatives—my father—our family

friends? You claim the rights of a mother: the right to call
me fool and child; to speak to me as no woman in authority
over me at college dare speak to me; to dictate my way of
life; and to force on me the acquaintance of a brute whom
anyone can see to be the most vicious sort of London man
about town. Before I give myself the trouble to resist such
claims, I may as well find out whether they have any real
existence.

The question "Who was my father?" follows inexorably,
and Vivie quickly divines that her mother has been too
promiscuous to know the answer. Relentlessly, she calls
her on it, and Mrs. Warren "buries her face in her hands."

In the romantic and sentimental "courtesan play" (the
most renowned being *La Dame aux Camélias* and *The
Second Mrs. Tanqueray*, both performed with great success
just before Shaw began *Mrs. Warren's Profession*[41]), the
chief figure, whatever her attributes, invariably puts the
audience at ease sooner or later by deploring her past mis-
deeds. The person who listens to her repentance usually
represses his own horror and treats the outcast with mag-
nanimous sympathy and forgiveness. Two postulates rule
the uncritical spectator: first, a repentant courtesan is
necessarily a reformed one, and second, her discomforting
presence will not have to be endured very long. After her
confession, a show of submissive gentility and an atoning
suicide are the norms. When Mrs. Warren soulfully buries
her face in her hands, she acts out one of the tip-offs to
this pattern.

According to Vivie's consistent point of view, however,
the fact that her mother has been a promiscuous woman is
not in itself a crucial indictment; rather, it clinches the more
basic indictment that she is a woman of no purpose, character, or grit. Reacting with contempt rather than horror,
Vivie spots the sheer theatricality of her mother's gesture
and clips: "Don't do that, mother: you know you don't
feel it a bit." Still following the course that her vitalism

logically dictates, she abruptly dismisses the subject from her mind and asks her mother what time she would like breakfast. This glaring obliviousness to conventional feelings (the kind we observed in Charteris) subsequently leads Vivie to state her point of view with an equally oblivious clarity:

> MRS. WARREN (*wildly*). My God, what sort of woman are you?
> VIVIE (*coolly*). The sort the world is mostly made of, I should hope. Otherwise I don't understand how it gets its business done.

For Vivie, the "battle royal" has come to an end: she has reduced her mother to submission. After granting her a token of condescension, she suggests going to bed. For spectators, however, a sequel is mandatory, and Mrs. Warren's reactions encourage them to suppose that the sequel will be a typical one. Every line hints an impending collapse into confession and repentance.

> MRS. WARREN (*querulously*). You're very rough with me, Vivie.
> VIVIE. Nonsense. What about bed? It's past ten.
> MRS. WARREN (*passionately*). What's the use of my going to bed? Do you think I could sleep?
> VIVIE. Why not? I shall.
> MRS. WARREN. You! You've no heart.

Indeed, it is Vivie rather than her mother who apparently will not break down; Mrs. Warren seems ready to. Vivie's departure from the type demanded at this point, that of a sympathetic confessor, becomes an irritant which transfers a degree of favor to her mother. The audience, relishing its coming fare, nods agreement that Vivie has no heart.

But Shaw neither permits Vivie to go to bed nor gratifies the spectator's conventional wishes. At precisely this key moment, he convicts both of a meanly false judgment. He employs Mrs. Warren to show emphatically, first, that a prostitute can indeed be a woman of character, and second, that capitalist society as a whole is to blame for her choice of profession. The agent of this propaganda brazens her way through her function so forcefully that she carries Vivie overboard into diametrically opposite false judgments. Far from considering her mother a waster as she did before, Vivie comes to believe that she is "stronger than all England." And far from regarding her choice of profession as a conclusive sign of weakness, she finally attributes it to circumstances alone.

Shaw accomplishes this dual object by using the power of raw emotion, not primarily that of lucid ideas. What he refers to in his *Apology* (p. 45) as the "remorseless logic and iron framework of fact" underlying Mrs. Warren's defense is, in technical terms, a necessary but not sufficient condition of the desired effect. Mrs. Warren "suddenly breaks out vehemently in her natural tongue—the dialect of a woman of the people—with all her affectations of maternal authority and conventional manners gone, and an overwhelming inspiration of true conviction and scorn in her." The immediate result is that Vivie becomes "no longer confident; for her replies, which have sounded convincingly sensible and strong to her so far, now begin to ring rather woodenly and even priggishly against the new tone of her mother." Mrs. Warren prepares to relate the circumstances that led her into prostitution: "she plants her chair farther forward with brazen energy. . . . Vivie is impressed in spite of herself." One climax in the progression of "remorseless logic" which Mrs. Warren propels across the footlights comes when she rails against prostitutes who also happen to be wasters. She proclaims with great energy: "I despise such people: they've no character." The second comes when Vivie, "more and more deeply moved," offers what is actually the acid test of her mother's position: "Mother: suppose we were both as poor as you were in those wretched old days, are you quite sure that you wouldn't advise me to try the Waterloo bar, or marry a labourer, or even go into the factory?" Mrs. Warren passes the test: "Of course not. What sort of mother do you take me for!" At the end of her rigorously organized and superbly conducted defense— a contemporary novelty in drama which prompted one critic to dub Shaw "Euclid" and the play "mere theorem"— the vindicated prostitute "yawns" and "stretches herself lazily, thoroughly relieved by her explosion, and placidly ready for her night's rest." Shaw refuted the misapprehending critic as follows:

> I promise my flatterer that when he is sufficiently accustomed to and therefore undazzled by problem on the stage to be able to attend to the familiar factor of humanity in it as well as to the unfamiliar one of a real environment, he will both see and feel that *Mrs. Warren's Profession* is no mere theorem, but a play of instincts and temperaments in conflict with each other and with a flinty social problem that never yields an inch to mere sentiment.
>
> I go further than this. I declare that the real secret of the cynicism and inhumanity of which shallower critics accuse me is the unexpectedness with which my characters behave like human beings, instead of conforming to the romantic logic of the stage.
>
> .   .   .   .
>
> Far from ignoring idiosyncrasy, will, passion, impulse, whim, as factors in human action, I have placed them so nakedly on the stage that the elderly citizen, accustomed to see them clothed with the veil of manufactured logic about duty, and to disguise even his own impulses from himself in this way, finds the picture as unnatural as Carlyle's suggested painting of Parliament sitting without its clothes. (*Apology*, pp. 47–49)

The "idiosyncrasy, will, passion, impulse, whim" in Mrs. Warren's defense give it a distinctive and compelling power. The audience as well as Vivie stands, if not convinced, at least inescapably convicted.

Chapter 3

Sean O'Casey on Shaw: "We Irish, when we think,
and we often do this, are just as serious and sober
as the Englishman; but we never hesitate to give a serious
thought the benefit and halo of a laugh. That is why
we are so often thought to be irresponsible, whereas,
in point of fact, we are critical realists, while
Englishmen often mistake sentimental mutterings
for everlasting truths."[1]

Critical Comedies

The method of convicting the audience of a meanly false judgment is especially appropriate to Shaw's general strategy in the propaganda plays, that of attacking ideals by means of unpleasant effects. The chief method of his critical comedies is to make his characters seem ridiculous when they act in accord with ideals and sympathetic when they behave naturally. The resulting "conflict of unsettled ideals," a conflict that takes place in the minds of spectators as well as on stage, is eminently appropriate to a strategy of ideal-destroying through *pleasant* effects; and in contrast to the *Unpleasant Plays*, this is the strategy of *Arms and the Man* (1893–94), *Candida* (1894–95), and *You Never Can Tell* (1895–96).* Yet when Shaw compared these plays with his previous efforts, he spoke of them as "works of dramatic art purely" (*CL*, I, 698). In 1896, he complained about the preference of his friends at the Independent Theatre, once a vanguard of Ibsenite drama, for "those plays of mine which have no purpose except the purpose of all poets & dramatists as against those which are exposures of the bad side of our social system."[2] A precise understanding of these somewhat exaggerated statements is vital before

* The other play in the *Pleasant Plays* volume, *The Man of Destiny* (1895), will be treated as a humanization of an heroic type of drama.

examining the ethical tactics of the *Pleasant Plays*. We cannot simply dismiss Shaw's distinction on the grounds that he was peeved at the Independent Theatre managers for becoming "wretchedly respectable," though he certainly was.[3] It is best to go along with him temporarily and agree that the purpose of these plays is in some respects more aesthetic than ethical.

All three, for one thing, reveal close affinities with well-known traditional genres: romantic comedy, sentimental or "tearful" comedy, and the comedy of manners. *Arms and the Man*, despite similarities to military melodrama, derives most of its lasting effects from a series of near-farcical events which alternately advance and impede a pair of amusingly interlocked love affairs. In the manner of Shakespearean romantic comedy, the play tickles the spectator's sense of mental superiority, flutters his romantic impulses, and leaves him fully gratified at the end. Shaw's standard epithet for *Candida* is "sentimental." First subtitled a "domestic play" to indicate its contemporary alliances and then later called a "mystery," the play is undeniably much more than a latter-day *comédie larmoyante*.[4] Nevertheless, it bears some of the unmistakable marks of that genre: its story of a high-minded middle-class couple facing "tribulations" caused by the intrusion of an adolescent poet; its recurring atmosphere of mother-love; its final image of new-found manhood for the boy and restored domestic bliss for the couple. Shaw wrote *You Never Can Tell* as a "humanized" farcical comedy of the fashionably witty type prescribed by a specific theatre. But he also came very close to the pattern of the comedy of manners, with its gulling scenes, love intrigues and wit combats, and its distinctive sense of fellow-feeling with the intellectual ingroup and mockery of the outgroup. Through his attempt to enrich the form of farcical comedy, Shaw humanized the traditional genre as much as the currently popular one; but the play, like *Arms and the Man* and

Candida, still approximates the typical features and effects of a major comic genre to a surprising degree. Whatever else these three plays may be, they are first of all modern "classic" comedies.

Shaw himself liked to find a classic vein of comedy in all his plays, and his rationale is revealing. As we might expect, he even warps his aesthetic definitions toward his ethical aims. "It is the business of the writer of a comedy," he said in 1924, "to wound the susceptibilities of his audience. The classic definition of his function is 'the chastening of morals by ridicule.' "[5] During his early period, he gave the same idea an added twist: "The function of comedy . . . is nothing less than the destruction of old-established morals."[6] Note that this function, as Shaw conceives it, is also a self-destructive one. As it gradually succeeds in its work of destroying outmoded ideals, it gradually disintegrates. The very attempt to eliminate ideals therefore ceases to have its intended effect the moment that effect has come about. Furthermore, the incidental by-products of this function also cease to occur. Few spectators are now shocked, scandalized, or otherwise emotionally stricken when Morell's idealistic view of the reasons for his wife's fidelity receives its comeuppance; they no longer share his ideals. Actually, few of the "old-established morals" Shaw attacked have completely lost face in the last seventy years (much less his final target, the basic tendency to cherish ideals); but from a long-term literary point of view, the specific ethical effects he sought must be recognized as transitory, ephemeral things. What we have ultimately are effects close to those of classic comedy: an arousing and purging away of sympathy and ridicule.

Even from the standpoint of ultimate artistic form, however, his ideal-destroying intentions are highly important. Because of them his comedies, classic or not, are undeniably unique in organization, emphasis, and tone. Their distinctive and enduring qualities that derive from his ethical aim can be singled out by comparing his type of comedy with satire. Shaw, first of all, does not attack departures from widely accepted norms of conduct, as the satirist typically does; he attacks the norms as such. But since norms are changeable, this is not an ultimate difference. More crucially, he rejects the satirist's technique of ridiculing not only the vices and follies of his characters, but the characters themselves. To assault ideals more efficiently, he combines sympathy for his ideal-ridden characters with ridicule of their ideals, thus isolating his real targets and avoiding waste. Sympathy, used strategically or not, is rarely an ingredient of satire. Most significant of all, his comedies feature explicit and genuine dissections of ideals. Although these analyses occur only sporadically, they are still deliberate "criticisms of false intellectual positions which, being intellectual, are remediable by better thinking" (Shaw's words).[7] Such elements are hardly conspicuous in satire. Shaw once distinguished between the satire in Molière's plays and the "criticism" in his own; we might well take his clue and identify the three early comedies as a special breed, "critical" comedy.[8] The term at least conveys that Shaw was willing to have them become "mere" classic comedies if they first served their ground-clearing evolutionary purpose.

COMEDY IN THE CONTROVERSIAL STAGE OF DRAMA

Spectators in the nineties were by no means prepared to respond to *Arms and the Man*, *Candida*, and *You Never Can Tell* as classic comedies, or even as comparatively pleasant plays. To all but Shaw's most advanced contemporaries, they were satires. The Prince of Wales walked out of a performance of *Arms and the Man* in a huff, muttering that Shaw must be a madman. A critic called the play "an offensive caricature and an apparent attack upon a nation, chiefly known . . . for her gallant struggle against tyranny and oppression." The real object of *Candida*, one critic presumed, "is to enable Mr. Shaw to expound his cynical philosophy and satirise the foibles of humanity."[9] The discrepancy between these estimates of the plays and Shaw's own (which we might roughly equate with present estimates) clearly springs from the susceptibility of his critics to codified ideals and romantic illusions.

Let us see how this discrepancy pertains to *Arms and the Man*. Preparing to write the play, Shaw read documents relating the experiences of military men.[10] Having formed a picture of military life based on first-hand information, he conceived a play in the traditional mode of romantic comedy. The conception involved several types of soldiers, several points of view toward them, and several disillusionments brought about by revelations of their actual nature. Shaw was perfectly aware that his comedy, as far as its effect was concerned, would initially amount to a "comedy of the collision of the realities represented by the realist playwright with the preconceptions of stageland"; and he even made this collision, "in a sense, the subject of the play" (*Shaw on Theatre*, pp. 23–24). In fact, given the decision to write a romantic comedy, Shaw had little reason to choose the military profession as the focal center of his play unless he sought, at least collaterally, to attack the preconceptions of stageland. Still, his ideal-destroying aims did not prevent him from composing a "work of dramatic art purely." He built his ethical purpose into an artistic design that exhibits "the purpose of all poets & dramatists." As a result, *Arms and the Man* has alternative subtitles, "a romantic comedy" and "an anti-romantic comedy," and both are fully justifiable. The first is appropriate in all

stages of the evolution of drama, the second in its "controversial" stage.

Shaw defines this stage as a period in which the higher
drama begins to gather momentum but is obstructed by the
prevalence of "false intellectual positions." About the time
he was finishing *Candida*, Shaw wrote an illuminating letter
to Henry Arthur Jones, a playwright he wanted to seduce
into his own camp. By way of defending himself against the
charge that he was a doctrinaire in drama, he explained his
predicament as a dramatist far ahead of his time:

> The conception of me as a doctrinaire . . . is a wrong one.
> On the contrary, my quarrel with the conventional drama
> is that it is doctrinaire to the uttermost extreme of dogma-
> tism. . . . I find that when I present a drama of pure feeling,
> wittily expressed, the effect when read by me to a picked
> audience of people in a room is excellent. But in a theatre,
> the mass of the people, too stupid to relish the wit, and too
> convention-ridden to sympathise with real as distinct from
> theatrical feeling, simply cannot see any drama or fun there
> at all; whilst the clever people feel the discrepancy between
> the real and theatrical feeling only as a Gilbertian satire on the
> latter, and, appreciating the wit well enough, are eager to
> shew their cleverness by proclaiming me as a monstrously
> clever sparkler in the cynical line. . . . Here and there, of
> course, I come across a person who was *moved* by the play.
> (*CL*, I, 462)

The higher drama, in other words, provokes bafflement,
indignation, or unintended hilarity because conventional
doctrine is so pervasive. Shaw goes on to say that despite
these perverse reactions he continues to write plays, partly
because they develop in his mind "out of their own vitality,"
but also because he is sure that in twenty years the public
will "see feeling and reality where they see nothing now
but mere intellectual swordplay and satire. . . . That is
what always happens."

The controversial stage of drama which Shaw describes

here and elsewhere involves, first, the overriding impulse of a genius to express himself in dramatic form. (At one point in the letter he apologizes for having assumed he is a genius.) Shaw attributes this impulse to the evolutionary prompting of the world will; thus from his point of view, he is the opposite of doctrinaire. In *The Sanity of Art*, written a few months later, he outlines recent controversial stages in art, music, and drama, and to account for them, proceeds inexorably into discussions of Schopenhauer and the master passions. To Shaw, the evolution of drama, like that of all social phenomena, derives from the will.

He proposes, second, that drama's controversial stage will inevitably dissipate after an inescapable clash with the public. Twenty years hence, people will accept without question things they repudiated earlier because they were unaccustomed to them. In an 1895 letter to the actor Charles Charrington, Shaw uses a favorite metaphor to explain this phenomenon: "I will let emotion and passion have all the play I can in my characters. But you must recollect that there is distinction [i.e., singularity] even in emotion and passion; and that the finer kinds will not run through the wellworn channels of speech. They make new intellectual speech channels; and for some time these will necessarily appear so strange and artificial that it will be supposed that they are incapable of conveying emotion. They said for many years, remember, that Wagner's endless melody was nothing but discord" (*CL*, I, 493).

Finally, Shaw divides the unaccustomed public's responses to the higher drama into two broad categories: an inability to "sympathise with real as distinct from theatrical feeling" and shallow hilarity at what seems like idle topsy-turviness. The latter reaction is as "convention-ridden" as the former, Shaw implies, since it derives from a Pavlovian expectation of the conventional or "theatrical" view. In the case of the comedy that Shaw is referring to (*Arms and the*

Man), both responses combined to cancel out those he had intended.

The responses that Shaw wanted to evoke are what he describes in various essays of 1894–96 as considerate sympathy and humane ridicule. The constructive side of his campaign to supplant ideals with realities was to make people sense the value of humanity as it naturally is, as opposed to what it allegedly should be. His experience as a propagandist playwright told him that artistically induced impressions—dramatic effects—could be just as useful in this effort as persuasive arguments, if not more so. He therefore worked into his critical comedies a subtle fabric of elements designed, first, to stimulate only "human" rather than "animal" emotions, and second, to prod the spectator into impulsively favoring natural over ideal behavior. Shaw presents the general theory behind this tactic in *The Sanity of Art*. Demonstrating the "solid usefulness" of art, he posits that "art should refine our sense of character and conduct, of justice and sympathy, greatly heightening our self-knowledge, self-control, precision of action, and considerateness, and making us intolerant of baseness, cruelty, injustice, and intellectual superficiality or vulgarity." He then defines the worthy and the great artist:

> The worthy artist or craftsman is he who serves the physical and moral senses by feeding them with pictures, musical compositions, pleasant houses and gardens, good clothes and fine implements, poems, fictions, essays, and dramas which call the heightened senses and ennobled faculties into pleasurable activity. The great artist is he who goes a step beyond the demand, and, by supplying works of a higher beauty and a higher interest than have yet been perceived, succeeds after a brief struggle with its strangeness, in adding this fresh extension of sense to the heritage of the race. (*MCE*, pp. 315–16)

To satisfy Shaw's minimum standard, then, the artist must

appeal only to the "heightened senses and ennobled faculties"; and to achieve greatness, he must make a tangible contribution to evolution by transcending the degree of cultivation that has already been attained.

Shaw pictures Ibsen and himself as avant-garde dramatists currently waging the great artist's evolutionary struggle against the lagging sensibilities of ordinary men. The way to close the gap, he says in a *Saturday Review* article, is for the dramatist to avoid "thriving parasitically" on spectators' "moral diseases," and to concentrate on "purging their souls and refining their senses" (*OTN*, I, 142). These moral diseases are of two kinds. One springs simply from man's most rudimentary responsive chords: his inherent tendencies, for instance, to cry over the death of a baby or to guffaw at a bit of horseplay. The other, more serious kind derives from his carefully nurtured habit of reducing complex situations to the simplistic terms of ideal codes of conduct. Shaw considers both types—the "lifeless" codes as well as the "mechanical" emotions—essentially inhuman. In another *Saturday Review* piece, he declares that the most striking and important quality in the attitude of the avant-garde dramatists is an "assertion of human worth" in opposition to these prevailing moral diseases (*OTN*, II, 143). It is precisely this assertion of human worth that underlies the dominant effects of his critical comedies.

Shaw's conception of sympathy emerges most clearly in his famous essay comparing Sarah Bernhardt and Eleonora Duse. The art of Sarah Bernhardt, he asserts, "is not the art of making you think more highly or feel more deeply, but . . . the art of finding out all your weaknesses and practising on them." She excels in the "brute" passions; Duse excels in the "distinctively human" ones. In Shaw's words:

> When it is remembered that the majority of tragic actors excel only in explosions of those passions which are common to man and brute, there will be no difficulty in understand-

ing the indescribable distinction which Duse's acting acquires from the fact that behind every stroke of it is a distinctively human idea. In nothing is this more apparent than in the vigilance in her of that high human instinct which seeks to awaken the deepest responsive feeling without giving pain. In La Dame aux Camélias, for instance, it is easy for an intense actress to harrow us with her sorrows and paroxysms of phthisis, leaving us with a liberal pennyworth of sensation.

.   .   .   .

As different from this as light from darkness is the method of the actress who shews us how human sorrow can express itself only in its appeal for the sympathy it needs, whilst striving by strong endurance to shield others from the infection of its torment. That is the charm of Duse's interpretation. . . . It is unspeakably touching because it is exquisitely considerate: that is, exquisitely sympathetic. No physical charm is noble as well as beautiful unless it is the expression of a moral charm; and it is because Duse's range includes these moral high notes . . . that her compass . . . so immeasurably dwarfs the poor little octave and a half on which Sara Bernhardt plays such pretty canzonets and stirring marches. (*OTN*, I, 150–52)

Moral charm, considerateness, withdrawal from the animal passions in man are the vital components of Shaw's brand of sympathy.

The same attentiveness to human worth determines the nature of his brand of ridicule. Just as Shaw requires moral charm in attempts to stir the passions, he requires moral earnestness in attempts to provoke laughter. He consistently rebukes William S. Gilbert for being no more than a virtuoso of the idle paradox. Shaw thought Gilbert clever enough to ridicule ideals, but also artistically immoral enough "to depend for the piquancy of his ridicule on the general assumption of the validity of the very things he ridiculed." Such a trick is "morally unjustifiable."[11] Shaw also insists that ridicule, like sympathy, should avoid merely triggering the spectator's tropistic reactions. Echoing his disparaging 1895 review of *The Importance of Being Earnest,* he once called Wilde's delectable farce "essentially hateful" because it lacks "that proximity [to] emotion without which laughter, however irresistible, is destructive and sinister."[12] In view of his aesthetic theories, his dislike for the play seems inevitable. *The Sanity of Art* calls the artist who exploits the physical and moral senses a "pandar" or a "prostitute"; the worthy artist must refine, not merely play upon, these senses. To Shaw, *The Importance of Being Earnest* violates this fundamental requirement. Therefore he says in his review: "It amused me, of course; but unless comedy touches me as well as amuses me, it leaves me with a sense of having wasted my evening. I go to the theatre to be moved to laughter, not to be tickled or bustled into it; and that is why, though I laugh as much as anybody at a farcical comedy, I am out of spirits before the end of the second act, and out of temper before the end of the third, my miserable mechanical laughter intensifying these symptoms at every outburst" (*OTN*, 1, 42–43). Shaw repeatedly condemns the inhumanity of plays which "tickle" the spectator into laughing. His most consummate attack appears in "The Farcical Comedy Outbreak":

> To laugh without sympathy is a ruinous abuse of a noble function; and the degradation of any race may be measured by the degree of their addiction to it. In its subtler forms it is dying very hard: for instance, we find people who would not join in the laughter of a crowd of peasants at the village idiot . . . booking seats to shout with laughter at a farcical comedy, which is, at bottom, the same thing—namely, the deliberate indulgence of that horrible, derisive joy in humiliation and suffering which is the beastliest element in human nature.
>
> .   .   .   .
>
> I class the laughter produced by conventional farcical comedy as purely galvanic, and the inference drawn by the audience that since they are laughing they must be amused

or edified or pleased, as a delusion. They are really being more or less worried and exhausted and upset by ill-natured cachinnation; and the proof is that they generally leave the theatre tired and out of humor with themselves and the world. (*OTN*, II, 118–20)

Concern for the distinctively human in man—what Shaw often speaks of as "our common humanity"—must be an ingredient in the ridiculous as well as the sympathetic side of comedy. In short, ridicule must also be humanely sympathetic.

Shaw's requirements for the serious writer of comedy, then, are entirely commensurate with his aesthetic theories, and equally stringent. It is illuminating to juxtapose the two. The worthy dramatist, to Shaw, will remain within the "wellworn channels of speech" for the responses that he evokes; however, he must address this appeal only to the "heightened senses and ennobled faculties." Neither his ridicule nor his sympathy should cater to man's "moral diseases": both should adhere to the distinctively human, whether popularly recognized as such or not. The great dramatist, a step above the worthy one, will incorporate into his plays an advance in artistic form or, more often, in current morality. Such an advance will represent both an expression of personal will and an assertion of human worth. These integrated forces will result in a power of artistry which will enable the dramatist to "make new intellectual speech channels" so that, after a brief struggle, he will succeed in adding a "fresh extension of sense to the heritage of the race." Meanwhile, he must expect to strike the public as a baffling, scandalous, or—worse yet—merely paradoxical writer. Since he fully intends to have his way in the long run, he will oppose resistance by using strategies which are sometimes overt and polemic, sometimes underground and permeative. Whatever the strategy, his acute awareness that the higher drama is presently engaged in evolutionary warfare will notably affect his work. Not at all surprisingly, this Shavian image of the great dramatist at work closely resembles Shaw's own activities during the middle eighteen-nineties.

He reflected much later: "I lived in a world unknown to the actors, playwrights, and narrowly specialised playgoers of that day, and had to create my audiences as well as my plays."[13] By 1894, only one of his propaganda plays had reached the stage, and that for only two performances. Obviously Shaw could not create his audiences, much less recreate English drama, by wilfully continuing to write problematic and unpleasant plays. First he had to gain at least a tenuous foothold in the English theatre. Accordingly, to the extent that he could bring himself to bend his dramaturgy toward a more popular theatrical form, he did so. The result was a series of plays which avoid grim facts and feature pleasing effects, but which are still thoroughly conditioned by the purpose Shaw revealed to Ellen Terry in 1897: "The theatre is my battering ram as much as the platform or the press" (*CL*, I, 722).

The aggressiveness of Shaw's determination at this time, as reflected in such statements, can be accounted for to some extent by the fact that his interest in the English theatre itself had greatly increased. He began writing weekly drama critiques for the *Saturday Review* in January 1895. By this time he had completed five full-length plays, all of which he intended to stage whenever he could secure competent acting companies for them without compromising his delicate position as critic of their performances. In 1892 and again in 1894 he supervised the production of his own plays; and from 1890 on—not at all a negligible side-light—he spent innumerable hours communicating (in one way or another) with Florence Farr, Janet Achurch, Ellen Terry, and other actresses of an intellectual sort.

More significant factors than these, however, caused the

compelling sense of mission that Shaw brought to his theatrical activities after 1893. A combination of ideas, most of them rarely found in his writings before this date, convinced him finally that the theatre could perhaps be more of a battering ram than the other outlets for his "public work." First, he came to believe that the theatre itself, whatever its standards might be, exerted a vast influence on human conduct. In the mid-nineties, Shaw urged this view upon his readers again and again.[14] His preface to a 1906 selection of the *Saturday Review* articles gaily announces that, of all things, a comparison of theatre and church attendance has indicated that he was right: "Only the ablest critics believe that the theatre is really important: in my time none of them would claim for it, as I claimed for it, that it is as important as the Church was in the Middle Ages and much more important than the Church was in London in the years under review" (*OTN*, I, vi). Shaw is not exalting the theatre; he is affirming its potential power as a source of motivation for men's actions, good or bad. His object in the *Saturday Review* and in his plays was ultimately to steer this power in a direction that would hasten world-betterment. By laying siege to the theatre "at the point of the pen," as he says, he tried to transform it into "a factory of thought, a prompter of conscience, an elucidator of social conduct, an armory against despair and dullness, and a temple of the Ascent of Man" (*OTN*, I, vii). Fundamentally, "Ascent" is what he was after.

Shaw's rationale for these opinions is far from perverse. In 1894 he summed up its basic tenet as follows: "It is feeling that sets a man thinking, and not thought that sets him feeling." Or, stated another way: "You cannot witness *A Doll's House* without *feeling*, and, as an inevitable consequence, thinking."[15] A well-known passage in his *Apology* for *Mrs. Warren's Profession* elaborates upon this idea: "I am convinced that fine art is the subtlest, the most seductive, the most effective means of moral propagandism in the world, excepting only the example of personal conduct; and I waive even this exception in favor of the art of the stage, because it works by exhibiting examples of personal conduct made intelligible and moving to crowds of unobservant, unreflecting people to whom real life means nothing" (p. 25).

The second set of ideas that led Shaw to regard the theatre as a battering ram relates to the growth of his outlook on social evolution. By 1894, his anticapitalist zeal had apparently relaxed to a marked extent. Not that he labored less for the Fabian cause; but he shifted the center of his attention away from economic problems and closer to the broad base of social evolution. For one thing, he evidently decided that glaring literary images of the "social horrors" under capitalism (like those that jolt Harry Trench and Vivie Warren) often produced only an enervating pessimism because of the way they conflicted with still-unquestioned assumptions about what life ought to be like. Even more essentially, he felt with increasing conviction that the collective will of the capable masses—that force which would bear society forward and upward if it were unobstructed—was effectively blocked by the inhibiting influence of social codes. Concluding his preface to the *Pleasant Plays*, Shaw declares: "To me the tragedy and comedy of life lie in the consequences, sometimes terrible, sometimes ludicrous, of our persistent attempts to found our institutions on the ideals suggested to our imaginations by our half-satisfied passions." In other words, the constricting presence of social conventions—the strong tendency to follow the line of least resistance and do what others do—closes the natural outlet of the will-driven passions. The passions thus feed on imaginary ideals, and by default these ideals become the fragile building blocks of social institutions. Shaw says in an 1896 article: "Nothing is more significant than the statement that 'all the world's a stage.' The whole world *is* ruled by theatrical illusion. . . . The case is not one of fanciful similitude but of identity" (*OTN*, II, 267). Later he relates the English theatre itself to this idea; taking issue with a critic of the Walkley type, he asserts: "[Augustin Filon] writes about the theatre as if it were merely a self-contained artistic contrivance. . . . But the theatre is also a response to our need for a sensible expression of our ideals and illusions and approvals and resentments. As such it is bound to affect our ideas, and finally our conduct, even to the extent of setting on foot the strangest functional adaptations in society to the morality it imposes on us through our imaginations" (*OTN*, III, 152).

The constructive side of this anti-idealist conviction is the third and conclusive set of ideas which prompted Shaw to besiege the English theatre as he never had before. After proclaiming in his preface to *Pleasant Plays* that the tragedy and comedy of life lie in the consequences of our attempts to found our institutions on theatrical ideals, he adds, "instead of on a genuinely scientific natural history." The alternative to illusion is of course reality, and Shaw is championing reality as the basis for social institutions. But he goes beyond this truism: he is mainly clamoring for people to *respect* reality, especially that of their own aspirations. What baffles critics when they deal with his plays, Shaw says elsewhere in the preface, is his "conception of romance as the great heresy to be rooted out from art and life—as the root of modern pessimism and the bane of modern self-respect" (p. xv). Farther on, he eloquently states his major point:

> the real issue between my critic and myself . . . [is whether idealism] will survive the general onslaught on idealism which is implicit, and indeed explicit, in *Arms and the Man* and the realistic plays of the modern school. For my part I

hope not; for idealism, which is only a flattering name for romance in politics and morals, is as obnoxious to me as romance in ethics or religion. . . . I can no longer be satisfied with fictitious morals and fictitious good conduct, shedding fictitious glory on overcrowding, disease, crime, drink, war, cruelty, infant mortality, and all the other commonplaces of civilization which drive men to the theatre to make foolish pretences that these things are progress, science, morals, religion, patriotism, imperial supremacy, national greatness and all the other names the newspapers call them. On the other hand, I see plenty of good in the world working itself out as fast as the idealist will allow it; and if they would only let it alone and learn to respect reality, which would include . . . respecting themselves, . . . we should all get along much better and faster. At all events, I do not see moral chaos and anarchy as the alternative to romantic convention; and I am not going to pretend that I do to please the less clear-sighted people who are convinced that the world is only held together by the force of unanimous, strenuous, eloquent, trumpet-tongued lying. (p. xviii)

In his defense of *Arms and the Man*, "A Dramatic Realist to His Critics" (1894), Shaw remarks that the play is essentially a drama of real life. Then he exhorts his readers much as he does above: "I now plead strongly for a theatre to supply the want of this sort of drama. I declare that I am tired to utter disgust of imaginary life, imaginary law, imaginary ethics, science, peace, war, love, virtue, villainy, and imaginary everything else, both on the stage and off it. I demand respect, interest, affection for human nature as it is" (*Shaw on Theatre*, pp. 38–39). Three years later, in the process of reviewing Louis Parker's *Vagabond King*, Shaw described his intentions in shaping *Arms and the Man* for the contemporary stage. Critics have largely abused Parker's play, Shaw says, but they have also found something "beautiful and true" in it. He proceeds to lash both the critics and Parker:

To me this bit of romantic beauty and truth is a piece of

immoral nonsense that spoils the whole work. If Mr Parker wishes to get on safe ground as a dramatist, he must take firm hold of the fact that the present transition from romantic to sincerely human drama is a revolutionary one, and that those who make half-revolutions dig their own graves. Nothing is easier than for a modern writer only half weaned from Romance to mix the two, . . . [and] this is precisely what has happened to Mr Parker. . . . If this were done purposely, with the object of reducing the romantic to absurdity, and preaching the worth of the real, there are plenty of works, from Don Quixote to Arms and the Man, to justify it as the classic formula of the human school in its controversial stage. (*OTN*, III, 225)

The greatest credit to these works, Shaw concludes, is their "affirmation of the worth of reality."

All three of the critical comedies are conceived as "revolutionary" works whose object, as Shaw says above, is to reduce the romantic to absurdity and to preach the worth of the real. In this sense, all three follow "the classic formula of the human school in its controversial stage." *Arms and the Man, Candida,* and *You Never Can Tell* are not only "realistic" but also "controversial" plays; they feature conflicts between elements of romance and elements of "a genuinely scientific natural history." The romantic elements become the targets for Shaw's sharpshooting; he handles them like clay pigeons, setting them up before the audience for the express purpose of shooting them down. The realistic elements—those which project the value of life as it is—are Shaw's conceptual weapons. From the standpoint of dramatic effect, he attacks with that intermingled combination of considerate sympathy and humane ridicule which he prefers. By carrying out this strategy within bounds dictated by the requirements of contemporary theatres, Shaw does everything currently in his power, restricted as it is, to destroy romantic ideals and to preach the worth of the real through the medium of drama.

THE *PLEASANT PLAYS* AND
RESPECT FOR REALITY

Arms and the Man

The most clear-cut example of this strategy occurs in *Arms and the Man*. Shaw arouses the conventional expectations of romantic drama, deliberately violates them, and finally exults in his triumph by having the utterly prosaic professional soldier, Captain Bluntschli, declare with sincerity that he has "an incurably romantic disposition." This naturally astounds the deposed romantic hero, Major Sergius Saranoff, who has wondered whether Bluntschli is a man or a machine; but even he comes to conclude that the values Bluntschli represents are better than his own unattainable ideals. At the curtain, the former idealist hails the realist with the meaningful words: "What a man! What a man!"[16]

An atmosphere of heavily theatrical romance that would appeal to most Victorian spectators emerges at the start of the play when the beautiful heroine, Raina Petkoff, responds rapturously to the news that Sergius, her fiancé, has led a victorious cavalry charge. Raina admits that she had been skeptical about her heroic ideals, a symptom of weakness that the audience—cued by her mother—would tenderly rebuke. The news of Sergius's gallantry has convinced her, however, that "the world is really a glorious world for women who can see its glory and men who can act its romance." Just before the antitheatrical hero, Bluntschli, sneaks into her bedroom, Raina gazes at a picture of Sergius and reverently murmurs, "My hero!"

From this point on, Shaw systematically deromanticizes Raina, along with those spectators who share her point of view. He does so largely by evoking favor for Bluntschli at the expense of idealist preconceptions. As the moments pass in Act I, the grimy, exhausted "chocolate cream soldier" engenders more sympathy than derision; and meanwhile he unwittingly exposes Sergius's deed as that of a lucky Don Quixote. The irresponsible nature of the deed is verified in Act II by Sergius himself, who also reveals startling nonidealist tendencies with a pretty maid (while Raina is peeking) and inadvertently informs Raina of Bluntschli's good sense in battle. On stage again in the third and final act, the realist stirs direct admiration as a vigorous, competent military officer, and displays the immense advantages of behaving naturally, as compared to emulating megalomaniac visions of oneself. (This gradual process of deromanticizing Raina and the audience reaches a high point early in the last act.) When Bluntschli resists believing that Raina has told no more than two lies in her entire life, she is first incensed, but then suddenly undergoes "a complete change of manner from the heroic to the familiar" and asks him, "How did you find me out?" Later, she proves that she has become clear-sighted by spotting his unconscious application of romantic premises about the way marriages are made. Figuring that no grown woman would abandon propriety in pursuit of a husband to the extent that Raina has, he mistakes her for a girl of seventeen (she is twenty-three). In response, she calls him "a romantic idiot." By the end of the play, Shaw has induced even his idealist spectators to prefer Bluntschli over Sergius as a husband for Raina. With a glint of irony, he gratifies their wishes in the traditional mode of romantic comedy. Bluntschli, a typical *jeune premier* for once, proposes marriage "with confident mastery"; Raina succumbs "with a shy smile"; and the Captain, before snapping back into his businesslike manner, reacts "with a boyish laugh of delight." These broad ideal-destroying tactics are supplemented by Shaw's treatment of the minor characters, particularly the servants Louka and Nicola, who show themselves worthy of higher stations in life mainly because of their Philistine immunity to ideals.

Most of the elements of character and action in *Arms and the Man* are clearly designed for the limited purpose of exploding a few highly vulnerable ideals, and are thus notably lacking in richness and complexity. Given an audience free of drastic illusions about war, "the higher love," defending one's honor, and marrying below one's station, the play becomes a straightforward (and somewhat thin) romantic comedy in the traditional vein. Indeed, by now most of the ideal points of view expressed with conviction by Sergius, Raina, and her parents are so amenable to caricature that performers tend to misrepresent them as such. When they do, Shaw's comedy becomes little more than an hilarious "galvanic" farce.[17] By 1904, Shaw himself "was startled to find what flimsy, fantastic, unsafe stuff it is."[18]

This estimate is belied to some extent by the play's elaborate handling of Sergius. Shaw's word "unsafe," in fact, may very well refer to the difficulty of this role: he told Richard Mansfield in 1894 that "all Sergius's scenes are horribly unsafe in second rate hands, whereas Bluntschli and Raina *cannot* fail" (*CL*, 1, 442). In any event, it is certain that Shaw gave Sergius the most important and complicated function in the play. The hero, Bluntschli, embodies an extreme, single-minded attitude toward ideals: the prosaic, businesslike, indulgent attitude of the professional realist. Unlike Sergius, he possesses only that degree of vitality which a generous and capable man needs, and he is for the most part passionless, if not quite a "machine." The heroine, Raina, changes her mind about ideals, but still exhibits another elementary extreme. She clings to them precariously, stifling her doubts and hopefully looking for verification; and when the doubts rather than the ideals are verified, she is converted with ease (besides, she now loves →

a realist). After her conversion she adopts an attitude toward her former ideals which can only be called negligible. The attitude that Sergius maintains, on the other hand, demands an intricate and concerted attack: he is the key figure in the antiromantic comedy. From the standpoint of Shaw's ethical intentions and artistic strategies alike, the main course of action in the play involves the gradual repudiation of Sergius's attitude through the combined forces of ridicule and sympathy.

To comprehend this course of action, we must first understand exactly what kind of target Sergius represents. Some of his qualities are not firmly linked to the outlook on life that the play is debunking; his "infallibly quick observation" and "acute critical faculty" (not to mention his vitality and courage) even contribute to the debunking process.[19] Indeed, a talent for perceiving reality characterizes Sergius as much as it does the person he is measured against, Bluntschli. The Major is a highly problematic target precisely because, barring experience, he has everything Bluntschli has except freedom from slavery to ideals. He is a man who sees life for what it is, but who exalts the ideal at the expense of life, not life at the expense of the ideal. To Shaw, he is thus a typical romantic pessimist.[20] Shaw condenses the Major's attitude into an epigram halfway through the last act of the play. When Raina charges Sergius with betraying their "higher love" by flirting with Louka, he confesses the fact, then avows cynically: "Raina: our romance is shattered. Life's a farce." Spelled out, his absurdly compressed statement means that people unquestionably should live up to their cherished ideals; but since they almost never do, "life's a farce" and cynicism is all it deserves. A moment later, Shaw has Bluntschli express the preferred alternative in his best shopkeeper's manner: "Life *isn't* a farce, but something quite sensible and serious."

Sergius is described in a long stage direction as a Byronic

hero on the model of Childe Harold. "By his brooding on
the perpetual failure, not only of others, but of himself, to
live up to his imaginative ideals, his consequent cynical
scorn for humanity, the jejune credulity as to the absolute
validity of his ideals and the unworthiness of the world in
disregarding them, . . . he has acquired the half tragic, half
ironic air, the mysterious moodiness] . . . by which Childe
Harold fascinated the grandmothers of his English contemporaries." That is, he is a victim of "the root of modern
pessimism and the bane of modern self-respect," romantic
ideals. Above all, he is a hero *manqué*, as Shaw calls him;
"man clings to the old pose, the old cheap heroism; and
[Sergius] . . . , whose life aspiration it has been to embody
that pose, feels, with inexpressible misgiving, the earth
crumbling beneath his feet as the enthusiasm his heroism
once excited turns to pity and ridicule" (*Shaw on Theatre*,
p. 50).

Shaw's inclusion of "pity" in this statement derives from
his belief that the ridicule necessary in an anti-idealist comedy should be humanely sympathetic. In his preface to the
Pleasant Plays, he says that he has made some of his key
stage effects depend on a "profoundly pitiful attitude
towards ethical conceptions which seem to [most people]
validly heroic or venerable" (pp. xiv–xv). *Arms and the
Man* clearly exhibits this policy in action for the first time
in Shaw's works. The chief agent of his ethical purpose in
the play, Bluntschli, is incurably frank and of course bluntly
realistic] Yet Shaw makes him remarkably considerate,
kind, and apologetic toward the people whose ideals fall in
his wake. Bluntschli transmits the effect of ridicule consistently: his practical, natural manner contrasts sharply
with the theatricality of Raina and Sergius, and his "professional point of view" gathers authority as the play
progresses. Yet he virtually never conveys this effect by
ridiculing a human being. Indeed, he shies away from

mockery, remains alert to the possible discomfiture of others, and only makes fun of someone—Sergius in the opening scene, for instance—when he is using him to exemplify a delusion.

The best illustrations of Bluntschli's sympathy involve the people who need it most, Sergius and Raina. In the first act, Bluntschli pictures the Major's foolish cavalry charge to Raina before he learns that she knows him. Raina, "steadfastly loyal to her ideals," shows him Sergius's portrait indignantly and says:

> That is a photograph of the gentleman—the patriot and hero—to whom I am betrothed.
>
> [BLUNTSCHLI] (*looking at it*). I'm really very sorry. (*Looking at her.*) Was it fair to lead me on? (*He looks at the portrait again.*) Yes: that's him: not a doubt of it. (*He stifles a laugh.*)
>
> RAINA (*quickly*). Why do you laugh?
>
> [BLUNTSCHLI] (*shamefacedly, but still greatly tickled*). I didn't laugh, I assure you. At least I didn't mean to. But when I think of him charging the windmills and thinking he was doing the finest thing—(*chokes with suppressed laughter*).
>
> RAINA (*sternly*). Give me back the portrait, sir.
>
> [BLUNTSCHLI] (*with sincere remorse*). Of course. Certainly. I'm really very sorry. . . . Perhaps I'm quite wrong, you know: no doubt I am. Most likely he had got wind of the cartridge business somehow, and knew it was a safe job.
>
> RAINA. That is to say, he was a pretender and a coward! You did not dare say that before.
>
> [BLUNTSCHLI] (*with a comic gesture of despair*). It's no use, dear lady: I can't make you see it from the professional point of view.

His point of view exposes the fact that Raina's white-black alternatives, admirable heroism and shameful cowardice, do not fit the picture that reality offers. Sergius has actually been a shamefully indiscreet hero, but by no means a cowardly one. Shaw brings about this exposure by applying the gentle, disillusioning comic touch that he typically employs in his early comedies. Moreover, he heightens the efficiency of his attack on ideals by making his destructive agent humane and sincerely remorseful, qualities that disarm the idealist's resistance and make his final surrender bearable.

A different kind of example of Bluntschli's sympathy occurs in Act III when he confronts Raina in another one of her self-righteous dudgeons. After she has heard directly from Sergius of his interest in Louka, she becomes so angrily sarcastic that the kindly realist steps in and acts as mediator between the two. Raina chides Sergius that he must fight a rival for Louka's hand, since she is already engaged to Nicola. The Major, adopting the manner of Othello, "rushes to and fro, raging," and calls the drab, middle-aged Nicola "Viper! Viper!" Bluntschli warns him that he is simply attracting further sarcasm from Raina, but instead of cooling down he responds by screaming "Tiger cat!"

> RAINA (*running excitedly to Bluntschli*). You hear this man calling me names, Captain Bluntschli?
> BLUNTSCHLI. What else can he do, dear lady? He must defend himself somehow. Come (*very persuasively*), don't quarrel. What good does it do? (. . . *after a vain effort to look vexedly at Bluntschli, [Raina] falls a victim to her sense of humor, and is attacked with a disposition to laugh.*)

Sergius is also infected with the laughter prompted by Bluntschli's down-to-earth attitude; then Raina says perceptively:

> I daresay you think us a couple of grown up babies, don't you?
> SERGIUS (*grinning a little*). He does, he does. Swiss civilization nursetending Bulgarian barbarism, eh?
> BLUNTSCHLI (*blushing*). Not at all, I assure you. I'm only very glad to get you two quieted. There now, let's be pleasant and talk it over in a friendly way.

The Captain blushes because Raina and Sergius have stung

him with the truth: his comments are much like those of the Mother Woman, Candida. In fact, his function throughout this scene is the maternal one of tempering painful, childish sarcasm and invective with sympathy and common sense.

This dramatic moment is the first in a concentrated series of effects by which Shaw artistically repudiates the cynical outlook of the romantic pessimist. From this moment until the curtain, Sergius's attitude is progressively reduced to its smallest elements, which are allowed to stand alone in all their glittering absurdity ("SERGIUS [folding his arms]. Nothing binds me."). Two specific developments provoke the Major to comprehend, bit by bit, that his characteristic attitude is a ludicrous and even incredible one. First, his conclusion that "life's a farce," quietly opposed by Bluntschli, comes to seem absurd to him as changes are rung upon it. Second, his sudden humanization from a caricature of Othello shouting "Viper!" and "Tiger cat!" into a self-confessed "baby" infected with laughter, again through the agency of Bluntschli, gradually impresses Sergius as respectably "pleasant" and "friendly." These two developments toward decreased cynicism and increased humanity are juxtaposed four times. When Sergius is first made to laugh, he remarks: "Ah, well, Bluntschli, you are right to take this huge imposture of a world coolly." That is, he drops his theatrics and wittily overstates his cynical position. Somewhat later, Raina's father discovers that she gave Bluntschli a portrait, and Petkoff exclaims to Sergius: "Do you mean to tell me that Raina sends photographic souvenirs to other men?" Sergius replies enigmatically: "The world is not such an innocent place as we used to think, Petkoff." Again, we sense a growing self-consciousness. The third juxtaposition occurs when Nicola sets Louka free from her engagement to him. After Nicola remarks that he became betrothed to her only to protect her, Sergius turns to Bluntschli and consults him according to the same white-black alternatives that Raina had posed: "This is either the finest heroism or the most crawling baseness. Which is it, Bluntschli?" The Captain, ever pragmatic, responds in terms that Sergius (who, after all, wants Louka) can readily accept: "Never mind whether it's heroism or baseness. Nicola's the ablest man I've met in Bulgaria." This artful dodge satisfies Sergius—a further sign of his personal rejection of his intransigent idealist point of view. Finally, after Sergius expresses astonishment at Bluntschli's declaration that he has "an incurably romantic disposition"—the peak of the antiromantic comedy—and witnesses the Captain's stupefaction when Raina proclaims her real age, he chortles with "grim enjoyment": "Bluntschli: my one last belief is gone. Your sagacity is a fraud, like all the other things. You have less sense than even I have." This open admission of the absurdity of his own views marks the end of his conversion, and also of Shaw's repudiation of romantic pessimism. Symptomatically, [Sergius discards one of his defining mannerisms—"I never apologize"]—and he does so for a practical reason: in order to win Louka. Soon afterwards, moreover, he refuses to discard "I never withdraw" —in order to keep her.

Along with the promised double marriage, the bounty heaped upon Bluntschli by his father's timely death, the final "What a man!" and the other trappings of traditional romantic comedy, the humanizing conversion of Sergius fulfils the audience's expectations and gratifies its carefully manipulated desires. In this sense, *Arms and the Man* is a "classic comedy," as Shaw dubbed it.[21] Nevertheless, the play is still a somewhat elementary product of Shaw's conscious involvement in the "controversial stage of drama"; and although it is undeniably delightful, it remains a work of comparatively minor stature. If we except *The Man of Destiny*, *Arms and the Man* is the least imposing of the

Pleasant Plays, however successful it may be as a deliberately antiromantic play.

Candida

    Just as successful, and greater in scope and intensity, is Shaw's next attempt to bring Victorian drama and morality up to date: *Candida: A Domestic Play* or *A Mystery.* Here, the conflict of ideals does not depend upon a convention-ridden audience for much of its effect: it takes place within the play itself, openly and tumultuously. Following Shaw's lead in the 1913 *Quintessence of Ibsenism,* we can say that this conflict has three stages: exposition, situation, and discussion. In the sense that ideals are introduced and clarified, the first act is wholly expository. The energetic minister James Morell, after surprising the audience with his broad-mindedness when he confronts his scoundrelly father-in-law, Burgess, shows that even a sophisticated parson can harbor precarious illusions about his wife, marriage, and family life in general. These ideals are exposed by an unlikely agent, the neurotic, self-styled competitor for Candida, Eugene Marchbanks. In so doing, Eugene pits his own poetic illusions against the ministerial ones of Morell; therefore his ideals are also brought to the fore in the act. The completely illusionless lady about whom the two men argue, Candida, suggests by her actions during her brief appearances that both views probably conflict as much with reality as they do with each other.

    The second and final acts, except for the concluding discussion, establish the situation that will have to be resolved. Morell comes to believe that his wife may indeed "belong" to Eugene, as the young poet has claimed. Candida herself reinforces this state of mind by inadvertently echoing some of the poet's denunciations of her husband,

then by picturing Eugene as a boy who may learn about
love from the wrong kind of woman if he does not from
her. In the third act, Morell misconstrues Eugene's symbolic
explanation of what happened when he was alone with
Candida, with the result that the tortured husband insists
on settling the matter at once. Candida settles it by committing herself to Morell. She does not stop after reconciling
herself with her husband, however; she must also resolve
the conflict of ideals. This she accomplishes by detailing the
needs of her two "babies," and in the process deftly punc-
turing Eugene's illusions about women, domesticity, and the
place of happiness in a poet's life. Thus the final discussion
becomes the crux of Shaw's ideal-destroying strategy.

Shaw says in *The Quintessence of Ibsenism* that a conflict
of unsettled ideals generally accounts for the dramatic
power of Ibsen and post-Ibsen plays. At first glance, it
might seem that the *Unpleasant Plays* feature conflicts of
this kind. Works such as *Mrs. Warren's Profession*, however, encourage the audience to concern itself less with the
validity of certain ideals than with the villainy of certain
characters. In this type of play the spectator is induced
to adjust and revaluate his punitive responses to Sartorius,
Mrs. Warren, and the like, not to wonder if he should prefer
Bluntschli's outlook to the contrasting one of Sergius or—a
trickier question—Eugene's ideals to Morell's. The technique
that recurs in the propaganda plays is that of convicting the
audience of a meanly false judgment, and this requires an
apparent villain (Sartorius, Mrs. Warren) or a false hero
(Charteris). Furthermore, nearly every character is made to
share a particular type of villainy, that of the capitalist system; thus there are always villains—or rather groups of reprehensible people much like those in the audience—and
never heroes. It is in the critical comedies that a conflict of
unsettled ideals becomes the dominant organizing principle.
The characters act on the basis of false ideals or mistakenly

consider other characters ideal, and these false intellectual positions provoke the conflict.

Shaw marks the borderline between the two strategies and at the same time throws an oblique light on *Candida* in the original *Quintessence* (1891). Ibsen's *Pillars of Society*, he says, is "disabled" as an ideal-destroying play because the hero "would hardly be accepted as a typical pillar of society by the class he represents." This remark applies to the cohorts in municipal jobbery of *Widowers' Houses*, the philandering and vivisecting men in *The Philanderer*, and the various "prostitutes" in *Mrs. Warren's Profession*. Shaw goes on to say that "Ibsen took care next time to make his idealist irreproachable from the standpoint of the ordinary idealist morality. In the famous Doll's House, the pillar of society who owns the doll is a model husband, father, and citizen. In his little household, . . . we have the sweet home, the womanly woman, the happy family life of the idealist's dream. Mrs Nora Helmer is happy in the belief that she has attained a valid realization of all these illusions . . . and that Helmer is an ideal husband" (*MCE*, p. 64). Substitute Morell for Nora, making him a "manly man" as well as the "doll" with illusions about his wife, and you have the starting point of *Candida*. Shaw recalled, late in life, that he had visualized the play as "a counterblast to Ibsen's *Doll's House*, showing that in the real typical doll's house it is the man who is the doll."[22] Moreover, audiences of 1897 were evidently surprised by the contrast (*HMC*, p. 544). But these are sidelights; what matters is that Shaw chose an "irreproachable" protagonist for the first time.

In fact, Morell is a sizable step above Helmer in irreproachability.[23] He recognizes that no law will bind Candida if she wishes to leave and that nothing in the conventional sense makes him master in his home. His ideals are not the kind that grant him an illusory position of

superiority to his wife, but the kind that mislead him about
the nature of the family unit itself. G. M. Young, in *Victorian England: Portrait of an Age*, poses the question:
"Who are these Victorians? By what mark are we to know
them? What creed, what doctrine, what institution was
there among them which was not at some time or other
debated or assailed?" He concludes that one of the very
few was "The Family"—precisely, "monogamic idealism."[24]
This observation aptly describes Morell's type of idealism
and implies its irreproachability at the time the play was
written.

Combining the angle of vision peculiar to his profession
with this unquestioned ideal, Morell visualizes his family
life as a microcosm of heaven. "Get married to a good
woman . . . ," he tells Lexy Mill, his curate. "That's a foretaste of what will be best in the Kingdom of Heaven we
are trying to establish on earth." The domestic analogue of
heavenly perfection that Morell suggests by such platitudes
takes its particular shape from his belief that the earth will
some day become a new heaven. This conviction is the root
of his illusions in the play. Shaw makes him an advocate of
Christian Socialism, a doctrine which had gained a large
following by 1894 partly because of the belief that Morell
expresses.[25] Shaw's Fabian meliorism postulates a very gradual, unending process of world-betterment; Morell's contrasting view is set forth in one of his capsule sermons to
Marchbanks: "I will help you to believe that God has given
us a world that nothing but our own folly keeps from being
a paradise. I will help you to believe that every stroke of
your work is sowing happiness for the great harvest that
all—even the humblest—shall one day reap." This is the
Marxian apocalyptic view of socialism, the view that Shaw
opposed in the *Fabian Essays*, in articles on Marx, and in a
brief paper written in 1894, the year he began *Candida*.[26]
Morell's restoration of God to this Marxian image explains

the popularity of his Christian Socialism; the image itself—
that of a heaven on earth—accounts for his ideal of family
life. It is not surprising, then, that he rounds out his speech
to Marchbanks by immediately shifting this image to the
domestic plane: "Last, but trust me, not least, I will help
you to believe that your wife loves you and is happy in her
home." Again, the illusion that marriage per se is a foretaste
of heaven on earth stands out conspicuously.

Shaw notes in a stage direction that Morell is "void of
subtlety," and his occasional parsonic orations to Marchbanks, Candida, and Lexy Mill may lead the modern reader
to place too much emphasis on this judgment.[27] It is extremely important to realize, however, that Shaw makes the
strongest case he can for Morell, given the nature of his
major illusion. Even his Christian Socialist idealism, according to the preface, is admirably "clear, bold, sure, sensible,
benevolent, *salutarily* shortsighted" (p. ix; my italics). A
stage direction describes him as vigorous, genial, pleasant,
hearty, and considerate: "a first rate clergyman, able to say
what he likes to whom he likes, to lecture people without
setting himself up against them, to impose his authority on
them without humiliating them, and to interfere in their
business without impertinence." His handling of Burgess
early in Act I is designed to enforce this impression.

In a letter written for Archibald Henderson, Shaw uses
Morell as an illustration in distinguishing between "the
satire of Molière and the criticism of Shaw":

> Molière does not criticise his doctors: he guys them. He
> represents them as humbugs who discuss their professional
> expenses with one another when they are pretending to dis-
> cuss their patients' symptoms. . . . The tradition of satire
> which vilifies what it criticises lasted well up to Shaw's time.
> . . . These lampoons are funny; but "they prove nothing,"
> though they are offered as valid evidence against the defen-
> dants' professions. Drunkenness or unctuous windbaggery

occur among Free Church ministers just as they occur among atheist lecturers: there is no organic connection in either case; and the suggestion that they are commonly associated is false: in fact the fun of the caricatures lies in their scandalous incongruity.

Shaw reverses the procedure. He strikes at Hector or Achilles, not at Thersites. Morell in *Candida*, though he is the butt of the piece, is "a first rate clergyman" without a single mean trait, who generously and affectionately owns up when he is convicted by his wife of being a little spoilt by his very pardonable masculine self-satisfaction. His gifts are genuine; and his character corresponds to them. (*HMC*, p. 740)

Aiming at "a really powerful and brilliant Morell," Shaw selected the highest type of clergyman he knew and attacked only those qualities which were organically connected with his profession, including a lack of subtlety.[28]

An urge for happiness, or more basically an assumption that happiness is the goal of human activity, lies beneath Morell's ideal of a domestic heaven on earth. In his speech to Marchbanks, he equates "paradise" with social and domestic bliss, and after his confrontation with him in the first act, he laments that an hour ago he was the happiest of men. Again, Shaw does not indict the man, Morell, by making his view sentimental or useless: Candida blames it on his upbringing, and it manifests itself in a prodigious amount of "salutary" work. On the contrary, he indicts the view itself, the ideal of supreme happiness, one which leads Morell and similar idealists to preach the worth of the unreal rather than that of the real. For one thing, Morell's urge for happiness and attendant desire for perfection in family life expose him to fears which would not exist if he had not implicitly left reality behind. Thus he is compelled to plead with the obdurate Marchbanks: "Even at home, we sit as if in camp, encompassed by a hostile army of doubts. Will you play the traitor and let them in on me?" Marchbanks will, of course: knowing how vulnerable Morell is, despite his physical superiority, he perceives that the clergyman is actually "the weaker of the two," and determines to crush his ideas.

Just as Morell's ideas are really ideals, however, so are those which the poet will pit against them. Morell has a clergyman's false ideals about his wife because he assumes that happiness is the proper goal of mankind; on exactly the same assumption, Marchbanks has a poet's false ideals about Candida. Shaw links *Don Quixote* to "the human school" of literature in its "controversial stage," and in *Arms and the Man*, chides the mock-heroic Sergius for tilting at windmills. He puts Marchbanks in the same tradition: "To Eugene, the poet living in a world of imagination and abhorring reality, Candida was what Dulcinea was to Don Quixote."[29] The world of imagination that Eugene dwells in revolves about the sentiment that he expresses in the second act: "To be beautiful and free and happy: hasn't every man desired that with all his soul for the woman he loves? That's my ideal." In Act III, he wants nothing more for himself than the happiness of being in love with Candida in the way that he is, and he proclaims to Morell: "I am the happiest of men. I desire nothing now but her happiness. (*With dreamy enthusiasm.*) Oh, Morell, let us both give her up." His conversion at the end of the play is tagged by Candida's comment that "he has learnt to live without happiness," and by his response: "I no longer desire happiness: life is nobler than that." He adds: "Parson James: I give you my happiness with both hands."

The rather maudlin poetic atmosphere in which Eugene bathes his ideal tended to mislead early spectators into accepting his position as valid without question, and it has even misled recent critics.[30] But the sentimentality which this atmosphere conveys is actually calculated to throw suspicion on Eugene's ideal. Instead of buying Candida the

new scrubbing brush that she needs, he wants to buy her
"a boat—a tiny shallop to sail away in, far from the world,
where the marble floors are washed by the rain and dried
by the sun, where the south wind dusts the beautiful green
and purple carpets. Or a chariot—to carry us up into the sky,
where the lamps are stars, and don't need to be filled with
paraffin oil every day." Morell intervenes with the harsh
but accurate moral thrust: "And where there is nothing to
do but to be idle, selfish and useless." These are the words
that Eugene abruptly translates into the adjectives "beautiful and free and happy." In contrast to Morell, Eugene is
indeed useless.[31] To be sure, he demonstrates some of the
"intensely utilitarian" virtues of the "highest genius"—for
example, the ability to sweep away the rubbish of cant—
and Shaw can therefore insist that the poet is "fiercely
practical."[32] But it is only after he decides that *life* is nobler
than happiness (this is the import of his conversion) that
the spectator discards his reservations about Eugene's impending value as an artist. The poet must first demonstrate
his own worth by affirming the worth of reality.[33]

Eugene's poetic apotheosis of a life of beauty, freedom,
and happiness prompts him to take an absurdly romantic
point of view toward Candida. He sincerely believes that he
and Morell should set her free. He comes to this conviction
not only because he is a person (to adapt Shaw) who
"imagines a treasure of tenderness and noble wisdom in the
beauty of a woman" (*MCE*, p. 264), but also because he
holds the quasi-Shelleyan notion that certain people, given
total freedom, are capable of enjoying a constant state of
unmitigated bliss. His reaction to Candida's beauty, along
with his ideal of liberated ecstasy, have led him in the past to
give her an autotype of Titian's Virgin of the Assumption.
They lead him during the play to talk ludicrously about her
as an angel who would continually dwell on the "highest
summits" drinking in "the silent glory of life" if she were

only turned loose from ugly household chores like peeling onions, from her husband's preaching, and even from that "wretched little nervous disease," himself. Worse, he rhapsodizes that the only worthy lover for her would be "some beautiful archangel with purple wings" ("Some fiddlestick," Morell fires back). Candida is partly wrong when she classes Eugene as one of those "poetic men, who imagine all women are angels"—he treats Prossy unexaltedly enough; but he cannot help viewing anything that does not belong in a heavenly realm as terribly inappropriate to Candida. Just as Morell's "monogamic idealism" exposes him to unwarranted fears, so Eugene's vision of a woman of supernal beauty makes him susceptible to what Burgess calls "the poetic 'orrors."

Obviously Morell has more at stake than Eugene, however; Candida is his wife (and "mother and three sisters"). His drastic illusions about her, products of the happiness that he derives from Candida but links to "paradise" in his clergyman's mind, carry much more dramatic weight than an adolescent poet's idle dreams. Specifically, he confides in her "goodness and purity," not in her love and her realization that he needs her. More broadly, he lacks a conscious awareness that he, not she, is the "doll" in the house. He protests distractedly to Eugene: "Oh, if she is mad enough to leave me for you, who will protect her? Who will help her? who will work for her? who will be a father to her children?" His parsonic bid for Candida in the final "auction scene" is in the same vein. In short, he totally misconceives the nature of the tie that binds them together.

Morell and Eugene are the main active participants in the conflict of unsettled ideals which supplies most of the drama in *Candida*. It is now necessary to sketch in a revised picture of Candida herself, the passive and conciliatory agent who unwittingly prompts this conflict. The picture that several critics have drawn bears little resemblance to the one Shaw encourages us to see, and the play will be incomprehensible if she remains fundamentally misunderstood. Marchbanks, despite his illusions, divines her essential character when he attacks Morell's notion that she must have someone to protect her. In a poetic fury—"snapping his fingers wildly" and dancing about—he rants: "It is she who wants somebody to protect, to help, to work for—somebody to give her children to protect, to help and to work for. Some grown up man who has become as a little child again. Oh, you fool, you fool, you triple fool! . . . You don't understand what a woman is."[34] Shaw immediately sends Candida in to verify this revelation: she hurries to her husband, "quite forgetting her wifely tact" in her annoyance at Eugene's attack on Morell, and insists: "My boy shall not be worried: I will protect him." In the concluding scene, Morell actually becomes "as a little child again," a symbolic action that Shaw humorously accentuates by seating him in a child-size chair. After Candida reminds him that he has been "spoiled from his cradle" and that she serves as "mother and three sisters and wife" for him, he admits "with boyish ingenuousness" that she is "the sum of all loving care" to him. In this manner, Candida is explicitly defined in the text itself.

But this is only a rough definition, and at any rate Shaw has issued a number of statements about her. These must be dealt with at some length, since they have confused many critics. Arthur Nethercot is the most imposing example; he goes beyond many commentators by taking full account of what Shaw says, and his interpretation of the play has been highly influential.[35] After noting that he has seen many performances of *Candida*, he presents his most extreme judgment: "I have watched the women in the audience wipe their eyes unashamedly and heard the men sigh secretively over their idol of womanly perfection. And yet I am confident that if the actresses had acted the part as Shaw wrote it and that if the audiences had known Shaw's real opinion of Candida there would have been hisses and boos instead" (*Men and Supermen*, p. 10). Shaw's real opinion of Candida, then, is crucial to Nethercot's argument.

He begins this argument by restating what he terms Shaw's "formula" in *The Quintessence of Ibsenism* for dividing up humanity into the classes of realist, idealist, and Philistine according to their points of view toward marriage. In Nethercot's rewording of Shaw, the Philistines are "the satisfied persons" who neither conceal the truth behind masks to preserve their ideals "nor bother themselves about realities, but vegetate contentedly as they are" (p. 3). He relegates Candida to "the static Philistine" class. The Shaw statement with which he supports this estimate occurs in a well-known 1904 letter to James Huneker.[36] Nethercot banks on such passages as the following: "Candida is as unscrupulous as Siegfried. . . . She seduces Eugene just exactly as far as it is worth her while to seduce him." "Nothing can be more coldbloodedly reasonable than her farewell to Eugene: 'All very well, my lad: but I don't quite see myself at fifty with a husband of thirty-five.' " Enlightened at last, Eugene considers the Morell home a "greasy fool's paradise." And Shaw concludes: "I should certainly be lynched by the infuriated Candidamaniacs if this view of the case were made known" (pp. 14–15). Near the end of his argument, Nethercot concedes that Candida "is both the mother-woman and the Philistine," and therefore "a Philistine, plus." But he counterbalances this slight reservation by extracting from the play the only estimate of Candida that another woman offers. Morell's secretary, Prossy, has been irritated by the way he glorifies his wife, and she snaps to Lexy Mill: "It's enough to drive anyone out of their *senses* . . . to hear a perfectly commonplace woman raved about in that absurd manner merely because she's got good hair, and a tolerable figure." This is Nethercot's trump card.

It is actually his weakest point, however. Prossy continues: "She's very nice, very good-hearted: I'm very fond of her and can appreciate her real qualities far better than any man can." The men, that is, appreciate only the unreal, ideal qualities they mistakenly grant her. Furthermore, Prossy calls her "perfectly commonplace" for two main reasons: first, because Candida *is* commonplace in contrast to the paragon men make her (poems "addle" her, for instance), and second, because Prossy is infatuated with Morell and thus jealous of his wife.[37] In any event, Shaw eliminated the words "perfectly commonplace" from the standard edition of the play.

As for Candida being "a static Philistine," according to *The Quintessence* Philistines are those who "comfortably accept marriage as a matter of course, never dreaming of calling it an 'institution,' much less a holy and beautiful one, and being pretty plainly of opinion that Idealism is a crackbrained fuss about nothing" (*MCE*, p. 27). They are the "satisfied" ones, as Nethercot says, but they do not necessarily "vegetate contentedly." It would be more in line with Shaw's "formula," in fact, to say that Candida is a realist rather than a Philistine. She is "strong enough to face the truth" (part of Shaw's definition) and she "insists on tearing off . . . masks, in order to expose the reality underneath" (part of Nethercot's). But then in Shaw's eyes, only one person in a thousand is a realist. Surely it would be best to assume that the quintessence of Shavianism, like that of Ibsenism, is that there is no formula.

What tells even more heavily against Nethercot's judgment are the passages from Shaw's letter which he reproduces but misinterprets. Shaw describes Candida as "that very immoral female, . . . a woman without 'character' in the conventional sense. . . . She is straight for natural reasons, not for conventional ethical ones." The import of these statements should be clear by now: Candida is simply an embodiment of realities, not ideals. She has no corrupting "morals" (a view that would infuriate "Candidamaniacs"—spectators who shared Eugene's idealized vision of Candida). As Shaw says further, she is "as unscrupulous as Siegfried." But Wagner's hero, to the Shaw of 1898, is the "perfectly naive hero upsetting religion, law and order in all directions, and establishing in their place the unfettered action of Humanity doing exactly what it likes, and producing order instead of confusion thereby because it likes to do what is necessary for the good of the race" (*MCE*, pp. 215–16). And Candida, though as "unscrupulous" as Siegfried, is by no means as "naive." If Nethercot had not omitted the chief clue to this in Shaw's letter to Huneker, he might not have misinterpreted Candida so drastically and led several other critics to do the same.[38] He omits the phrase I have italicized in the following: "It is just this freedom from emotional slop, *this unerring wisdom on the domestic plane*, that makes [Candida] so completely mistress of the situation."[39] Candida's "immorality"—her affinities with Siegfried—and her "unerring wisdom on the domestic plane" are in fact key elements in Shaw's conception of her. She "seduces" Eugene, the letter states, "just exactly as far as it is worth her while to seduce him": that is, enough to keep a hold on him so that she can apply her maternal wisdom to his youthful inadequacies.

After all, Eugene is only a "poor boy" to Candida. She is thirty-three; he is eighteen. In her long explanatory speech after he and Morell make their bids, she states in a "calm, sane, tender tone": "You remember what you told me about yourself, Eugene: how nobody has cared for you since your old nurse died: . . . how your father is trying to starve you into returning to Oxford: how you have had to live without comfort or welcome or refuge, always lonely, and nearly always disliked and misunderstood, poor boy!" Because he is a "poor boy" in this sense, Candida extends her vast sympathies to him and mothers him until she "makes a man of him." Her standard epithet for him throughout the play is "boy": in Act I she refers to him as "poor boy," "a dear boy," "a very nice boy," a "great baby," and "a good boy"; in Act II he is again a "poor boy" ("Did I make it slice nasty little red onions?" she adds); and in Act III he is a "bad boy," "a good little boy," "a foolish boy," and, finally, "poor boy!" Indeed, she mothers her husband almost as blatantly as she does Eugene: the play concludes with Morell in the child's chair being lectured to as "this other boy here—*my* boy." Her characteristic expression, Shaw says in a stage direction, is an "amused maternal indulgence."

Shaw's frequent comments on the play, especially those he made in the eighteen-nineties, lay stress on Candida's "unerring wisdom on the domestic plane." According to Stephen Winsten, he explained in late 1894 that "the person who was to play Candida must meditate and pray, must read the gospel of St. John and the *Lives of the Saints*, to be worthy of such a part. And the indispensable quality of all was dignity." He went on to present "his conception of fine womanhood: the calm dispassionate queen who hands out her favours to those who need her most."[40] Early in 1895, he told the actress whom he had in mind for the part, Janet Achurch: "You must part your hair in the middle, and be sweet, sensible, comely, dignified, and Madonna like. If you condescend to the vulgarity of being a pretty woman, much less a flashy one . . . you are lost" (*CL*, I, 502). Janet Achurch was, significantly, one of the two women Shaw knew "whose ideal of voluptuous delight was that life should be one long confinement" (*CL*, I, 645). In April 1896 Shaw wrote to the other maternal genius, Ellen Terry, that "Candida, between you and me, is the Virgin Mother and nobody else"; and, in August: "It is all very well for you to say that you want a Mother Play; but why didn't you tell me that in time? I *have* written THE Mother Play—'Candida' " (*CL*, I, 623, 641–42). He informed a drama critic in the same year that *Candida* is "the poetry of the Wife & Mother—the Virgin Mother in the true sense; & so on & so forth" (*CL*, I, 632). If Henderson is right, Shaw nearly always referred to the play in this manner.[41]

Shaw conceives of Candida, it appears, as a composite of two main ideas: a quasi-religious concept of "the Virgin Mother in the true sense" and an ethical concept of woman as Wife and Mother. Since the character of Candida bears almost the full weight of Shaw's affirmation of reality, and also since the play, as a sentimental comedy, leans heavily on the side of sympathy rather than ridicule, these two ideas require further clarification. Neither the Candida-maniacs nor the critics who reacted against them have done much more than confuse her image.

A large autotype of the chief figure in Titian's Virgin of the Assumption hangs at eye-level on the center wall throughout the entire play. Marchbanks presented this picture to Candida because "he fancied some spiritual resemblance" between her and the Virgin, as Shaw says in a stage direction. Any "wisehearted observer," he implies, would see that her "serene brow, courageous eyes, and well set mouth and chin" testify to this spiritual resemblance. To Shaw, they "signify largeness of mind and dignity of character." Eugene's dreamy effusions cannot all be trusted, but he seems to convey Shaw's idea when he sighs to Morell: "A woman like that has divine insight: she loves our souls." By means of this insight, Candida had previously made Eugene realize that his passion for her as a woman was in fact adoration for her as an angel.[42] Later, through the same insight, she prepares him to live without adoring an illusion, and thus without the happiness based on it. She smashes the illusion by unangelically detailing her maternal concerns about the "great baby," Morell, then by posing a question: "Am I *your* mother and sisters to you, Eugene?" (He responds with disgust, "Ah, never.") She makes him perceive, in other words, that she is the Virgin Mother in the *true* sense, not the ideal one.[43]

Shaw outlines his idea of "Woman as Wife and Mother" in *The Intelligent Woman's Guide to Socialism and Capitalism*. Approaching the subject from an economic point of view, he says: "The bearing and rearing of children, including domestic housekeeping, is woman's natural monopoly. As such, being as it is the most vital of all the functions of mankind, it gives women a power and importance that they can attain to in no other profession, and that man cannot attain to at all. In so far as it is a slavery, it is a slavery to Nature and not to Man: indeed it is the means by which women enslave men" (p. 176). This is much more than a rationale for Candida's "immoral" mothering; it is a glorification of it. As the "slavery to Nature" passage hints, in Shaw's eyes the basis of Motherhood is not primarily love. "I do not know whether women ever love," he avowed to Ellen Terry; "I rather doubt it: they pity a man, *mother* him, delight in making him love them; but I always suspect that their tenderness is deepened by their remorse for being unable to love him" (*CL*, I, 622).

The tie that really binds Candida to Morell and her children is not love but awareness of need. Shaw anticipates the famous oratorical period of the preface to *Man and Superman* ("This is the true joy in life, the being used . . . ") in another letter to Ellen Terry that analyzes love:

> Mind, I am not to be your lover, nor your friend; for a day of reckoning comes for both love and friendship. You would soon feel like the Wandering Jew: you would know that you *must* get up and move on. You must enter into an inexorably interested relation with me. My love, my friendship, are worth nothing. Nothing for nothing. I must be *used*, built into the solid fabric of your life as far as there is any

usable brick in me, and thrown aside when I am used up. It is only when I am being used that I can feel my own existence, enjoy my own life. . . . Everything real in life is based on need. (*CL*, I, 676)

Candida has entered into "an inexorably interested relation" with Morell because he obviously needs her—and also because she loves him, at least in the way a mother loves her baby.

The basis of Candida's affinity with the Virgin Mother and of her domestic wisdom is what Shaw terms "the primal republican stuff out of which all true society is made." This catholic idea is closely related to his distinctive view of sympathy. The role of Candida is one of those "sympathetic parts properly so called" which Shaw refers to in the *Saturday Review* as parts "where wisdom of heart, and sense of identity and common cause with others—in short, the parts we shall probably call religious as soon as we begin to gain some glimmering of what religion means—" communicate a sense of "reality" to the audience (*OTN*, III, 127). Two letters, again to Ellen Terry, clarify this idea considerably. "You boast that you are a fool," Shaw exhorts her, " . . . but you have the wisdom of the heart." He goes on to say that she may not be able to talk about philosophy or literature, "but one does not get tired of adoring the Virgin Mother" (*CL*, I, 623). A few weeks later he returns to his distinction between the fool and the wise of heart:

> We may all admire one another, enjoy one another, love one another, enter into all sorts of charming relations with one another; but all this is the mere luxury of human intercourse: behind it all, if it is to be really worth anything, there must be a certain deep and sacred respect for one another that we are free neither to give nor to withhold. It stands as an inexorable condition that we must not violate. It does not vary according to brains or beauty or artistic talent or rank

or age or education; and the difference between the wise of
heart and the fool is nothing but the difference between the
person who feels it & acknowledges it and the person who
doesn't. It is the primal republican stuff out of which all
true society is made. (*CL*, I, 643)

This "deep and sacred respect for one another," the mark
of "the wise of heart," is what Candida possesses to a degree that Shaw encourages us to call "divine." He has
Eugene say: "A woman like that has divine insight: she
loves our souls." To Shaw the soul is the will ("our old
friend the soul or spirit of man"); thus respect for the individual human soul is "an inexorable condition." His object
in *Candida* is to accomplish as effectively as possible the
destruction of ideals which violate this condition, and his
principal strategy involves the "divine" degree of sympathy
that Candida exudes. He manipulates her artistically so that
she creates proper channels for the ridicule which these
ideals alone deserve and so that she awakens sympathy to
the point of tears for the persons who uphold them. Moreover, the affirmation of reality represented by Candida
herself acts as an ideal-destroying undercurrent throughout
the play and provides a constant foil for Morell's and
Eugene's attractive delusions, especially their ministerial
or poetic advertisements of otherworldliness.

The two high points in this repudiation of ideals by
"laughter and tears" are Candida's talk with her husband
in the second act and the auction scene at the end. Eugene's
clash with Morell early in the play is not a central part of
the conflict of unsettled ideals; the illusions of these two
men concerning Candida, domesticity, and happiness are
introduced, but not really tested. Lesser romantic ideals
come into contention: for instance, Eugene turns Morell's
"cant" against him and wrecks his confidence in the power
of physical strength to overcome fear. Furthermore, conventions such as those regarding the behavior of clergymen

are toppled by better alternatives: when Morell grants Burgess the right to act as a scoundrel if he will only stop pretending to be anything else, the effect on Burgess is "to remove the keystone of his moral arch." But the main ideals do not meet challenging opposition; they merely face each other in battle array. Eugene signals the preparatory nature of Act I when, near the end, he proclaims to Morell: "I'm not afraid of a clergyman's ideas. . . . I'll pit my own ideas against them." Early in Act II this preparation is completed when Eugene learns from Prossy that it is indeed possible for a woman to love Morell. From the time he sits dejectedly in the child's chair after this discovery until Morell takes it over at the end of the play, nearly every piece of business is directly involved in an open war on ideals.

Candida's talk with her husband, which follows Eugene's revelation about him almost immediately, comes precariously close to engendering the kind of ridicule that Shaw considers inhumane. The graphic reduction to absurdity of Morell's delusion that his wife fits the best idealist molds, or that his practiced rhetoric is capable of meeting any challenge, evokes derisive and at times contemptuous laughter. Whatever Candida happens to say that casts ridicule on his naive views amounts to a double blow, since she unknowingly echoes the sense of Eugene's outright verbal assault in the preceding act. Furthermore, even though Candida's statements reflect a mood of levity rather than fervor, they carry great authority in contrast to those of Eugene, who opposes a clergyman's ideals only with a poet's, and who suffers from such theatrical infirmities as poetic puerility, disabling shyness, and "anarchic" clothes. Eugene manages to jolt the minister's self-assurance severely, but Candida prompts him to utter: "What soul-destroying cynicism!" Even to some influential critics, the scene is a "ruthless analysis" in which Candida is "cruel" to Morell.[44]

But Shaw has handled the crucial confrontation so that the ridicule aimed only at Morell's ideals is kept strictly on target. Candida's unconsciously barbed words serve as the instruments of ridicule, but her consciously maternal feelings enclose her husband—the human being himself— within a protective wall of sympathy. The critics who find her cruel during the scene have been misled (like Morell) by its sheerly verbal content. The nonliteral, subjective, atmospheric content of the scene reveals that Candida does as much as she can to temper her unintentionally hard-hitting words with her characteristic motherly tenderness. Bearing in mind that Morell has encouraged her repeatedly to think for herself "and never to hold back out of fear of what other people may think," let us focus for a moment on Candida's actual feelings and motives.

The scene begins soon after Morell's clash with Eugene. Left alone, Morell shakes his head resignedly, "sighs, and goes wearily to his [desk] chair, . . . looking old and care-worn." Candida enters, "at once notices his dejected appearance, and posts herself quietly at the spare chair, looking down at him attentively." She attempts a joke, but it concerns Eugene and therefore fails. Going nearer to him and "putting her hand down softly on his," she says, "Come here, dear. Let me look at you"; then she makes him stand for inspection in front of the window. "Looking at him critically all the time," she remarks: "My boy is not looking well. Has he been overworking? . . . He looks very pale, and grey, and wrinkled, and old." She notices that "his melancholy deepens," so "she attacks it with wilful gaiety." After seating him in the easy chair (a sentimental touch) she commences her "ruthless analysis." The beginning of this exchange in the standard edition tones down the original version, but the original will do:

> CANDIDA. . . . You've done enough writing for to-day. Leave Prossy to finish it and come and talk to me.
> MORELL. But—

CANDIDA. Yes, I *must* be talked to sometimes. [She *has* been away for three weeks.] . . . Now (*patting his hand*) you're beginning to look better already. Why don't you give up all this tiresome overworking—going out every night lecturing and talking? Of course what you say is all very true and very right; but it does no good: they don't mind what you say to them one little bit.

The trick of plot that makes these and the following words exert an increasingly devastating effect on Morell has apparently tripped up interpreters as much as it misleads Morell. Of course Candida knows nothing about her husband's clash with Eugene. She assumes that he has followed his natural bent unchecked in her absence and has worked to the point of exhaustion. Not that she is simply jesting: despite the fact that she refers to her banter as a "jest" near the end of the play, here she is using exaggeration and sympathetic levity to express the gist of what she believes. But she by no means implies a cynical attitude. Like most wives or mothers confronted with enthusiastic husbands or children, she wants to bring him down to earth a step or two. In this sense, Candida is primarily deflating the balloon of her husband's enthusiasm a bit so that he will stop overworking—at least for her homecoming night. She is a little worried about him, and she combines typically maternal gestures of comfort with a mood calculated to restore his buoyancy. She fully expects him to be pleasantly amused by her, interested in vindicating his position with his usual mastery, and above all, distracted from his work by her banter. If he had not been jolted by the astonishingly perceptive verbal onslaught of a queer young boy, he surely would have responded in the way she meant him to. But because she exaggerates her debunking appraisal in order to attain the effect of levity that she desires, the appraisal coincides directly at several points with the fierce one that Eugene has just made. Morell, understandably misled by this coincidence, somewhat incredulously reads Eugene's

attitude into Candida's words. Not surprisingly, he becomes more and more shocked and hurt as the scene
progresses.

Candida, in reaction, experiences "growing wonder and
misgiving." When Morell implies that he prefers her goodness and purity to her love, she calls him a thorough clergyman, and not seeing his "heart-stricken" condition because
he has turned away, she responds "with lively interest"
when he mutters that Eugene calls him the same. Her
words are significant: "Eugene's always right. He's a
wonderful boy." During the famous "shawl" speech,
Candida realizes how "stupid" her husband is about poetic
and maternal love, and she is "a little disappointed" in him,
"though quite tenderly so." She finishes the speech "with
the fondest intimacy." Once more her terms coincide with
Eugene's, and Morell bitterly notes the fact; again she is
"delighted," and in a moment, she "laughs, and kisses him
to console him" because he understands "nothing." When
he recoils at her kiss, however, she arises, "alarmed," and
is "amazed" at his demand not to touch him. But her father
comes in, and a joke sets her laughing again ("Candy mad
too!"). The standard edition states: "She sits gaily on the
arm of the chair"; obviously she is not taking Morell's discomfiture seriously. Perhaps she is enjoying her first momentary triumph over the virtuoso of rhetorical swordplay.
"Still in a bantering humor," she hears Eugene accuse her
of torturing Morell, and she replies "incredulously": "*I
torture James! Nonsense.*" In a word, she knows he can
take it. Finally she learns that her husband has actually
given up an engagement to speak, and she begins "to suspect something wrong." When he shouts at Prossy, she
starts "watching his movements all the time with growing
wonder and misgiving." Their last exchange in Act II
follows:

    CANDIDA (*with anxious misgiving*). But—but—Is anything
the matter, James? (*Greatly troubled.*) I can't understand—

MORELL. Ah, I thought it was *I* who couldn't understand, dear. (*He takes her tenderly in his arms and kisses her.*)

Even Morell now senses that she has not been voicing "soul-destroying cynicism."

The second high point in the conflict of unsettled ideals, in the final act, further stresses the importance of Candida's sympathy toward her husband, and in this case, also toward Eugene. Morell informs her decisively that she must resolve his doubts about her love for him by choosing between himself and Eugene. To Shaw, this is an honorable and sensible thing to do;[45] but it takes Candida by surprise, and its veneer of rhetoric disconcerts her. She asks the two with a kind of haughty dignity to place bids for her choice. Morell's bid, on a purely literal plane, is an idealistic clergyman's howler: "I have nothing to offer you but my strength for your defence," and so forth; "that is all it becomes a man to offer to a woman." Even Candida later mocks it, although "caressingly" and "fondly." From the standpoint of dramatic effect, however, Morell's actual bid comes immediately after she requests it:

CANDIDA. . . . Pray, my lords and masters, what have you to offer for my choice? I am up for auction, it seems. What do you bid, James?
MORELL (*reproachfully*). Cand— (*He breaks down: his eyes and throat fill with tears: the orator becomes the wounded animal.*) I can't speak—

This is the turning point in the scene: it establishes an indelible impression of the man beneath the clergyman's mask, the "wounded animal" beneath the "orator." Candida retreats, "chilled," from the formal bid that follows, but after this one she goes to him "impulsively" and sighs, "Ah, dearest." Just as the above is Morell's real bid, so the superlative "dearest" is her real indication of choice: as far as dramatic effect is concerned, the competition is over. Indeed, after the formality of Eugene's bid is carried out (he exclaims: "My weakness! my desolation! my heart's need!"), Morell utters still another wounded animal's plea: *"(in a suffocated voice—the appeal bursting from the depths of his anguish).* Candida!" She proceeds to give herself to "the weaker of the two"—that is, to the man who projected his heart's need without divining that a true, expressive bid would be stronger than an ideal, parsonic one. For Shaw's audience, the parsonic ideal has been sharply distinguished from the genuine Morell. It has also been exposed as the only real threat (with Eugene proven an illusory one) to the renewal of domestic tranquillity. Therefore even spectators ruled by the sentimentalities of domestic drama have been led to wish that Morell would forget his idealistic image of himself and act naturally. Candida's "sweet" mockery of the image later on intensifies the wish, and her husband's entirely natural "boyish" response brings a pleasureful gratification. The conflict within Morell between real feelings and mistakenly applied ideals thus comes to an end. Not that his marriage will "never be the same again" (Eric Bentley's notion[46]), but he has certainly gained a degree of respect for the realities of home life that he lacked before. And Shaw has taken every measure to communicate that degree of respect to the audience.

Two of Shaw's many explanations of "the secret in the poet's heart" give the best clues to his artistic strategies in the finale of the play. The first describes Eugene's rejection of his greatest ideal and suggests the part that Candida plays in bringing him to it:

> In *Candida* the poet begins by pursuing happiness with a beloved woman as the object of his life. When at last under the stress of a most moving situation she paints for him a convincing picture of what that happiness is, he sees at once that such happiness could never fulfill his destiny. "I

no longer desire happiness—life is nobler than that. Out,
then, into the night with me." That is, out of this stuffy little
nest of happiness and sentiment into the grandeur, the maj-
esty, the holiness that night means to me the poet. Candida
and Morell do not understand this.[47]

The second explanation sets Eugene in contrast to Morell
and again stresses Candida's role:

What business has a man with the great destiny of a poet
with the small beer of domestic comfort and cuddling and
petting at the apron-strings of some dear nice woman?
Morell cannot do without it: it is the making of him: without it he would be utterly miserable and perhaps go to the
devil. To Eugene, the stronger of the two, the daily routine
of it is nursery slavery, swaddling clothes, mere happiness
instead of exaltation—an atmosphere in which poetry dies.
To choose it would be like Swinburne choosing Putney.
When Candida brings him squarely face to face with it,
his heaven rolls up like a scroll; and he goes out proudly into
the majestic and beautiful kingdom of the starry night.[48]

Taken together, these statements imply that the audience's wishes and expectations are purposely gratified on
two distinct levels: the sentimental and the mystic. The
playgoer who neither understands nor sympathizes with a
poet's rejection of "the small beer of domestic comfort"
at least acknowledges that such an occurrence is plausible
and accepts its presentation in dramatic form. He does so
for many reasons, of course, but primarily for the sentimental reason that he wants to see Eugene leave—if possible,
gracefully. For this kind of spectator, the play remains a
sentimental comedy, with all its domestic wishes gratified
and its domestic realities affirmed.

A spectator on another level, however, will resist the
"tears of happiness" that derive from Morell's return to the
family bosom and his heightened awareness of its nature.[49]
This more advanced (and probably unmarried) spectator
will respond most acutely to Eugene's "fierce gesture of

disgust" in reply to Candida's leading question ("Am I *your* mother and sisters to you, Eugene?"); to the "ring of a man's voice—no longer a boy's" in his assertion that life is nobler than happiness; and, finally, to the intimation of imaginative superiority in his enigmatic retort to Candida: "In a hundred years, we shall be the same age. But I have a better secret than that in my heart."[50] For this spectator, the play is "a mystery"—its standard edition subtitle —much more than a domestic or sentimental play. Its gratifications are indefinite, private, poetic: they exist on a "higher" aesthetic plane. And they involve a repudiation of Happiness in general for the sake of Life in general. The term "a mystery" defines the total effect as well as any.

Notably, the last moment of the play fortifies both its sentimental and mystic aspects. Candida takes Eugene's face in her hands; "he divines her intention and bends his knee"; and she kisses his forehead before "he flies out into the night." In effect, the poet ready to pursue his destiny first receives the blessing of the Virgin Mother. Candida then turns to Morell, holds out her arms, and they embrace. "Ah, James," she utters, adding a concluding touch of poignancy. It is by no means a sentimentalized poignancy: Candida is not a sentimentalized woman. Like the entire play, she is an implicit affirmation of reality on the domestic plane.

You Never Can Tell

Shaw considered *Candida* a "charming work of art" filled with "strange fascinations" that might possibly tempt a progressive acting company to venture a few matinees (*HMC*, p. 432). Viewed as one attempt to gain a foothold in the English theatre, it stands far from Shaw's next two plays, *The Man of Destiny* and *You Never Can Tell*.

Besides derogatively subtitling *The Man of Destiny* "a trifle," Shaw dismissed it as "hardly more than a bravura piece to display the virtuosity of the two principal performers" (Pref., *Pleasant Plays*, p. ix). He downgraded the play in this manner chiefly because he had written it to tempt a specific actor and actress, Richard Mansfield and Ellen Terry.[51] In the same vein, Shaw referred to *You Never Can Tell* as "a frightful example of the result of trying to write for the theatre de nos jours" (*CL*, I, 801), and he once confessed that he was "ashamed of its tricks and laughs and popularities."[52] Not only had he designed it as a fashionable West End comedy, but he had also tried to observe the constricted requirements of a particular theatre, the Haymarket.

Never before had Shaw deliberately sought performances at popular theatres. After completing *Widowers' Houses* for a promised two-day stand at J. T. Grein's Independent Theatre, he had remained satisfied to aim at this tiny stronghold of the higher drama in his other two propaganda plays. After them, he finished *Arms and the Man* for the Avenue Theatre during its season of exclusively advanced plays; and he anticipated little contemporary stage success with *Candida*. In *The Man of Destiny*, however, Shaw began concentrating on the limited objective of infiltrating the popular theatre. This preoccupation strongly affected the dramaturgy of the three plays he wrote in 1895 and 1896: the Napoleon one-act, *You Never Can Tell*, and *The Devil's Disciple*, planned expressly as an Adelphi Theatre melodrama.

At this time Shaw regarded permeation of the theatre as a vital part of his ideal-destroying campaign. By early 1897, he had changed his mind and concluded that a more feasible way to exploit drama for his purposes was to publish his plays in strikingly attractive form. This decision first led to the highly readable 1898 volumes, *Plays Pleasant and Unpleasant*, then influenced the tactics of his last early-period works, *Caesar and Cleopatra* and *Captain Brass-bound's Conversion*. For the present, therefore, we are dealing with an interim in Shaw's development during which, however lofty his ulterior motives remained, he virtually prostituted his art to the commercial theatre.

The Man of Destiny was partly contrived to disarm the resistance of Ellen Terry, leading lady at Henry Irving's Lyceum Theatre, and Richard Mansfield, the American actor-manager. The background of Shaw's frustrating relations with these two key figures clearly indicates why he resorted to extreme measures in his abortive efforts to reach the general public with his plays. The chief obstacles in his path were the theatre managers themselves. Such men as Irving, Mansfield, and Cyril Maude were rarely hostile toward his plays; rather, they were simply unable to overcome their deeply rooted habits and preconceptions. In early 1895, Shaw offered *Candida* to Mansfield, who had already staged *Arms and the Man* ostensibly because he hoped to "awaken intelligence and advance taste" (*HMC*, p. 429). Mansfield tentatively accepted the play and struggled through a few rehearsals before deciding that the play was "of the impossible," as he told Shaw in a remarkable letter. If we realize that within the next two years Irving and Maude, less daring theatre managers, also rejected plays that they nearly produced (*The Man of Destiny* and *You Never Can Tell*), Mansfield's apologia takes on an ominous import:

> *Candida* is charming—it is more than charming—it is delightful, and I can well see how you have put into it much that is the best of yourself—but—pardon me—it is *not* a play—at least *I* do not think that it is a play—which thinking does not make it any more or any less of a play—it's just only what I think and I happen to be skipper of this ship at this time of thinking. Here are three long acts of talk—talk—talk—no

matter how clever that talk is—it is talk—talk—talk. . . .
   It isn't right to try and build a play out of a mere incident.
Candida is only an incident. . . . All the world is crying out
for deeds—for action! When I step upon the stage I want to
act—I'm willing to talk a little to oblige a man like you—but
I must act. . . . Shaw—if you will write for me a strong, hearty
—earnest—noble—genuine play—I'll play it. . . .
   You'll have to write a play that a *man* can play and about
a woman that heroes fought for and a bit of ribbon that a
knight tied to his lance.
   The stage is for romance and love and truth and honor.
To make men better and nobler. To cheer them on the
way—
   Life is real. Life is earnest. And the grave is not its goal. . . .
   Be not like dumb, driven cattle
   Be a hero in the fight! (*CL*, I, 523–24)

Such were the sentiments that Shaw had to expect from
the closest thing to an avant-garde theatre manager in the
United States. He aimed *The Man of Destiny* at the English market through Ellen Terry, probably the most ac-
complished English actress of the nineties. Shaw's view of
her situation as an actress reflects some of the conditions
that had blocked his previous attempts to permeate drama
without bending considerably to the level of the contemporary theatre. As early as 1892 he had berated Ellen for
wasting her "sacred fire" on mutilated, Irvingized Shakespeare and on the clockwork plays of Scribe, Sardou, and
Augier (*CL*, I, 349). In his third *Saturday Review* piece
(January 19, 1895) he groaned: "As to Miss Ellen Terry,
it was the old story, a born actress of real women's parts
condemned to figure as a mere artist's model in costume
plays which, from the woman's point of view, are foolish
flatteries written by gentlemen for gentlemen. . . . What a
theatre for a woman of genius to be attached to!" (*OTN*,
I, 17). In June he returned to the attack, blasting "Sardoodledom" and imploring Ellen to play Ellida in Ibsen's

Lady from the Sea, then in the next article commending her "irresistible personal charm" and pleading for someone to supply her with a challenging part (*OTN*, I, 133–46).

Meanwhile, not these supplications but an announcement that Bernard Shaw was to address the Women's Progressive Society at the Ideal Club on the subject of "Feminine Meanness" (an odd sequel to *Candida*) prompted Ellen to renew their correspondence in March 1895 after a three-year lapse. No letters are extant between March and November, when Shaw completed *The Man of Destiny*.[53] But on the first of November he admonished her as he had in his articles: "I utterly refuse to concern myself with your Beatrices & Portias and the like. *Anybody* can play Shakspere: you are wanted for other things." Then he issued a veiled suggestion that she might want to reserve *The Man of Destiny* for herself: "To my great exasperation I hear that you are going to play Madame Sans Gene. And I have just finished a beautiful little one act play for Napoleon and a strange lady—a strange lady who will be murdered by someone else whilst you are nonsensically pretending to play a washerwoman."[54] Shaw's hint at first bore fruit: Ellen asked him to save the play for her and talked Irving into all but promising a future performance. Finally, however, she never starred as the Strange Lady since Irving, to no one's surprise, found an excuse to break his gentleman's agreement.[55] Thus *The Man of Destiny*, a deliberately simplified product of Shaw's attempt to gain a foothold in the theatre, failed him no less decisively than its more creditable predecessors.

With managers on the order of Mansfield and Irving to satisfy if he was to infiltrate the theatre, Shaw adopted different tactics in writing *You Never Can Tell*, his most complex dramatic work since *Mrs. Warren's Profession.* Rather than limit his scope severely as he had done in *The Man of Destiny*, Shaw instead took the elaborate materials of a popular dramatic form, farcical comedy, and tried to fashion them into a modern comedy of manners in the Shavian mode. Unfortunately, he not only failed to get the play performed; he also failed to accomplish—at least to his own satisfaction—the extremely difficult artistic task that he had set for himself. The title of the play, more or less logically extended, discloses its affiliations with the comedy of manners and points to its ambitious theme: *You Never Can Tell . . . The Way of the World*. The melodic waiter sounds this keynote when he remarks: "It's the unexpected that always happens, isn't it? (*Shaking his head.*) You never can tell, sir: you never can tell." Moreover, for the first time in Shavian drama "the way of the world"—here called Nature—plays an important role, as it does later as the Life Force in *Man and Superman*. Indeed, Shaw anticipates *Man and Superman* by showing how Nature treats the Duellist of Sex: Valentine mourns, "Nature was in deadly earnest with me when I was in jest with her." As a comedy of manners, however, *You Never Can Tell* fails to generate the comic power of such a model as Congreve's *The Way of the World*. It is still a richer play than *Widowers' Houses* or *The Philanderer*, to be sure. Nevertheless, it bears the scars of a campaign that Shaw largely abandoned when he decided to gear his further efforts to the reading public.

The main reasons for the artistic shortcomings of *You Never Can Tell* are not difficult to establish. To quote Shaw himself, the play is at once "*tout ce qu'il y a de plus Shawesque*," requiring "a brilliant company—eight parts, all immense," and at the same time a "frightful" product of aiming at immediate production in a popular theatre.[56] While the play was still incomplete, Shaw triumphantly informed Ellen Terry that it "brings life and art together and strikes showers of sparks from them as if they were a knife and a grindstone"; but after he had read the finished product to a group of friends, he told her that "the reading tonight was an appalling failure. The play's no use: I looked for my gold and found withered leaves." He concluded that "number seven is a phantom" (*CL*, I, 623, 695). To the extent that *You Never Can Tell* is artistically unimpressive, it is so mainly because Shaw was writing with the theatre of his day too prominently in mind. This narrowed focus played a large part in determining his selection and handling of dramatic materials, and ultimately accounts for his failure to mold them into a fully effective artistic unit. It was not just that he looked forward to a possible run at the Haymarket, which had allegedly (but not really, as Shaw knew) adopted an enlightened policy toward advanced drama.[57] He also wanted to humanize the two varieties of farcical comedy that attracted West-End audiences in the mid-nineties: not only the lowbrow "galvanic" type in the vein of James Albery's *Pink Dominos*, but also the aristocratic, intellectually witty kind typified by Wilde's recent successes, *Lady Windermere's Fan* and *The Importance of Being Earnest*. Both varieties, according to Shaw's theories of ridicule, required humanizing because they appeal to the "beastly" rather than the "distinctively human" elements in man. Referring to *You Never Can Tell* in his preface to the *Pleasant Plays*, Shaw says: "Far from taking an unsympathetic view of the popular demand for fun, for fashionable dresses, for a pretty scene or two, a little music, and even for a great ordering of drinks by people with an expensive air from an if-possible-comic waiter, I was more than willing to shew that the drama can humanize these things as easily as they, in undramatic hands, can dehumanize the drama."[58]

Regarded as an attempt to permeate the English theatre via the Haymarket, *You Never Can Tell* stands in a complementary relation to *The Man of Destiny*. In the Mansfield-Terry "bravura piece," Shaw tempted influential performers to make small concessions to the higher drama for the sake of displaying their surefire qualities and skills in a relatively simple, short, and conventional dramatic vehicle. In *You Never Can Tell*, instead of trying to seduce only a single actor or actress, he aimed at an entire company, beginning with the actor-manager in power and reaching far down the line. Since he was well aware that the prevailing West End system required an excellent part for the actor-manager, he gave Cyril Maude a choice between the lovable sixty-year-old waiter William and the thirty-year-old romantic lead, Valentine. Further calculating that the supporting actors and actresses would be grateful for challenging roles, he planned on "a brilliant company—eight parts, all immense." The result is a spacious gallery of extraordinary individuals, all capable of serving major functions, but faultily integrated (if, indeed, not wholly intractable) as elements in a total design. To a certain extent, several of the characters are "cut flowers stuck in sand."

Considered as a humanization of farcical comedy, *You Never Can Tell* marks a minor turning point in Shaw's development. So far, the relation between a specific popular genre of drama and the materials of a Shaw play has not assumed much significance in itself. For instance, *The Philanderer* employs farcical effects, but mainly because they bolster the strategy of permeation through unpleasantness; and *Arms and the Man* evokes the expectations of romantic drama, but for the chief purpose of battering the romantic delusions they are founded upon. Shaw had borrowed effects and broad patterns of action from contemporary genres, but never a large packet of identifiable materials. In composing *You Never Can Tell*, however, he definitely seems to have begun with a recommended list of farcical comedy items before him. Martin Meisel shows that audiences for many years overlooked Shaw's humanizing features and saw only "the manifest emblems of farcical comedy" underneath. These include the outrageous coin-

cidence which brings the Crampton-Clandon family together; the "volatile, amoral hero bent on sexual conquest";
the "bluestocking," Mrs. Crampton (which she changed
to Clandon); the "haughty feminine prig," her daughter
Gloria; the "crusty old curmudgeon," her long-separated
husband Crampton; above all, the comic waiter and the
typical setting at the generically-named Marine Hotel.[59]
These distinguishing features were fixed in the tradition of
farcical comedy before 1896. Shaw's use of them all resulted
in a plethora of unwieldy materials which are unsuccess-
fully fused. The Comedy of *Man and Superman* proves
that he was capable of manipulating a wide variety of materials with imposing success if he gave himself free rein;
but *You Never Can Tell,* yoked to farcical comedy as it
is, does not seem in comparison even a magnificent failure.

In *Candida,* Shaw's dominant sharpshooting technique
involves a careful mingling of sympathy with ridicule. The
power of this ridicule, springing as it does from the attack
of a contemptuous young genius and from a trick of plot
that redoubles the force of his assertions, is so obviously
destructive that it has often misled critics. To apply Shaw's
distinction, commentators have mistaken "criticism" for
"satire." I have therefore stressed the function of sympathy
in the play, especially its role in separating the man, Morell,
from the ideals under assault. In *You Never Can Tell,* the
interaction of ridicule and sympathy is again important;
but in this case the kind of ridicule that Shaw tempers with
sympathy is more akin to the ludicrousness of farce than
to the derision of satire. Moreover, the kind of sympathy
he employs does not radiate from anything like an embodiment of humane, considerate motherhood; for the most
part, it emerges under pressure from characters who have
inhumane attitudes. Even William the waiter, for all his
disarming drollery and levelling reasonableness, does not
serve the directly sympathetic functions of Bluntschli and

Candida. From the standpoint of dramatic effect, his function is almost exclusively a musical one; he possesses only that power which allows him to restore a tranquillity of *tone* to individual scenes. Indeed, his mellifluous voice, which prompts Dolly to liken him to Shakespeare, accounts for his pervasive influence on others much more than what he actually says or does.[60] Aside from William, the effusions of sympathy or respect for reality in the play strike the audience as revelations of the carefully suppressed humane feelings of rigid characters. Bergson's phrase, the "mechanical encrusted on the living," suggests the impression that these characters normally convey; their moments of spontaneous humanity therefore come across dramatically as "breakthroughs." Since Shaw's dramaturgy throughout is keyed to the humanization of the mechanical materials of farcical comedy, his metaphor of the breakthrough describes his method appropriately.

The strategy of humanization in the play extends over a huge territory. At one pole is the theoretical humanization of the duel of the sexes, whereby Nature determines the outcome rather than the better duellist. The *jeune premier*, Valentine, is strongly attracted to Gloria Clandon, who has previously remained cool and controlled in the face of many lovers' advances. At the end of the second act, he skilfully overcomes her powers of resistance by turning her own defensive weapon, rational argument, against her. The experience of losing control of herself horrifies Gloria, who, although over twenty, has never been swept away by Nature before. Still, Nature's main victim is Valentine. Near the end of the play, he recaps from his own point of view Shaw's treatment of the sex duel. Using the key metaphor of the breakthrough, he says to Gloria:

> You thought yourself very safe, didn't you, behind your advanced ideas! I amused myself by upsetting *them* pretty

easily. . . . But why did I do it? Because I was being tempted
to awaken your heart—to stir the depths in you. Why was
I tempted? Because Nature was in deadly earnest with me
when I was in jest with her. When the great moment came,
who was awakened? who was stirred? in whom did the
depths break up? In myself—*myself*: *I* was transported: *you*
were only offended—shocked. You were only an ordinary
young lady.

When Valentine adds that he still has the Gloria of
"depths"—the human rather than the "ordinary" Gloria—
stored safely in his imagination, she is moved to express
her own point of view:

> Keep your own Gloria—the Gloria of your imagination.
> (*Her emotion begins to break through her pride.*) The real
> Gloria—the Gloria who was shocked, offended, horrified—
> oh, yes, quite truly—who was driven almost mad with shame
> by the feeling that all her power over herself had broken
> down at her first real encounter with—with— (*The color
> rushes over her face again* [the trademark of her break-
> throughs in the entire play]. *She covers it with her left hand,
> and puts her right on his left arm to support herself.*)
>   VALENTINE. Take care. I'm losing my senses again. (*Sum-
> moning all her courage, she takes away her hand from her
> face and puts it on his right shoulder, turning him towards
> her and looking him straight in the eyes* [the breakthrough
> is complete]. *He begins to protest agitatedly.*) Gloria: be
> sensible: it's no use: I haven't a penny in the world.

Nature still requires brainwork ("sense") to fulfil its
purpose by overcoming the economic difficulty. This is
supplied in the last act by the "incarnation of intellect,"
the lawyer Bohun. Appearing only when Nature needs
him, Bohun perceives at once that since Gloria has plenty
of money, Valentine should insist on a financial settlement.
Before the terrified lover can say a word in defense of his
cherished bachelorhood, Gloria proudly assents. We are of
course reminded of the action and theoretical background
of *Man and Superman*, but in this case Gloria initially op-

poses marriage much more than Valentine does, and a veritable *deus ex machina*, Bohun, intrudes to resolve the dilemma. In his own right, Bohun creates an impression of "absolute tremendousness," as Shaw says; and in alliance with Nature, he proves irresistible. In effect, a force of will external to the destined pair summons the aid of another external force, that of intellect, in order to get its way.[61]

Gloria's abandonment of a fixed, reasoned decision to resist love and marriage introduces another element of the play's complicated ethical strategy, in which rationalistic poses are upset by natural actions. The "inhuman" intellectual positions of the self-styled rationalists, Gloria and Mrs. Clandon, are shown to be false by their own spontaneous acts—by breakthroughs which dramatically expose and affirm reality. Gloria, the feminine prig of farcical comedy and an "incarnation of haughty highmindedness," tries to behave in accord with her mother's comprehensively coded rationalism.[62] But because Gloria is fundamentally "all passion," conflict rages within her between obstinate pride in her self-control and the insidious forces she is sensing in the presence of Valentine (and reading about in Schopenhauer). At the end of the second act, after he first stirs the "depths" in her, she reproaches her mother and conveys Shaw's point: "Why didn't you educate me properly? . . . You taught me nothing—*nothing*." That is, she taught her nothing about the nature of her irrational, wholly natural self.

Partly in contrast to Gloria, Mrs. Clandon is not priggish but "entirely kindly and humane." Furthermore, though her nature is a passionate one, "passion in her is humanitarian rather than human: she feels strongly about social questions and principles, not about persons." Still, she also involuntarily violates the principles that she never ceases to uphold. She is especially susceptible to such breakthroughs when her maternal instincts are stimulated. For instance, she has spoiled her eighteen-year-old daughter, Dolly, by always scolding her in an excessively tender manner. During the play, Mrs. Clandon often exposes herself to the gay mockery of Dolly and her twin brother, Philip, by failing to follow rationalistic doctrines which they aptly cite against her from her own Twentieth Century Treatises on Creeds, Conduct, Cooking, and so forth. On one important occasion, her strong conviction that everyone has the right to privacy in his own affairs breaks down conspicuously. When she learns to her astonishment that Valentine has engineered a kiss from Gloria, she not only invades his privacy by questioning him about his intentions; she also obtrusively juggles her doctrines to give herself a theoretical precedent for questioning him. Through the mild ridicule evoked by actions of this kind, Shaw leads the audience to chide the notion that reason should be exalted and to perceive that all thinking is basically wishful thinking, even in a paragon of principle.[63]

Still another type of humanizing strategy attracts sympathy rather than ridicule toward a character. The central figure in this complex phase of the play is Mrs. Clandon's unrefined and ill-tempered husband, Fergus Crampton. Eighteen years before, he had provoked her to get a legal separation on grounds of extreme cruelty, and she had gained custody of all three children. Ever since, she has kept them out of his reach and unaware of his surname. The audience, after observing Crampton in the first and second acts, is inclined to feel that this is a fortunate thing. Near the end of the third act, however, Shaw uses the technique of the persuasive long speech to command sympathy for the crude man. The argument is voiced by an apostle of respectability, the solicitor Finch M'Comas, who effectively drops his usual reticence to defend Crampton against his cold opponents, Mrs. Clandon and Gloria. As a preliminary, M'Comas notes that Crampton was not en-

tirely to blame for the separation and that Mrs. Clandon
has perhaps treated him more cruelly since they parted
than he had treated her before. His most telling point
follows:

> Mrs. Clandon: believe me, there are men who have a good
> deal of feeling, and kind feeling, too, which they are not
> able to express. What you miss in Crampton is that mere
> veneer of civilization, the art of shewing worthless atten-
> tions and paying insincere compliments in a kindly, charming
> way. . . . But think of the other side of it! Think of the
> people who do kind things in an unkind way—people whose
> touch hurts, whose voices jar, whose tempers play them
> false, who wound and worry the people they love in the
> very act of trying to conciliate them, and yet who need
> affection as much as the rest of us. Crampton has an abom-
> inable temper, I admit. He has no manners, no tact, no
> grace. He'll never be able to gain anyone's affection unless
> they will take his desire for it on trust. Is he to have none—
> not even pity—from his own flesh and blood?

M'Comas's impassioned plea undoubtedly succeeds in
arousing the audience's sympathy for Crampton. It also
melts the already flexible twins, Dolly and Philip, and
softens Gloria, whose heart is beginning to show under her
rational shield. But M'Comas fails to move the inflexibly
heartless Mrs. Clandon, in spite of his perceptive criticism
of her unwillingness to look beneath her husband's "veneer"
for his "common humanity." By the same stroke that Shaw
attracts sympathy toward his crusty old curmudgeon,
therefore, he also evokes scorn for his rigid rationalist.

Nevertheless, Shaw does not want the audience to retain
its generalized sympathy for Crampton. In the fourth and
final act, Crampton's repulsive qualities are intensified by
his crass insistence on living away from his wife but with
his children, no matter what they might prefer. By means
of this development, Shaw prompts the audience to retract
its soft, indiscreet sympathy for the whole galling indi-

vidual, Crampton, whose own rigidity has led him to demand an unpleasant and unfeasible arrangement. At the same time, however, the audience retains sympathy for the feelings he shares with humanity, since it is his craving for affection which in a sense underlies his extreme obstinacy. This kind of sympathy is free of "galvanic" ingredients; it is, in fact, the "considerate sympathy" for the "distinctively human" in man that Shaw regards as the most worthy kind. After Crampton resigns himself to occasional visits from his children and even joins in the high-comedy dance (the feast has already taken place), our aversion to his "crust" disappears, and Shaw's job with him is done.

You Never Can Tell also includes many lesser strands of humanizing and ideal-destroying action. Dolly, first representing "youth personified (having no soul)" (*CL*, I, 671), reacts to her newly identified father by exhibiting one dehumanizing attitude, amiable indifference, until M'Comas's apologia for Crampton inspires her to adopt another, sentimental pity. But finally she too experiences a breakthrough: in a moment of fright she instinctively seeks her father's protection and calls him Papa. Her equally soulless brother Philip serves a variety of functions. For example, by ludicrously claiming a vast knowledge of human nature seven times in the first act and a half—spurious wisdom he obviously acquired not from life but from his rationalistic mother—he inadvertently hammers into the audience's mind a clear sense of the disparity between the deductions of reason and the revelations of real life. Moreover, he is Shaw's chief scandalizer in the play. But even the person most easily scandalized, M'Comas, is granted a debunking capacity: fully aware of his own conventionality, he is one up on Mrs. Clandon, and at one point he delicately exposes her as an "old fogey" who persists in clamoring for her once-advanced opinions without realizing that they are passé (except, he notes, in the theatre).

Still, the most significant thing about the "eight parts, all immense" in the play is the fact that Shaw conceived them with performance at the Haymarket as his immediate goal. He rejected the play as a "phantom." If he meant anything in an artistic sense, he meant that the total integration of his complicated, intertwining movements, keys, and themes finally eluded him. Because of this, several characters—Philip and M'Comas indisputably, and perhaps William the waiter—contribute much less to the entire sequence of effects than is justified by the great interest they arouse as distinctive individuals. Philip and M'Comas have only a negligible stake in the major conflicts, and both merely evaporate from the play at the end. From a conceptual standpoint, they fill in corners of a huge mold; but in more crucial dramatic terms, they do little more than arouse and gain pleasure from largely superfluous ridicule. For the most part, therefore, they are dangling particles in an already grand design. Again because Shaw failed to coordinate his full orchestra of effects, the astonishing "incarnation of intellect," Bohun, upstages the more genuinely natural, life-affirming characters; and he does so in the act that bears by far the greatest burden of the total effect in the play—the last. His powerful presence can be rationalized on conceptual grounds, but not quite accepted in dramatic terms.

I have barely mentioned the most glaring deficiency in the play: the recurring spots of farcical comedy "business" that Shaw seems to have included for the sake of Cyril Maude and his acting company, the various "tricks and laughs and popularities." Symptomatic enough is Valentine's first-act advice to the twins after they have asked him out to lunch:

Will you excuse my frankness? (*They nod.*) Thank you.

Well, in a seaside resort there's one thing you *must* have
before anybody can afford to be seen going about with you;
and that's a father, alive or dead. (*He looks at them alternately, with emphasis. They meet his gaze like martyrs.*) Am
I to infer that you have omitted that indispensable part of
your social equipment? (*They confirm him by melancholy
nods.*) Then I'm sorry to say that . . . it will be impossible
for me to accept your kind invitation to lunch.

This is no Shavian jest in earnest; Valentine soon learns that
the twins have a respectable grandfather, and he remarks,
"That makes it all right, of course." The best that can be
said for this segment of silliness is that it is rhythmic, cute,
and mildly reminiscent of *The Importance of Being Earnest*.
Examples of the same sort occur on every fourth or fifth
page of the text.

However endearingly delightful *You Never Can Tell*
may seem in performance, and however complex, serious,
and uncompromisingly Shavian it may indeed be, the play
nevertheless invites the label that Shaw attached to it in
sober retrospect: "potboiler." If he had not originally
geared it to the exceedingly limited end of infiltrating West
End theatre, *You Never Can Tell* might have excelled as a
modern comedy of manners to the degree that *Candida*
excels as a modern sentimental comedy. The play might
also have transcended the actual materials of a discredited
type of popular drama to the extent that its predecessors
do. Because of its greater magnitude and complexity, moreover, it would have ranked first among the critical comedies
as an artistic achievement instead of meriting the mildly
damning tag that Shaw gives it.

Chapter 4

C. S. Lewis on the sixteenth-century Puritan,
William Tyndale: "In reality Tyndale is trying
to express an obstinate fact which meets us long
before we venture into the realm of theology; the
fact that morality or duty (what he calls 'the
Law') never yet made a man happy in himself or
dear to others. It is shocking, but it is undeniable.
We do not wish either to be, or to live among,
people who are clean or honest or kind as a matter
of duty: we want to be, and to associate with,
people who like being clean and honest and kind.
The mere suspicion that what seemed an act of
spontaneous friendliness or generosity was
really done as a duty subtly poisons it. In
philosophical language, the ethical category is
self-destructive; morality is healthy only when it
is trying to abolish itself. In theological
language, no man can be saved by works. The whole
purpose of the 'gospel', for Tyndale, is to deliver
us from morality. Thus, paradoxically, the 'puritan'
of modern imagination—the cold, gloomy heart,
doing as duty what happier and richer souls do
without thinking of it—is precisely the enemy
which historical Protestantism arose and smote.
What really matters is not to obey moral rules but
to be a creature of a certain kind."[1]

Humanizations
of Heroic
Types of Drama

Shaw's next play, *The Devil's Disciple* (1896), reveals the same humanizing purpose as *You Never Can Tell* and the same intimate relation to the contemporary form that it humanizes. Remaining within the narrow bounds of Adelphi Theatre melodrama, Shaw substituted a "genuinely scientific" theory of human motivation for a theatrical, romantic, ideal one. Shaw notes in his preface to *Three Plays for Puritans* that ordinary dramatists accept a romantic metaphysic which postulates, among other things, that a blackguard can be redeemed only by love; but the metaphysic he accepts is the realistic one of Schopenhauer, as updated by himself. Thus his Diabolonian hero, Dick Dudgeon, almost hangs for a mere acquaintance solely because of "the law of his own nature," his domineering and virtuous will. This is the play's "genuine novelty" (pp. xxiii–vi). With different degrees of elaboration, the same antiromantic theory of wilful motivation is also the most notable feature of *The Man of Destiny* (1895) and of Shaw's last two early-period plays, *Caesar and Cleopatra* (1898) and *Captain Brassbound's Conversion* (1899). All four plays approximate forms of drama that were familiar to playgoers in the nineties, yet all humanize these forms by undermining their idealistic notions of motivation and supplanting them with Shavian premises reflecting the distinctiveness and primacy of the individual will.

Shaw deliberately makes these humanizing premises conspicuous. For one thing, he deals with the motives underlying crucial, melodramatic actions: matters of life and death. Dick Dudgeon's self-sacrifice and eleventh-hour rescue, Ftatateeta's murder of Pothinus and subsequent death at Rufio's hands, the various threats of violence and humiliation in *Captain Brassbound's Conversion* are incidents without parallel in earlier plays. The characters involved are also given extravagant dimensions. Measured on the Shavian scales of virtue and vice, potential benefit or harm, none of the earlier characters evokes nearly as much unqualified admiration as Caesar, Lady Cicely, Dick Dudgeon, or Anthony Anderson. Except for Sir George Crofts, moreover, none is as blameworthy or contemptible as the host of "animals" and "fools" who provide these admirable characters with a contrasting backdrop: the sub-lieutenant in *The Man of Destiny;* Mrs. Dudgeon, her younger son Christy, and Major Swindon in *The Devil's Disciple;* Ftatateeta, Pothinus, Lucius Septimius, and Theodotus in *Caesar;* Sir Howard Hallam and several of the brigands in *Brassbound*.[2] This new use of extremes enables Shaw to convey graphically his theory that a person's motives for doing significant things, whether good or bad, are dictates of his dominant inner qualities.

In these plays, appropriately, Shaw exploits the popular forms of drama that specialized in extremes of action and character, the melodramatic genres. *The Devil's Disciple* is a comic melodrama; *Captain Brassbound's Conversion* is a melodramatic comedy; and the Napoleon and Caesar plays are allied to historical melodrama. Shaw's desire to permeate the theatre also affects these plays in other ways. *The Man of Destiny* is largely a "bravura piece," a vehicle for Richard Mansfield and Ellen Terry. Furthermore, in this play Shaw concentrated on humanizing the image of Napoleon recently implanted in the minds of English playgoers through Sardou's thin melodrama, *Madame Sans-Gêne*.[3] The connections of *The Devil's Disciple* with the contemporary stage are almost as direct. When Shaw wrote the play in 1896, the Adelphi Theatre had reached its apex as the home of melodrama. According to him, in March of that year William Terriss, the Theatre's leading man, "proposed that we should collaborate in a play which should contain every 'sure-fire' melodramatic situation." Although the proposal came to nothing, Shaw developed an urge to "revive" melodrama and finished the play on his own. As a result, he says, it was still "stuffed with everything from the ragbag of melodrama," but it also included "just that little bit of my own that made all the difference."[4] Unlike *The Man of Destiny*, therefore, the play is much less a vehicle for actors than a humanization of typical Adelphi melodrama.

The current theatre influenced Shaw's next two plays much less than his previous three (including *You Never Can Tell*), partly because he had decided to stop anticipating immediate production. Although he planned the roles of Caesar and Lady Cicely for Johnston Forbes-Robertson and Ellen Terry, he did so because he considered them the two finest classical performers of the time, and thus the actors best equipped to play his exemplars of heroic virtue.[5] His principal concern in these plays is heroism, male and female. *Caesar and Cleopatra* is accordingly a humanization of that type of history play which revolves around a figure of great historical import. It could be referred to as a modern "heroic drama," with the term used in a literal rather than seventeenth-century sense. *Captain Brassbound's Conversion* is its counterpart as a dramatization of feminine heroic virtue, and to a lesser extent, as an heroic drama. In some respects the play is an antitype of current adventure melodrama, and in others, of melodramatic comedy;[6] but to consider it a humanization of either would give undue prominence to a secondary factor. *Brassbound* is first of all a humanization of what might be called "great lady" drama, a type dominated by a nondomestic, nonhistorical heroine. To the playgoer, especially in a period when established leading ladies were valued for themselves more than for their parts, this kind of play would have constituted an identifiable genre, with its own set of conventions and expectations, as clearly as melodrama or bedroom farce.

The Man of Destiny and the *Three Plays for Puritans*, then, are all humanizations of definite heroic types of drama. To a certain degree, they are also critical plays, like the comedies that precede them, so that we might designate *The Devil's Disciple* a critical comic melodrama, *Caesar and Cleopatra* a critical heroic drama, and so forth. But these terms fail to convey Shaw's shift in emphasis. To him, drama in its controversial stage meant reducing romance to absurdity and preaching the worth of the real. His targets in the critical comedies are social conventions and romantic ideals; his weapons are ridicule and sympathy. Deliberately or not, by adhering to his conception of the function of comedy as "the destruction of old-established morals," he produced three examples of traditional comic forms. In the ensuing humanizations, the main stress falls upon Shaw's own ideas about motivation. The dramatic embodiment of his humanizing doctrine interests him more than anything else.

It is important to understand this doctrine thoroughly. Broadly speaking, Shaw's theory of motivation is his own realistic alternative to the romantic theory implicit in most popular plays of the nineties. In his comments on *The Devil's Disciple*, he declares that the average drama critic's constant exposure to conventional plays "so discourages any association between real life and the stage, that he soon loses the natural habit of referring to the one to explain the other." He refers instead to preordained codes of conduct, widely accredited simplifications of the complex relations between motive and act. These codes decree, among other things, that a heroic deed is inevitably a manifestation of a high ideal. Critics faced with Dick Dudgeon's act of self-sacrifice, which they could not attribute to any ideal, were thus left groping for a reason. Shaw says wryly: "On the stage, it appears, people do things for reasons. Off the stage they don't" (Pref., *Three Plays for Puritans*, pp. xxvi–xxvii). Such theatrical codes, he implies, ignore the elementary fact of existence—the primacy of the human will. In *The Sanity of Art*, written the year before he composed *The Devil's Disciple*, Shaw treats the will as a passion and describes it as "the true motive power in the world." Then he exhorts his readers to "look life straight in the face and see in it, not the fulfilment of a moral law or of the deductions of reason, but the satisfaction of a passion in us of which we can give no rational account whatever." Here he applies his basic premise to acts which are shameful: "It is natural for man to shrink from the terrible responsibility thrown on him by this inexorable fact. All his stock excuses vanish before it: 'The woman tempted me,' . . . 'I was not myself at the time,' 'I meant well,' 'My passion got the better of my reason,' 'It was my duty to do it,' 'The Bible says that we should do it,' 'Everybody does it,' and so on. Nothing is left but the frank avowal: 'I did it because I am built that way' " (*MCE*, pp. 310–11). In his preface to *Three Plays for Puritans*, Shaw applies the same premise to praiseworthy deeds. Dick Dudgeon's self-sacrifice was a spontaneous, involuntary, unreasoned act; he did it simply because he was "built that way." To Shaw, then, the root of all significant action, harmful or beneficial, is the distinctive individual will.

Napoleon in *The Man of Destiny* is wilful to the point of totally unscrupulous selfishness. Shaw considers him a "real hero" and in some respects a great man. Napoleon is not necessarily a *virtuous* hero, however; the question of whether his actions will finally prove beneficial remains an open one at the end of the play. All three leading characters in the *Three Plays for Puritans*, on the other hand, are not only "real heroes" but also exemplars of heroic virtue; they are "puritanical" as well as wilful. Shaw calls his devil's disciple "a Puritan of the Puritans" and explains, rather obscurely, that he is "a man impassioned only for saving grace" (Pref., *Three Plays*, pp. xxiv, xxvi). He means not only that Dick Dudgeon is a true Puritan among false ones such as his mother, but also that his will by its very nature is virtuous. In *The Quintessence of Ibsenism*, Shaw translates his doctrine of will into the terms of Puritan theology: "The will is our old friend the soul or spirit of man; and the doctrine of justification, not by works, but by faith, clearly derives its validity from the consideration that no action, taken apart from the will behind it, has any moral character: for example, the acts which make the murderer and incendiary infamous are exactly similar to those which make the patriotic hero famous. 'Original sin' is the will doing mischief. 'Divine grace' is the will doing good" (*MCE*, p. 20 n.). In other words, no action that merely complies with an ethical code deserves to be called either moral or immoral. Human actions have moral character only when they represent expressions of the will. An obviously beneficial action such as Dick Dudgeon's springs from "divine grace"—the will doing good—and the fact that it was a commitment to death, and thus an ultimate action, proves that he must be a genuine Puritan.

With this concept of Puritanism in mind, Shaw defines the true hero as "not an average Englishman miserably mortifying his natural badness, but a superior human be-

ing strenuously gratifying his natural virtue." The philosophic hero, Don Juan, "is a man who, though gifted
enough to be exceptionally capable of distinguishing between good and evil, follows his own instincts without
regard to the common, statute, or canon law." The heroic
statesman, Caesar, is *"naturally* great" because he acts with
"entire selfishness," and "having virtue, he has no need of
goodness."[7] Finally, Lady Cicely is "the great lady" because
she always does exactly what she likes to do, and what she
likes to do is beneficial for mankind.[8]

This is not to say that Shaw advocates wilful anarchy.
No constitutional socialist would. In his opinion, sensible
people will accept severe limitations in order to insure
getting what they ultimately want. Some will recognize that
they cannot possibly achieve their long-range goals without
suppressing some of their short-term desires; others will
act with restraint out of intelligent consideration for
others. Shaw says in *The Sanity of Art:* "The moral evolution of the social individual is from submission and obedi-
ence as economizers of effort and responsibility, and safe-
guards against panic and incontinence, to wilfulness and
self-assertion made safe by reason and self-control. . . .
Without high gifts of reason and self-control: that is,
without strong common-sense, no man dares yet trust himself out of the school of authority. What he does is to
claim gradual relaxations of the discipline, so as to have
as much liberty as he thinks is good for him, and as much
government as he thinks he needs to keep him straight"
(*MCE*, p. 308). In *Captain Brassbound's Conversion*,
Shaw conveys the same general idea in a lighter way. The
ignorant Italian brigand, Marzo, is so enthusiastic about
Lady Cicely that he twists a bit of Catholic dogma: "She
saint. She get me to heaven—get us all to heaven. We do
what we like now." Cicely supplies the Shavian corrective:

"Indeed you will do nothing of the sort, Marzo, unless you like to behave yourself very nicely indeed."

THE MAN OF DESTINY AND WILFUL VERSUS THEATRICAL MOTIVATION

The action of Shaw's first dramatization of heroism, *The Man of Destiny*, revolves around Napoleon's attempt to satisfy his immediate needs and desires without obstructing his ultimate goals. Shaw presents him as a young general on the threshold of his career, just after his ambition has been prodded by a success in battle which has made him famous overnight. The general learns that certain papers en route to him have been intercepted, among them private letters from Paris and dispatches informing him of enemy plans. He encounters a strange lady and easily discovers that she is the thief. His initial problem of recovering the papers is simple for a man who has no scruples against taking what he wants by force, even from a lady's bosom. When he convinces her that he is indeed such a man, she surrenders the papers. But he has so far assumed that she is an enemy spy assigned to steal the secret dispatches, whereas she is actually a friend of his wife's on a mission to destroy one of her seductive letters to his superior, Barras, which a conspirator has stolen and sent to Napoleon. When this becomes clear to him, he realizes that he is faced with a more intricate problem than his first one. He should read the dispatches, and he craves to read the incriminating letter. Yet if interested parties know that he received the letter, he will be forced into a domestic quarrel, a public scandal, a duel with his superior, and above all a disrupted career. Again unscrupulously, and this time inhumanely, he decides that he can save his career and still achieve his present ends simply by wrecking the career of the credulous sub-lieutenant who entrusted the documents to the lady. The details from here on are surprisingly trivial (for instance, the lieutenant and innkeeper must believe in witches). Suffice it to say that the lady upsets his solution for the second time; his last problem seems insoluble to everyone but himself; and he finally satisfies all his wishes through consummate "meanness and selfishness." At the curtain, he hints (though ambiguously) that he may give his wife reason to doubt his own fidelity.

From the standpoint of dramatic effect, this "trifle" of a plot amounts to a revelation of the historical Napoleon in action, the incipient man of destiny already driven by immense ambition, unhampered by scruples, and shrewd enough to get what he wants. The little intrigue and counter-intrigue he engages in, with their blatant improbabilities and startling lack of momentousness, by no means detract from Shaw's revised portrait of the man. On the contrary, they direct the spectator's focus away from the events and toward the character of Napoleon as a potential conqueror and ruler of half the world. By using this strategy, Shaw impresses upon his audience the two or three basic qualities of heroism which, in his mind, account for the real Napoleon's rise to greatness.

He also leaves himself room for two things that bulk large in the play: discussions of what motivates a hero and assaults on the currently accredited opinion. To a significant degree, *The Man of Destiny* is a dramatized essay on wilful versus theatrical motivation. Shaw gives Napoleon a penchant for Sergius-like heroics, and stresses his theatrical abilities almost as much as his self-centered vitality. The budding emperor is "imaginative without illusions, and creative without religion, loyalty, patriotism or any of the common ideals. Not that he is incapable of these ideals: on the contrary, he has swallowed them all in his boyhood, and now, having a keen dramatic faculty, is extremely clever at playing upon them by the arts of the actor and stage manager." To influence the strange lady, Napoleon occasionally strikes heroic attitudes and mouths the conventional precepts of popular idealism. Once he "pulls himself piously together, and says, like a man conducting a religious service," that he wins battles "for humanity—for my country, not for myself." Later, "composing himself into a solemn attitude, modelled on the heroes of classical antiquity, he takes a high moral tone" and utters: "Self-sacrifice is the foundation of all true nobility of character." These obviously affected displays nauseate the lady, who admires the thoroughly selfish Napoleon. By their marked incongruity with his usual manner, they also tempt spectators to ridicule ideals which would normally evoke thrills of affirmation. Thus the play is strongly antitheatrical.

It is also highly discursive, at least for an early Shaw play. *The Man of Destiny* lacks the sharp intellectual give-and-take of Shaw's middle-period plays; the character whom Napoleon talks to most, the strange lady, agrees with his convictions outright and shows her instinctive accord by reacting negatively to his sham attitudes and positively to his genuine ones. The dramatic conflict arises from the plot, not from any clash of ideas, and is put aside (at times with faint dramatic justification) when a point can be made explicitly. The most conspicuous example is Napoleon's 500-word set speech on English idealism. After solving his final problem, Napoleon gratuitously compliments the lady for beating him, credits it to her "scruples," and accounts for it by the fact that her grandfather was an Englishman. Then he says: "Listen to me: I will explain the English to you." We can virtually picture the man behind the play bending the dialogue toward one of his own favorite diatribes; this one comes almost straight from the 1891 *Quintessence of Ibsenism* (see *MCE*, pp. 26–28).

Napoleon divides mankind into three classes, two of which could never defeat him. The third is dangerous, however, because such people—among them all the English—are his equals in knowledge and purposefulness; and although "chained hand and foot by their morality and respectability," they are irresistible when they become possessed with "a burning conviction that it is [their] moral and religious duty to conquer those who have got [what they want]." Unintentional hypocrisy of this kind is a weapon that Napoleon, as a "true hero," must do without.

The other discussions in *The Man of Destiny* form a step-by-step discourse on the basic qualities necessary for true heroism. While still wrangling over the papers, Napoleon and the lady agree that although they have done brave things, they never have lost their sense of fear in doing them. Napoleon seizes the occasion to explain at length that fear and bravery are irrelevant to heroism; what really matters is a feeling that you absolutely must have what you want, a conviction so strong that fear actually tightens the "grip of your own purpose." The lady intervenes to distinguish between her "womanish" and his "real" heroism. "My courage is mere slavishness," she says; "it is of no use to me for my own purposes. It is only through love, through pity, through the instinct to save and protect someone else, that I can do the things that terrify me." (Shaw had invented his maternal genius, Candida, less than a year before.) On the other hand, the lady continues, Napoleon is entirely selfish: "What is the secret of your power? Only that you believe in yourself. You can fight and conquer for yourself and for nobody else. You are not afraid of your own destiny. You teach us what we all might be if we had the will and courage." Shaw, of course, is also teaching us.

A few moments later, he switches the subject to the vital quality of unscrupulousness. Napoleon threatens to take the documents from the strange lady by force, and she

delays him by posing as a defenseless martyr, whereupon
he spoils her attitude by coolly looking her up and down.
When she behaves naturally once more, he addresses her,
again at length:

> Now attend to me. Suppose I were to allow myself to be
> abashed by the respect due to your sex, your beauty, your
> heroism and all the rest of it? Suppose I, with nothing but
> such sentimental stuff to stand between these muscles of mine
> and those papers which you have about you, and which I
> want and mean to have: suppose I, with the prize within my
> grasp, were to falter and sneak away with my hands empty;
> or, what would be worse, cover up my weakness by playing
> the magnanimous hero, and sparing you the violence I dared
> not use[;] would you not despise me from the depths of your
> woman's soul? Would any woman be such a fool? Well,
> Bonaparte can rise to the situation and act like a woman
> when it is necessary. Do you understand?

Shaw has the lady give Napoleon the papers at once, thereby
making his point dramatically as well as discursively. The
same subject is touched upon just before the general's
Shavian oration on the reasons why the English will ultimately beat him. The strange lady praises Napoleon's
triumph by saying: "I adore a man who is not afraid to
be mean and selfish." When he is theatrically indignant in
response, she explains her remark: what he did was "the
meanest thing I ever knew any man do; but it exactly
fulfilled your purpose; and so you weren't a bit afraid or
ashamed to do it." He later attributes the intelligence of
this insight to her grandmother—an Irishwoman.

One more explanatory speech warrants attention. Speaking with the phlegmatic innkeeper, Giuseppe, Napoleon
is so struck by his lack of ambition that he is prompted to
describe his own inner compulsions: "You have no devouring devil inside you who must be fed with action and
victory—gorged with them night and day—who makes you

pay, with the sweat of your brain and body, weeks of Herculean toil for ten minutes of enjoyment—who is at once your slave and your tyrant, your genius and your doom . . . —who shews you all the kingdoms of the earth and offers to make you their master on condition that you become their servant!" Here, Shaw is presenting his interpretation of the historical Napoleon's ruling *daimon,* a quality crucial to the individual himself, not one he shares with the will-driven, antitheatrical Shavian hero in general. Some of Napoleon's minor characteristics also fall into the same limited class, especially his mildly lascivious vulgarity and his unqualified readiness to act inhumanely. Shaw does not treat his later heroes, Caesar in particular, as distinctive human beings who can be separated quite easily from the ideas of heroism that he is forwarding. To some extent the play is therefore one of his "works of dramatic art purely." At any rate, it is not an heroic drama on the order of *Caesar and Cleopatra,* in which Shaw deliberately introduces anachronisms and even alters recorded history for the purpose of conveying his fully developed conception of heroic virtue. *The Man of Destiny* is most precisely an updated Napoleon play: a radical humanization of the figure of Napoleon that appeared in the conventional theatre of the nineties.

From mid-1896 on, Shaw became increasingly absorbed in the ideas that he finally embodied in *Caesar and Cleopatra.* About the time he completed his second humanization, *You Never Can Tell,* he worked out a theory which may have steered him toward this central interest, since it unites his ideas about wilful motivation with apparently new ideas about the evolution of drama. In a *Saturday Review* article, Shaw presents a schematic outline of social and human evolution, then suggests its implications for the dramatic artist. "As the world goes on," he begins, "manners, customs, and morals change their aspect with revolutionary completeness, whilst man remains almost the same. . . . Nevertheless, men do change, not only in what they think and what they do, but in what they are." Moreover, "everything has its own rate of change. Fashions change more quickly than manners, manners more quickly than morals, morals more quickly than passions, and, in general, the conscious, reasonable, intellectual life more quickly than the instinctive, wilful, affectionate one." He then applies this scheme to drama:

> It follows, does it not, that every "immortal" play will run the following course? First, like London Assurance [1841, by Dion Boucicault], its manners and fashions will begin to date. If its matter is deep enough to tide it over this danger, it will come into repute again, like the comedies of Sheridan or Goldsmith, as a modern classic. But after some time—some centuries, perhaps—it will begin to date again in point of its ethical conception. Yet if it deals so powerfully with the instincts and passions of humanity as to survive this also, it will again regain its place, this time as an antique classic, especially if it tells a capital story. . . . Not until the change has reached our instincts and passions will [this play] begin to "date" again for the last time before [its] final obsolescence. (OTN, II, 166–68)

Shaw draws no further conclusions in this article, but he may have on his own. For several years he had been concerned about how to expose the obsolescence of plays by idealist dramatists. He had already produced a group of comedies that would make the ethical basis of conventional plays seem drastically out of date; possibly the Three Plays for Puritans were aimed at their dramatized instincts and passions. Ideas of wilful motivation, broadcast on the grandest scale, would perhaps put the romantic metaphysic to rout. Compelling images of natural heroic virtue causing the deeds normally attributed to patriotism, love, or honor might force idealist codes of conduct to lose face. Speculations of this kind seem to have spurred Shaw's desire to revive heroic types of drama, an ambition he expressed shortly before he started *The Devil's Disciple* in September 1896 (*CL*, I, 650).

Concurrently, Shaw came to believe that he did not need to rely upon performances of his plays to bring about the advances that he sought. He gradually realized the full import of the fact that Ibsen had managed to exert a great influence on public taste even though his plays, like Shaw's own, had rarely held the stage. Beginning a spray of comments in the *Saturday Review* that touch the same theme, three of Shaw's late 1896 articles focus on the "eclipse of the stagey drama" caused largely by people reading or hearing about Ibsen's plays (*OTN*, II, 237). Reviewing the published but unacted *John Gabriel Borkman* early the next year, he addressed backward theatre managers in terms that held a lesson for himself: "Already Ibsen is a European power: this new play has been awaited for two years, and is now being discussed and assimilated into the consciousness of the age with an interest which no political or pontifical utterance can command" (*OTN*, III, 29). Once again taking his cue from Ibsen, Shaw decided to concentrate on spreading his own influence by publishing his plays.

Announcing this decision to a drama critic, he explained:

I have resolved to accept an offer made me by Mr Grant Richards for the publication of my plays. I am not a disappointed dramatist, as the curiosity and interest shewn in my plays by managers, and their friendliness & accessibility for me, have exceeded anything I had any right to expect. But in the present condition of the theatre it is evident that a dramatist like Ibsen, who absolutely disregards the conditions which managers are subject to, and throws himself on the reading public, is taking the only course in which any serious advance is possible, especially if his dramas demand much technical skill from the actors. So I have made up my mind to put my plays into print and trouble the theatre no further with them.[9]

Accordingly, from May 1897 until a year later, Shaw devoted his mornings to preparing his first seven plays for publication. In doing so for the express purpose of advancing the drama, he made them far more attractive to read than plays had ever been before.[10] True, he did not literally stop troubling the theatre; but he kept his vow to ignore the restrictions peculiar to the English theatre of the day, and he wrote *Caesar and Cleopatra* and *Captain Brassbound's Conversion* with the *Three Plays for Puritans* volume primarily in mind.[11]

Plays Pleasant and Unpleasant came out in April 1898. In May, after an injury forced him to resign (not begrudgingly) from the *Saturday Review*, Shaw began writing a book on Wagner's *Der Ring des Nibelungen* and continued his new play, *Caesar and Cleopatra*. Early in *The Perfect Wagnerite*, describing the prefiguration of Siegfried that comes to Wotan (Godhead) in *Das Rheingold*, he reveals that his ideas of heroic virtue and Wagner's are basically the same: "Wotan has a great thought. With all his aspirations to establish a reign of noble thought, of righteousness, order, and justice, he has found . . . that there is no race yet in the world that quite spontaneously, naturally, and unconsciously realizes his ideal. . . . Erda, the First Mother, must travail again, and breed him a race of heroes" (*MCE*, p. 184). To explain what Wagner means by such a race, Shaw uses the analogy of an England full of Caesars:

> If the next generation of Englishmen consisted wholly of Julius Caesars, all our political, ecclesiastical, and moral institutions would vanish. . . . Caesars would no more trouble themselves about such contrivances as our codes and churches than a Fellow of the Royal Society will . . . listen to the village curate's sermons. This is precisely what must happen

some day if life continues thrusting towards higher and higher organization as it has hitherto done. As most of our English professional men are to Australian bushmen, so, we must suppose, will the average man of some future day be to Julius Caesar. (*MCE*, pp. 189–90)

At this time, Shaw regarded Caesar as the prime historical exemplar of heroic virtue, Siegfried as the prime literary exemplar. Both represent the most advanced offspring of "the First Mother," the world will, produced so far. Moreover, both possess the quality that Shaw considers indispensable to heroes of great plays: freedom from the affliction of morality, a total freedom springing from confidence in one's own impulses raised to "an intense and joyous vitality" (*MCE*, p. 213). He states it another way elsewhere: "Virtue, which is defiant and contemptuous of morality . . . , is the life-blood of high drama."[12]

THREE PLAYS FOR PURITANS AND NATURAL HEROIC VIRTUE

The Devil's Disciple

Shaw assigns Wagner's hero to the same Diabolonian position in literature that his own Dick Dudgeon shares with the mythical Prometheus, the devil in Blake's *Marriage of Heaven and Hell*, and "our newest idol, the Overman" (Pref., *Three Plays*, p. xxv). The age was "visibly pregnant" with this idea, Shaw asserts; "the most inevitable dramatic conception . . . of the nineteenth century [was] that of a perfectly naive hero upsetting religion, law and order in all directions, and establishing in their place the unfettered action of Humanity doing exactly what it likes, and producing order instead of confusion thereby because it likes to do what is necessary for the good of the race"

(*MCE*, pp. 215–16). It follows that by the end of the century, "there never was a play more certain to be written than The Devil's Disciple" (Pref., pp. xxv–vi).

Well before he wrote *The Perfect Wagnerite*—in fact, at the time he began *The Devil's Disciple*—Shaw was apparently turning Wagner's "inevitable" conception of *der reine Thor*, the pure fool, over and over in his mind. His reflections on the subject, for instance, intrude with little pretext into two letters of early 1896 (*CL*, I, 602–6, 623). In a Fabian document later that year, he approaches the idea from the angle of the "good of the race" that the "perfectly naive hero" accomplishes: "All human progress involves, as its first condition, the willingness of the pioneer to make a fool of himself. The sensible man is the man who adapts himself to existing conditions. The fool is the man who persists in trying to adapt the conditions to himself." He proceeds with an allusion to Wagner's pure fool.[13] This connection between human progress and spontaneous, unreasoned heroism is a rudimentary but essential part of Shaw's total concept of heroic virtue. He makes it a major element in the first play for Puritans, then supersedes it, perhaps deliberately, in the other two. The hero of the first becomes precisely what Shaw calls Wagner's hero: "a fool, enlightened by compassion" (*CL*, I, 603).

The suggestion of human progress in *The Devil's Disciple* arises from the success in the American Revolution that the play depicts, a minor victory engineered by the pastor, Anthony Anderson, but made possible by the spontaneous heroism of Dick Dudgeon. British soldiers decide to hang Anderson in order to intimidate the citizens of his town, but he is away on an unexpected call to the deathbed of Dick's mother when they come to imprison him. Because he was interrupted in his attempt to convert Dick, Anderson had instructed his wife, Judith, to keep him at their home until his return, despite her antipathy for the

self-professed "Devil's Disciple." Therefore the soldiers
find Dick instead of Anderson, and it is at this point that
the great act of heroic virtue occurs. With no motive except an instinctive inability to let another man die in his
place, Dick poses convincingly as the fated minister and
is taken to be hanged after a cursory trial. As a result,
Judith is stunned into a morbid infatuation for him. Another result of the noble deed involves Anderson: when
he comes home and learns what Dick has done, he too discovers the "law of his own nature" and becomes a hero.
Impetuously racing off to a nearby outpost, he summons
the militia, surrounds his town, and saves Dick from the
gallows at the last minute. To Judith's satisfaction, her
husband announces that he will remain a warrior; then he
hails Dick as the obvious choice for a new minister. The
townspeople concur in the celebrative finale by parading
the Diabolonian through the marketplace on their shoulders. A revelation of his true profession—that is, of his
natural heroic virtue—has thus induced Dick, seconded by
Anderson, to make a small contribution to a salutary war
for independence.

Shaw clarifies this relation between human progress and
"pure fool" heroism in the text of the play itself. In Act
III, after his arrest, Dick talks at length with Judith, who
clearly wants him to admit that his actual motive for sacri-
ficing himself was a secret passion for her. Before this
romantic notion becomes an issue, Dick suggests that another ideal commonly evoked in Adelphi melodrama, noble
patriotism, might have caused him to stand in her husband's
place. The British, he proclaims, "are determined to cow
us by making an example of somebody on that gallows
to-day. Well, let us cow them by showing that we can
stand by one another to the death. That is the only force
that can . . . make America a nation." Nothing in the play
tends to belie this sentiment; we are left to assume that

Dick's action has indeed aided America. In fact, at the gallows he cries: "Amen! my life for the world's future!"[14] On the other hand, the implication that a sentiment of this kind might have supplied the *motive* for Dick's heroic deed is immediately ruled out. Judith disparages his alleged patriotism by saying impulsively: "Oh, what does all that matter?" He is disarmed: "(*laughing*). True: what does it matter? . . . You see, men have these strange notions, Mrs. Anderson; and women see the folly of them." The notion that he was helping to make America a nation, we may assume, came into Dick's mind during his efforts to rationalize what he had done on sheer impulse.

When Judith confesses her passion for Dick, he explains his motivation in a manner that dramatizes the relation between his true Puritan virtue and the "folly" that links him to Shaw's version of Siegfried. Before, he had gallantly admitted that he must have carried out his heroic sacrifice a little for her sake ("You let them take me, at all events," he notes, leaving but a remnant of his compliment alive). Now, however, he drops his gallantry altogether:

> If I said—to please you—that I did what I did ever so little for your sake, I lied as men always lie to women. You know how much I have lived with worthless men—aye, and worthless women too. Well, they could all rise to some sort of goodness and kindness when they were in love. (*The word love comes from him with true Puritan scorn.*) That has taught me to set very little store by the goodness that only comes out red hot. What I did last night, I did in cold blood, caring not half so much for your husband, or (*ruthlessly*) for you (*she droops, stricken*) as I do for myself. I had no motive and no interest: all I can tell you is that when it came to the point whether I would take my neck out of the noose and put another man's into it, I could not do it. I don't know why not: I see myself as a fool for my pains; but I could not and I cannot. I have been brought up standing by the law of my own nature; and I may not go against it, gallows or no gallows. . . . I should have done the same for any other

man in the town, or any other man's wife. . . . Do you
understand that?
JUDITH. Yes: you mean that you do not love me.
RICHARD (*revolted—with fierce contempt*). Is that all it
means to you?

What it means to Dick, and to Shaw, and later to Anderson, is that he possesses the spontaneous impulses of a born
hero: thus his forthright statement that he sees himself as
a fool for his pains, and his "true Puritan scorn" of love
and "fierce contempt" for Judith's (and the audience's)
shallow view.

Shaw puts Anderson through a parallel course of pure
fool heroism. He does so partly, of course, to emphasize
his main point, but also for another significant reason.
One of the play's most telling strokes against the romantic assumptions of melodrama is the last-minute suggestion, growing out of this parallel, that totally unreasoned
heroism is not really adequate. When Anderson suddenly
grasps the fact that the British intended to hang him when
they took Dick by mistake, he disabuses Judith of her expectation that he would sacrifice himself in turn. "The
man of peace vanishes, transfigured into a choleric and
formidable man of war." He shouts "Blood an' owns!"
and "Minister be—faugh!" The startled Judith tries to kiss
him goodbye, but he exclaims, "Waste another half minute! Psha!" and "rushes out like an avalanche." Of course
he is not running away from danger, as Judith thinks; he
is hurrying to activate the Springtown militia and save
Dick from the gallows. After he has saved him, he spells
out the parallel situation that unifies the play: "It is in the
hour of trial that a man finds his true profession. This foolish young man [Dick] . . . boasted himself the Devil's Disciple; but when the hour of trial came to him, he found
that it was his destiny to suffer and be faithful to the death.
I thought myself a decent minister of the gospel of peace;

but when the hour of trial came to me, I found that it was my destiny to be a man of action." Nothing in the play has yet thrown a particle of doubt upon the greatness of Dick's heroic deed, and Anderson's lucid contrast between the martyr and the man of action does no more than set the stage for the expression of such a doubt. Notably, it is Dick himself who perceives the implication of the minister's words and accuses himself of a serious Shavian sin: impracticality.

> RICHARD. . . . I have behaved like a fool.
> JUDITH. Like a hero.
> RICHARD. Much the same thing, perhaps. (*With some bitterness toward himself*) But no: if I had been any good, I should have done for you [Anderson] what you did for me, instead of making a vain sacrifice.

Shaw does not press this point; he is writing an Adelphi melodrama, not a Court Theatre discussion play. Still, the long-term repudiation of the crux of heroic melodrama, a noble sacrifice, is sufficiently embodied in Dick's speech.

Precisely, Dick sees that he actually had two alternatives when the soldiers came for the minister, the one he took and the one Anderson's contrast implies. That is, he might have allowed Judith to tell the British that he was not the man they wanted, then rushed off to save Anderson in the same way that Anderson saved him. Preoccupied at the time with discovering the law of his own nature, it did not occur to him that he might do other than what he did: his virtuous impulse drove him toward a single goal, and he followed this impulse "like a fool," as he says—not quite like a hero. It is by no means an indictment to call him a Shavio-Puritan pure fool, but if he had been something more, he would have had sense enough to try to keep himself as well as Anderson away from the gallows. He would have reasoned out a better way to fulfil the will that was

driving him toward heroism: the will was in fierce operation, but its proper instrument, the intellect, remained
inactive. To anticipate a little, Dick, unlike Caesar and
Lady Cicely, is in Shaw's eyes "a prodigy of vitality without any special quality of mind."

This unintellectual kind of heroism suits the type of
drama that *The Devil's Disciple* represents, humanized
melodrama. Before settling down to write the play, Shaw
decided exactly what melodrama amounted to in his day,
what it could become in a master hand, and what ingredients were needed to revive it. An 1895 article presents his
acute and systematic definition of the genre (perhaps the
best ever written):

> It should be a simple and sincere drama of action and feeling,
> kept well within that vast tract of passion and motive which
> is common to the philosopher and the laborer, relieved by
> plenty of fun, and depending for variety of human character,
> not on the high comedy idiosyncrasies which individualize
> people in spite of the closest similarity of age, sex, and cir-
> cumstances, but on broad contrasts between types of youth
> and age, sympathy and selfishness, the masculine and the
> feminine, the serious and the frivolous, the sublime and the
> ridiculous, and so on. The whole character of the piece must
> be allegorical, idealistic, full of generalizations and moral
> lessons; and it must represent conduct as producing swiftly
> and certainly on the individual the results which in actual
> life it only produces on the race in the course of many cen-
> turies. (*OTN*, I, 93)

Martin Meisel has shown that this describes the formal
nature of Shaw's melodrama accurately.[15] Such a form,
according to Shaw in the same article, "only needs elaboration to become a masterpiece." His own elaboration is concentrated within "that vast tract of passion and motive
which is common to the philosopher and the laborer," but
which he considered sorely misunderstood by ideal-ridden
playgoers. Shaw's purpose in *The Devil's Disciple* was to

advertise natural as opposed to ideal motives for heroism and virtue. Referring to the play, he told Ellen Terry: "A good melodrama is a more difficult thing to write than all this clever-clever comedy: one must go straight to the core of humanity to get it" (*CL*, I, 617). *The Devil's Disciple* became a straightforward melodrama injected with a Shavian "core of humanity."

Shaw speaks of the play as his "attempt to substitute natural history for conventional ethics and romantic logic" (Pref., *Three Plays*, p. xxxvi). The hero that he conceives as the antithesis of his own consistently affirms prevailing ethical codes and behaves in strict accord with romantic notions of motivation. Shaw's attacking strategy involves repeated demonstrations that the irresistibly favorable characters are attractive precisely because they reject what the conventional hero affirms. Aside from Dick Dudgeon, the most attractive characters are Anderson and Dick's young worshipper, Essie (the inescapable "orphan chee-ild" of melodrama, here an illegitimate sixteen-year-old persecuted by Dick's mother). The heroic ideals they reject are evoked by the sentimental reactions of Judith Anderson.

In the highly dramatic moment when Anderson suddenly breaks away from his post at the very stronghold of religion and morality, he incites his wife's contempt because of her ideals. For spectators who adopt Judith's delusion that he is making a cowardly escape from his grim duty, the play contains a clear instance of the method commonly used in Shaw's unpleasant plays, that of convicting the audience of a meanly false judgment. This is perhaps why Shaw makes Anderson brutishly unsentimental toward his wife in his warlike haste, and also why the single thing he says to her with "his old quiet and impressive conviction" is entirely ambiguous ("You don't know the man you're married to"). Few spectators, however, would slip into Judith's delusion. Shaw's artistic object is not to

arouse antipathy toward Anderson among reasonably perceptive spectators; it is rather to throw suspicion upon
Anderson's wife. He says in a letter to an actress who played
Judith: "If the end of the second act produces the right
effect, the sympathy goes from the woman for her mistake
about Anderson: whenever I have read it here the women
have always been disgusted at her little faith" (*CL*, I, 830).
Spectators, in turn, are supposed to be impressed by Anderson's vital show of unorthodoxy, though they might retain
doubts about him until he wins Judith back in the last
scene with his boyish "Well, what do you think of your
husband, *now*, eh?—eh??—eh???"

Essie's most stirring moment also involves a spontaneous rejection of a conventional point of view toward
heroic virtue. When Dick dedicates his inherited house to
the devil, he avows: "From this day this house is his home;
and no child shall cry in it: this hearth is his altar; and no
soul shall ever cower over it in the dark evenings and be
afraid. Now . . . which of you good men will take this
child and rescue her from the house of the devil?" Once
again it is Judith who stands in the position of ideal goodness. She strikes a heroic attitude, tells Dick he should be
"burnt alive," and offers to rescue Essie. But the girl punc-
tures her self-righteousness by declaring unassailably: "I
don't want to." Dick points the moral: "Actually doesn't
want to, most virtuous lady!" Worse, she does want to be
rescued by Dick.

Shaw describes the principal line of ideal-destroying
action in a revealing letter to Ellen Terry: "It is not
enough, for the instruction of this generation, that Richard should be superior to religion & morality as typified by
his mother and his home, or to love as typified by Judith.
He must also be superior to gentility—that is, to the whole
ideal of modern society" (*CL*, I, 734). In other words,
Shaw allots three large segments of *The Devil's Disciple*

to successive rejections of more and more imposing ideals. The atmosphere of Dick's home reflects a bleak, naysaying moral orthodoxy that cannot compete in dramatic appeal with his own refreshing audacity, especially when Essie becomes the issue. The Diabolonian proves to be more humane as well as infinitely more interesting than the grim Puritans. Dick shows explicitly that he is superior to "love as typified by Judith" in his elaborate and scornful explanation of the real motive for his sacrifice. Moreover, the audience—always highly susceptible to the claims of love —is kept from sharing Judith's most extreme romantic palpitations by the severely realistic way they are dramatized (what Shaw would call a bit of "scientific natural history"). It is hard to sympathize with a person who exhibits, not passion or even admiration for a proven hero, but rather a beglamored fixation on his impending Sidney-Carton death. (In one sequence, "her eyes are steadfast with a mechanical reflection of Richard's steadfastness," then she "looks rigidly straight in front of her, at the vision of Richard, dying.")

Shaw's further use of Judith's love fortifies the third phase of his attack. At the trial and later at the gallows, the horror that springs from her infatuation serves as one of the chief instruments in the repudiation of gentility, the ideal embodied in the figure of General Burgoyne. Shaw writes in the letter to Ellen Terry quoted above: "Burgoyne is a gentleman; and that is the whole meaning of that part of the play."[16] In the last two scenes, "Gentlemanly Johnny" Burgoyne not only lives up to his nickname in a manner that holds great attraction for the audience; he also expresses gratitude toward Dick for upholding gentility in the face of death. Judith, by communicating horror at the exchange of polite, considerate pleasantries during the trial, and finally by rebuking Burgoyne outright, contributes significantly to Shaw's artistic exposure and vilification of "the whole ideal of modern society." She reacts with an almost physical revulsion, for example, in the following exchange:

> BURGOYNE [addressing Dick, who is posing as Anderson]. . . . We can hang you in a perfectly workmanlike and agreeable way. (*Kindly*) Let me persuade you to be hanged, Mr. Anderson?
> JUDITH (*sick with horror*). My God![17]

Later Burgoyne tells Judith: "I am sure we are greatly indebted to the admirable tact and gentlemanly feeling shewn by your husband." She retorts by admonishing him accurately: "Oh, you are mad. Is it nothing to you what wicked thing you do if only you do it like a gentleman?" An elusive instance in the final scene exemplifies how Shaw marshals such effects to accomplish his purpose. Just after Dick mounts the gallows, Judith falls on her knees "with a frightful shudder." Burgoyne's gentlemanly instincts preserve him from sympathy: he nods approvingly when she begins to pray, tells the chaplain not to disturb her, and remarks: "That will do very nicely." Shaw singles this out as "one of the most appalling things in the play" (*CL*, I, 830).

Dick Dudgeon contributes more than Judith to this attack, and in a different way. During the trial he displays the same gentlemanly qualities of urbanity and self-possession that distinguish Burgoyne, yet Dick is not afflicted with gentility. When he seizes Major Swindon by the neck for speaking harshly to Judith, or when he becomes "moody and disorderly" on his trip to the gallows, he leaves no doubt that all his actions are the offspring, not of an ideal, but of his real nature.[18] By standing on the same plane as Burgoyne for a while, then rising above it (or stooping below), he highlights the rigidity of his antagonist's ideal gentlemanly manner. At the foot of the gallows, he denounces Burgoyne in what is actually the peroration of the central argument in Act III: "Hark ye, General Burgoyne. If you think that I like being hanged, you're mistaken. I don't like it; and I don't mean to pretend that I do. And if you think I'm obliged to you for hanging me in a gentlemanly way, you're wrong there too. I take the whole business in devilish bad part; and the only satisfaction I have in it is that you'll feel a good deal meaner than I'll look when it's over."

The typical melodrama of the eighteen-nineties was grounded in thoroughly genteel assumptions. Shaw's assault on the whole ideal of modern society therefore fit snugly and advantageously within the restrictive bounds of the form. In his *Saturday Review* articles, he had already campaigned to eliminate the "ladylike" veneer which contemporary melodrama had developed, particularly the "conventional abstractions of gentility" that posed as dramatis personae. In opposition, he called for "a genuine drama, which, without being very subtle, [is] at least . . . a sincere story about real men, women, and events" (*OTN*, I, 205–7). As a further part of this campaign, he produced a model, *The Devil's Disciple*, which is purposely not very subtle. What sets it apart from the ordinary melodrama of the nineties more than anything else is its distinctively Shavian "core of humanity," heroic motives that are beyond ideals, especially gentility.

Caesar and Cleopatra

Shaw instructed an actress who had played the role of Judith: "You may NOT say that you like the Devil's Disciple better than 'C and C.' The D's D is a melodrama, made up of all the stage Adelphi tricks. . . . Anybody could make a play that way. But 'C and C' is the first and only adequate dramatization of the greatest man that ever lived. I want to revive, in a modern way and with modern refinement, . . . the projection on the stage of the hero in the big sense of the word" (*HMC*, p. 473). To Shaw *The Devil's Disciple* was most significantly an attempt to revive melodrama, the genre itself, while *Caesar and Cleopatra* was first of all an attempt to revive the stage hero. In his humanization of melodrama, he adopted a rigidly standardized dramatic form as his structural base, whereas in the history play he molded the form to fit the dimensions of his hero and bound himself only to a few traditional characteristics of a largely unconsolidated genre: the elaborate spectacle, flamboyant histrionics, and "amoristic intrigue" of historical drama.[19] These features are by no means crucial sources of effect in the play. Clearly *Caesar* is a humanization, not of a well-defined type of history play, but of heroic drama itself: drama built around a great hero.

Just as clearly, Shaw chose the historical personage Caesar to dramatize because to him Caesar was "the greatest man that ever lived," the highest achievement of the world will on the plane of actual humanity. Shaw measures greatness by applying four main ethical criteria. First, he gauges the degree of freedom from ideals that a given candidate exhibits. His favorite literary exemplar of this requirement is Wagner's Siegfried, the "pure fool" who expresses his will uninhibitedly. Shaw's Napoleon, whose power derives from hard-driving, unscrupulous personal ambition, also fulfils this rudimentary condition, though no others.

A step higher, Shaw examines the quality of the will as it manifests itself in a large range of activities over a long period of time. This test determines if the will is essentially beneficial rather than harmful—if it reflects "divine grace" rather than "original sin." Again, Siegfried becomes a model, since Wagner's opera reveals that in the long run the self-indulgent hero "likes to do what is necessary for the good of the race." The actions of Dick Dudgeon similarly prove that he is a "Puritan" as well as an ideal-rejecting Diabolonian; thus he also meets Shaw's first two conditions for greatness.

But neither hero lives up to the third condition. For the most part, they are both anarchic forces working toward good; and as Dick himself suggests, their heroism is too often impractical. In *The Perfect Wagnerite*, Shaw grants that anarchism in thought is "an inevitable condition of progressive evolution," but he warns that in social action it is "just as hopeless as any other panacea, and will still be so even if we breed a race of perfectly benevolent men" (*MCE*, p. 223). Society cannot attain higher forms of organization if its members refuse to accept any kind of order at all. Shaw therefore insists that a man will lack real greatness if he fails to put his organizing, will-directing faculty—his intellect—into useful operation. From the historical evidence Shaw infers that the real Caesar, as a creator of governments and civilizations, must have possessed this faculty to an extreme.

Shaw's final requisite of great heroic virtue is the one that he advertises more prominently than any of the others in *Caesar and Cleopatra*. Neither Napoleon, Dick Dudgeon, nor Siegfried (nor, by the way, Nietzsche's *Übermensch*) exhibits this quality to any conspicuous degree. Shaw's term for it is "the passion of humanity"; we have met it before as "heart wisdom," "respect for reality," "considerate sympathy," and broadly, "the primal republican stuff out of which all true society is made." Shaw makes Caesar "in the most accurate sense of the word, a kind character," and celebrates his kindness and clemency again and again in the play.[20] Obviously this quality bears little or no relation to heroic action, but it determines the height of virtue to which a man can rise. Over and above remarkable wilfulness and vitality, then, Shaw grants his own literary exemplar of greatness freedom from ideals, natural benevolence, an active intellect, and a passion for humanity.

In his various comments on Caesar, Shaw consistently heralds one or more of these qualities. Setting his own hero against Shakespeare's, he chuckles that in *Julius Caesar* we realize that "the apparently immortal author" is "a man, not for all time, but for an age only, and that, too, in all solidly wise and heroic aspects, the most despicable of all the ages" (*OTN*, III, 298). His biographer records the remark: "Shakespeare's Caesar is the *reductio ad absurdum* of the real Julius Caesar. . . . My Caesar is a simple return to nature and history."[21] Shaw says elsewhere that his Caesar also represents a humanized antitype of the prevailing hero of the day, the "gentlemanly hero." Shaw has a broader idea of gentility in mind than the one he conveys through Burgoyne in *The Devil's Disciple*; here he alludes to a man who is generally "irreproachable from the standpoint of the ordinary idealist morality," an heroic equivalent of Ibsen's Torvald Helmer. He declares:

> Our conception of heroism has changed of late years. The stage hero of the palmy days is a pricked bubble. The gentlemanly hero, of whom Tennyson's King Arthur was the type, suddenly found himself out, as Torvald Helmer in Ibsen's *Doll's House*, and died of the shock. It is no use now going on with heroes who are no longer really heroic to us. Besides, we want credible heroes. The old demand for the incredible, the impossible, the superhuman, which was supplied by bombast, inflation and the piling of crimes on catastrophes and factitious raptures on artificial agonies, has fallen off; and the demand now is for heroes in whom we can recognise our own humanity, and who, instead of walking, talking, eating, drinking, sleeping, making love and fighting single combats in a monotonous ecstasy of continuous heroism, are heroic in the true human fashion: that is, touching the summits only at rare moments, and finding the proper level of all occasions, condescending with humour and good

sense to the prosaic ones, as well as rising to the noble ones, instead of ridiculously persisting in rising to them all on the principle that a hero must always soar, in season and out of season.[22]

Caesar is above all "heroic in the true human fashion," and therefore a hero "in whom we can recognise our own humanity."

Shaw's Notes to *Caesar and Cleopatra* in the *Three Plays for Puritans* volume explain what he considers the immense significance of his conception of heroism. Above, he contracts the opposing idealist conception into its meager embodiment in the gentlemanly stage hero, but in the Notes he expands it to embrace the entire field of Christian religion and morality.[23] Shaw begins by establishing the direct relevance of the historical Caesar to the present day. In the scheme of social and human evolution that he had worked out in 1896, he had postulated that the instincts and passions of humanity would change less rapidly than anything else; and in a preliminary section of the Notes, he asserts that such evolution has not occurred to any significant extent since Caesar's time. In other words, the historical Caesar, as far as his instincts and passions are concerned, could very well represent the pinnacle of modern human development. Shaw then moves to the next plane of evolution, that of the "conscious, reasonable, intellectual life," and declares that no development of any note has taken place on that plane either. The current cliché about man's "increased command over Nature" is actually an illusion, he remarks, since "the only sort of command relevant to his evolution into a higher being" is his "increased command over himself" (Notes, *Caesar and Cleopatra*, p. 201). Again, Caesar's attainments in this respect, the reader gathers, can logically be held up as a goal for moderns.

Dealing with Caesar himself, Shaw plays down his obvious superiority in vital qualities in order to stress his less recognized intellectual superiority. He grants that Caesar must have deserved his reputation as a conqueror and prodigious worker, achievements which clearly derived from his indomitable will. But then Shaw reminds us that others have equalled Caesar in this respect: "half-witted geniuses" like Nelson and Joan of Arc were also conquerors, and "men with common ideas and superstitions" like Gladstone and Napoleon were also great workers. Shaw trumpets forth his point: "How if Caesar were nothing but a Nelson and a Gladstone combined! a prodigy of vitality without any special quality of mind!" Not very usefully, Shaw terms this quality "originality." But as his explanation reveals, the term encompasses two of his four requisites for greatness, freedom from ideals and an active intellect. Originality, Shaw says, enables a man "to estimate the value of truth, money, or success in any particular instance quite independently of convention and moral generalization." Because Caesar possesses originality, he can "act with entire selfishness," which is "perhaps the only sense in which a man can be said to be *naturally* great" (p. 206).

But since a man with originality in this sense might still be naturally evil, Shaw immediately turns to the requisites of greatness that indicate virtue: natural benevolence and a passion for humanity. In these respects, Shaw announces, Caesar stands in direct opposition to reigning English ideals: "Having virtue, he has no need of goodness. He is neither forgiving, frank, nor generous, because a man who is too great to resent has nothing to forgive; a man who says things that other people are afraid to say need [not be frank] . . . ; and there is no generosity in giving things you do not want to people of whom you intend to make use. This distinction between virtue and goodness is not understood in England" (p. 206).

Thus far in the Notes, Shaw has at least implied that the difference between virtue and goodness is the main point of *Caesar and Cleopatra*. While explaining Caesar's originality and virtue, he casually relates the qualities of the man to the effect that he produces on others. "Originality gives a man an air of frankness [and] generosity. . . . Hence, in order to produce an impression of complete disinterestedness and magnanimity, he has only to act with entire selfishness. . . . It is in this sense that I have represented Caesar as great" (p. 206). From here on, Shaw focuses on the impression of greatness that he has tried to produce in his play. If he has succeeded in communicating a powerful impression to the idealistic public, an impression which stems from virtue rather than goodness, then the implications are vast. "The really interesting question," Shaw states, "is whether I am right in assuming that the way to produce an impression of greatness is by exhibiting a man, not as mortifying his nature by doing his duty, . . . but as simply doing what he naturally wants to do." He follows with a sweeping finale:

> For this raises the question whether our world has not been wrong in its moral theory for the last 2,500 years or so. It must be a constant puzzle to many of us that the Christian era, so excellent in its intentions, should have been practically such a very discreditable episode in the history of the race. I doubt if this is altogether due to the vulgar and sanguinary sensationalism of our religious legends, with their substitution of gross physical torments and public executions for the passion of humanity. . . . It may have been the failure of Christianity to emancipate itself from expiatory theories of moral responsibility, guilt, innocence, reward, punishment, and the rest of it, that baffled its intention of changing the world. (pp. 207–8)

Shaw finds these expiatory theories incarnated in the innumerable theatrical heroes who place moral responsibility above the passion of humanity. Such heroes, he implies,

make a strong imprint on the public mind and foster the
ideals they uphold by inadvertently pointing the way to
"right" conduct. In *Caesar and Cleopatra*, to supplant this
appealing image of idealism and to recommend a new
mode of conduct, Shaw presents an alternative image of
natural heroic virtue. At bottom, it is his desire to improve
a world partially corrupted by Christianity that leads him
to create as compelling an image as he can.

From the standpoint of dramaturgy as well as world-
betterment, Shaw is clearly most concerned with the *impression* of greatness that his play conveys. Indeed, in all his
plays, the main aesthetic instruments that he employs for
his ethical ends are impressions—dramatic effects—rather
than ideas. It is necessary to emphasize this often-neglected
fact once more because the actual idea-content of *Caesar
and Cleopatra* exceeds that of all Shaw's previous plays
with the possible exception of *Mrs. Warren's Profession*.
Moreover, in *Caesar*, Shaw works with dramatized points
of view and outright discussion techniques more prominently than ever before. Yet here, as elsewhere, he bases his
ethical strategies not upon verbalized concepts, but rather
upon the complex of dramatic circumstance and personal
motive from which ideas emerge. His intention is to strike
the mind through the emotions.

In the *Saturday Review* articles of this period, Shaw
stresses that "people's ideas . . . are not the true stuff of
drama, which is always the naive feeling underlying the
ideas" (*OTN*, II, 192). Hamlet, says Shaw, is a great dramatic character because "he is none of your logicians who
reason their way through the world because they cannot
feel their way through it: his intellect is the organ of his
passion: his eternal self-criticism is as alive and thrilling
as it can possibly be" (*OTN*, III, 203). This passage echoes
an earlier article in which Shaw asserts that "in all the
[drama] that has energy enough to be interesting to me,

subjective volition, passion, will, make intellect the merest tool" (*OTN*, I, 6). In his dramatic projection of Caesar's greatness, Shaw follows this principle as conspicuously as he did in *Mrs. Warren's Profession*.

The ideal-destroying strategy of *Caesar and Cleopatra* involves a lopsided competition between a number of dramatized points of view, ideal and otherwise, and an impression of natural heroic virtue conveyed through the feelings that underlie Caesar's sophisticated ideas. Early in the play, Shaw establishes a schematic scale of motives and indicates that several characters belong in assigned places on that scale. Each of these characters is at least two-dimensional, but a designated type of motivation determines his function in the play. That is, each represents a dramatized point of view calculated to express, oppose, or contrast with the ideals that Shaw is attacking; and each derives his individual qualities from the particular role that he plays in the conflict. Lucius Septimius, who murdered Pompey before Caesar's arrival in Alexandria, is a clear-cut example. As a typically amoral professional soldier, he killed Pompey to win the approval of the leader who held the upper hand at the moment—a pragmatic motive. But when he confronts Caesar, he stupidly claims the accredited motive of dutiful vengeance and loses favor. It is not until his actual motive becomes apparent that Caesar, who recognizes his usefulness, finds an excuse to give him a minor command. Physically, Lucius is a middle-aged Roman athlete type with symmetrical features and a "resolute mouth." Nothing else is necessary to characterize him; his entire part in the play stems from his actual and professed motives.

The scale of motives that Shaw presents has two dividing lines, one separating natural vice from natural virtue ("original sin" from "divine grace"), the other separating natural motives from ideal ones ("goodness"). Obviously

Shaw ranks natural vice lower than natural virtue, but his primary point is the immense superiority of virtue over goodness. He throws this into sharp relief by showing respect for all natural motives, however vicious, and disrespect for all ideal motives. Shaw designates a vicious motive—personal vengeance, for example—by likening it to that of a wolf, dog, cat, or other animal. In other words, he defines natural vice as a manifestation of the beastly element in man. Such a motive deserves exposure and reproof, of course; but it "at least is human," since even a man who is "part God," as Caesar refers to himself in his opening oration, is also "part brute." Because vicious motives are inextricably human, they can never be totally destroyed; they can only be checked and discouraged.

What can and must be destroyed, Shaw implies, are the widely accredited disguises that these vicious motives assume: ideals of justice, honor, duty, and moral responsibility. He uses the term "fool" to indicate a person who acts upon an idealized motive of this kind, no matter who that person is. In Act II, Lucius reminds Caesar of the atrocities that he committed at Gaul, asking, "Was that vengeance?" Caesar replies: "No, by the gods! would that it had been! Vengeance at least is human. No, I say: those severed right hands, and the brave Vercingetorix basely strangled . . . , were (*with shuddering satire*) a wise severity, a necessary protection to the commonwealth, a duty of statesmanship—follies and fictions ten times bloodier than honest vengeance! What a fool was I then! To think that men's lives should be at the mercy of such fools!" Again, "fool" is a technical term in Shaw's vocabulary, here a fool in the Scriptural sense. Whereas the "pure fool" responds solely to the promptings of his will, the "genuine fool of Scripture" responds to anything but, usually to conventions or ideals.[24]

One of the qualities that contribute most to Caesar's

attractiveness is his ability to evaluate and respond to these different motives without resorting either to gentlemanly high-mindedness or to cold logic. His reactions to others have an irresistible appeal because they are spontaneous and thus strikingly natural. Moreover, they are humane: Caesar ranks natural motives above ideal ones and acknowledges that everyone is part brute. Finally, they are self-effacing: he derides no one in the play more than himself as he was at Gaul—a revelation of a flaw in his character which, though transcended, further humanizes him for the audience. In these respects, Caesar is the type of hero in whom the spectator can recognize his own humanity.

The two characters who usually accompany Caesar in the play, his secretary Britannus and his bodyguard Rufio, frequently point up his essential humanity because their motives and evaluations contrast sharply with his. Britannus maintains the idealist point of view in every way until the last act, when we learn that he is a creature of blood after all (he has hurled unseemly epithets at the enemy during the offstage battle). Shaw introduces Britannus in Act II as he enters the court of Ptolemy with Caesar: "His serious air and sense of the importance of the business in hand is in marked contrast to the kindly interest of Caesar, who looks at the scene, which is new to him, with the frank curiosity of a child." A moment later, Caesar remarks to Pothinus, Ptolemy's guardian: "Ah! that reminds me. I want some money"—the undisguised, actual motive. Britannus corrects him: "My master would say that there is a lawful debt due to Rome by Egypt. . . ; and that it is Caesar's duty to his country to require immediate payment"—the ideal motive masking the real one. But Caesar implicitly confesses that, duty or no duty, he would not ask for money if he did not want it: he states firmly, "I want 1,600 talents."

Duty as a motive is ridiculed in Act III by the manly

aesthete Apollodorus, who angers a sentry by saying: "When a stupid man is doing something he is ashamed of, he always declares that it is his duty." Later, Britannus himself unwittingly reduces the closely related ideal motive of honor to absurdity. In one of the several small incidents in the play that exist solely for the purpose of setting ideals against natural virtue, Britannus brings Caesar documents that incriminate the Romans who conspired with Pompey. Caesar orders him to put them in the fire.

> BRITANNUS. Put them—(*he gasps*)!!!!
> CAESAR. In the fire. Would you have me waste the next three years of my life in proscribing and condemning men who will be my friends when I have proved that my friendship is worth more than Pompey's was [?] ... O incorrigible British islander: am I a bull dog, to seek quarrels merely to shew how stubborn my jaws are?
> BRITANNUS. But your honor— the honor of Rome—
> CAESAR. I do not make human sacrifices to my honor. . . .
> BRITANNUS. Caesar: this is mere eccentricity. Are traitors to be allowed to go free for the sake of a paradox?

The blinding perversity of Britannus's ideal is highlighted by his congenital obliviousness to Caesar's humane and sensible motives.

Rufio, bluntly free of such ideals, provides a different kind of foil for Caesar's humanity. A "ruffian" acting consistently on the basis of brute motives, he stands a degree above Lucius Septimius only because Caesar in a sense acts as his guardian. For this reason, Rufio has never actually manifested "original sin"—the will doing mischief—although he has also never shown "divine grace"—the will doing good. (His final acceptance of Caesar's methods and the accompanying hint that he will govern Alexandria in accord with them reflect Caesar's greatness, not principally Rufio's nature.) In Ptolemy's court, when the Egyptians raise a brief clamor of mutiny, "Caesar remains unruffled; but Rufio grows fiercer and doggeder." Later, "Rufio bites his beard, too angry to speak," while "Caesar sits as comfortably as if he were at breakfast." Other dramatic moments in the play similarly contrast Rufio's readiness to act inhumanely with Caesar's freedom from such impulses.

Being a practical soldier, Rufio deplores his general's well-known clemency. By voicing his objections to it in character, he reveals the fact that Caesar sets his enemies free simply because he wants to. In Act IV, Caesar declares "imperiously"—a clue that he is fitting the speech to the man addressed—that Rufio should have made sure that Pothinus escaped: "Have I not told you always to let prisoners escape unless there are special orders to the contrary? Are there not enough mouths to be fed without him?" Rufio replies: "Yes; and if you would have a little sense and let me cut his throat, you would save his rations." In other words, there are two ways of saving rations, both of them practical: Caesar's and Rufio's. Rufio goes on to prove, even to the satisfaction of Caesar, that his way is the more practical one: "Anyhow, [Pothinus] *won't* escape. . . . He prefers to stay and spy on us. So would I if I had to do with generals subject to fits of clemency." Caesar is "argued down," Shaw notes, but the suspicion that he might have let Rufio cut Pothinus's throat does not arise.

Rufio's and Britannus's opinions collide again and again with Caesar's, nearly always without perceptible irritation on Caesar's part. His instinctive kindness and imperturbability toward his subordinates heighten the impression of his magnanimity at the same time that they clarify and discredit unworthy motives. Only once does Caesar become incensed at the narrowness of the two, and on this occasion Shaw intentionally manipulates the dramatic action so that the audience will sense without effort that Caesar is attacking illusions rather than men. Cleopatra commands Ftatateeta to kill Pothinus, who has justly accused her before Caesar of wanting to rule Egypt by herself. When Caesar learns of the murder, he exclaims: "Assassinated!—our prisoner, our guest!" Before he speaks again, five different points of view favoring the assassination are unfolded in a plainly contrived fashion. Rufio's emerges first, giving Cleopatra the courage to state hers, after which she formally requests Lucius, Apollodorus, and Britannus in turn to state theirs. The emotional pitch of the scene remains high throughout, but the symmetry of presentation conveys the effect that individual passions are not being expressed so much as impassioned ideas. This is another notable technique that Shaw employs to assault illusions efficiently while avoiding wasteful skirmishes with isolated personalities; it is the counterpart of the technique by which sympathetic characters like Bluntschli and Candida shield idealists from derision. It appears conspicuously for the first time in *Caesar and Cleopatra,* where it culminates in Caesar's unqualified triumph over a variety of "animals" and "fools." As Shaw increasingly exploits its possibilities after 1900, it becomes primarily an instrument to provoke thought, but he uses it first for the purpose of exposing illusions to attack.

Of course Shaw's object in *Caesar and Cleopatra* is to celebrate the virtue of the hero as well as to derogate vicious and ideal points of view. In the scene following Pothinus's murder, therefore, he puts bald, assailable contentions in the mouths of everyone but Caesar, and permits Caesar to tear them apart at length. The key lines of argument are prompted by the attitudes of Britannus and Rufio. Britannus defends Cleopatra's act of vengeance by voicing the attitude of the absolute idealist. This attitude is essentially pessimistic, in Shaw's opinion, since a person who has an absolute trust in fixed codes of conduct regards men as mere animals held in check by the power of these codes. To such a person, punishment assumes great importance. Thus Britannus opposes his master by saying:

"Were treachery, falsehood, and disloyalty left unpun-
ished, society must become like an arena full of wild
beasts, tearing one another to pieces. Caesar is in the wrong."
Caesar refutes him vehemently. Facing Cleopatra, he commences with a maxim directed at modern audiences: "If
one man in all the world can be found, now or forever,
to *know* that you did wrong, that man will have either to
conquer the world as I have, or be crucified by it." He then
takes advantage of the uproar that has arisen in the streets
over the death of Pothinus to drive home the logical flaw
inherent in the theory of punishment, justice, or whatever
idealists may call it:

> Do you hear? These knockers at your gate are also believers
> in vengeance and in stabbing. You have slain their leader: it
> is right that they shall slay you. If you doubt it, ask your
> four counsellors here. And then in the name of that *right*
> (*he emphasizes the word with great scorn*) shall I not slay
> them for murdering their Queen, and be slain in my turn by
> their countrymen as the invader of their fatherland? Can
> Rome do less then than slay these slayers too, to shew the
> world how Rome avenges her sons and her honor? And so,
> to the end of history, murder shall breed murder, always in
> the name of right and honor and peace, until the gods are
> tired of blood and create a race that can understand.

This is the first of the many powerful argumentative orations to come in Shaw's plays.

Typically, Rufio responds to Caesar: "Enough of preaching. The enemy is at the gate." Rufio has endorsed Cleopatra on the practical grounds that Pothinus was a threat
to Caesar's security. But Caesar rebukes him on exactly
these grounds:

> (*turning on him and giving way to his wrath*). Ay; and what
> has held [the enemy] baffled at the gate all these months?
> Was it my folly, as you deem it, or your wisdom? In this
> Egyptian Red Sea of blood, whose hand has held all your
> heads above the waves? (*Turning on Cleopatra*) And yet,

when Caesar says to such an one, "Friend, go free," you, clinging for your little life to my sword, dare steal out and stab him in the back? And you, soldiers and gentlemen, and honest servants as you forget that you are, applaud this assassination, and say "Caesar is in the wrong." By the gods, I am tempted to open my hand and let you all sink into the flood.

This threat, along with the threat outside the gate, brings home to the realistic but shortsighted Rufio the grave impracticality of Cleopatra's action. He therefore makes a desperate plea which reinforces the impression of Caesar's moral and intellectual superiority: "Will you desert us because we are a parcel of fools? I mean no harm by killing: I do it as a dog kills a cat, by instinct. We are all dogs at your heels; but we have served you faithfully." Notice the defining terms in this plea: Rufio has spoken in support of "fools" and calls himself a "dog"—Shaw's labels for the ideal and vicious points of view.

The last minutes of the play include another notable series of baldly stated ideals followed by Caesar's acute refutations. In this case, ideals stripped of virtually all personal reference are staked against Caesar's spontaneous reactions. At the end of the scene described above, Cleopatra had implied to Rufio that she might order Ftatateeta to kill him for calling her a fool before Caesar, and he had responded by immediately cutting the brawny servant's throat. After Rufio has been appointed governor, Cleopatra, "cunningly dressed in black," confronts Caesar, who does not yet know about Ftatateeta's death. He asks her why she is in mourning, and she answers:

> Ask the Roman governor whom you have left us. . . . He who is to rule here in Caesar's name, in Caesar's way, according to Caesar's boasted laws of life. . . .
> CAESAR (*puzzled*). What do you mean by my way?
> CLEOPATRA. Without punishment. Without revenge. Without judgment.

> CAESAR (*approvingly*). Ay: that is the right way, the great
> way, the only possible way in the end.

Shaw then has Rufio describe the killing of Ftatateeta by
concealing it in a parable, another method of keeping
ideas on an abstract rather than personal plane without
abandoning dramatic interest:

> Look you. You are sailing for Numidia to-day. Now tell me:
> if you meet a hungry lion there, . . . [what] will you do to
> save your life from it?
>   CAESAR (*promptly*). Kill it, man, without malice, just as it
> would kill me.

A moment later, Cleopatra rails: "[Rufio] has shed the
blood of my servant Ftatateeta. On your head be it as upon
his, Caesar, if you hold him free of it." Caesar retorts at
once: "(*energetically*). On my head be it, then; for it was
well done." Here Shaw deliberately rings a change on the
same phrase in order to convey all the more convincingly
the spontaneity of Caesar's response. Again, it is the manner of the response, not primarily its matter, which gives
force to Shaw's image of heroic virtue.

Shaw marks off the outer dimensions of this total image
in three highly compelling dramatic moments, each one of
which highlights an ingredient of Caesar's greatness. The
three disclose, respectively, the breadth of Caesar's sympathy, the extent of his instinctive respect for human
nature as it is, and—far removed from the first—the intensity of his will to conquer. Each of these dramatic
moments is impressed upon the audience by being causally
connected with a murder of some kind, so that an obviously stirring event reflects back upon the dramatized quality of greatness and draws further attention to it. Moreover, each occurs when the audience is engrossed in what
is clearly the most appealing line of action: the education
of Cleopatra.

In the course of his relations with Cleopatra, Caesar appears at first as a kind of Henry Higgins fortunately equipped with a large increment of wisdom and sympathy. He attempts to make a queen out of the sixteen-year-old girl, an educative process that reaches its height when Rufio pitches her into the sea at the end of the lighthouse scene in the third act. Caesar's progress with her before this act can be exemplified briefly: at the court of Ptolemy, she realizes that it would be silly to think that she already knows more than Caesar, but at one point she is "rent by a struggle between her newly-acquired dignity as a queen, and a strong impulse to put out her tongue at [Ptolemy]." It is in the first scene of the third act, when Cleopatra is motivated by a childish whim to join Caesar at the lighthouse, that we are prompted to regard her development as a serious rather than trivial matter. Previously, she has shown her destructive temperament in harmless ways, but now she wields her power as queen with no interference from Caesar and with willing help from the "huge, grim" Ftatateeta and the skilled duellist Apollodorus. When she orders them to kill a Roman sentinel (they are thwarted), her further progress takes on a marked degree of dramatic import.

Her education culminates in a series of emotional crises during the lighthouse scene.[25] After Caesar has wasted so much time on her that he has caused the death of some of his soldiers by paying too little attention to a battle, Cleopatra must learn that this was merely an isolated instance of his sometimes excessive maternal sympathy. He shocks her by making her realize that he cares at least as much for his soldiers as he does for her: his sympathy is not selective, but catholic. This disclosure is set against a background of sharply contrasted passions:

CLEOPATRA. . . . . Caesar, you will not leave me alone, will you?

RUFIO. What! not when the trumpet sounds and all our lives depend on Caesar's being at the barricade before the Egyptians reach it? Eh?

CLEOPATRA. Let them lose their lives: they are only soldiers.

CAESAR (*gravely*). Cleopatra: when that trumpet sounds; we must take every man his life in his hand, and throw it in the face of Death. And of my soldiers who have trusted me there is not one whose hand I shall not hold more sacred than your head. (*Cleopatra is overwhelmed. Her eyes fill with tears.*) Apollodorus: you must take her back to the palace. . . .

CLEOPATRA (*struggling with her tears*). . . . I will not go back. Nobody cares for me. . . . You want me to be killed.

CAESAR (*still more gravely*). My poor child: your life matters little here to anyone but yourself. . . . Come, Rufio.

To some extent, Caesar atones for the shock he has just given Cleopatra by offering to swim from the lighthouse with her on his back, but Rufio promptly gives her a new, equally humbling shock by tossing her ingloriously into the sea. Six months later (but in the following scene), Cleopatra shows that she has profited from these experiences. She can now define Caesar's type of sympathy: "His kindness is not for anything in *me:* it is in his own nature"; and she has grown up enough to admire him for it. True, the essential bent that she has revealed (briefly, an inclination toward "original sin"[26]) remains unaltered: she exclaims to a servant who has affronted Caesar, "If I were not ashamed to let him see that I am as cruel at heart as my father, I would make you repent that speech!" Still, she is trying hard to live up to Caesar's example—partly because she has come out of the water, as she says, with much conceit washed out of her.

Just as Caesar's sympathetic care for Cleopatra at the lighthouse results in what he calls the "murder" of his soldiers, so his respect for her natural bent, however threatening to his own welfare, leads to the murder of Pothinus. This time Shaw evokes horror by staging a literal rather

than figurative murder, perhaps because only well-indoctri-
nated spectators would respond to the characteristic he is
dramatizing without a disconcerting degree of perplexity.
Caesar's respect for reality involves an unqualified acceptance of everything natural in man, even the "part brute,"
and therefore replaces such familiar attitudes as resentment and righteous indignation. It is actually the passive
side of the quality of heroic virtue that Shaw calls "the
passion of humanity," the active side of which is catholic
sympathy. Caesar reflects this passion more prominently
than any other quality of greatness, and Shaw appropriately stresses both of its major aspects in moments of the
play that hold the audience's interest most securely.

The circumstances leading to Pothinus's death begin
when he comes to warn Caesar that Cleopatra is impatient
to reign alone, and Caesar compels him to repeat his warning in her presence. "Her heart is set on your departure,"
Pothinus declares fiercely. Cleopatra, stricken in part by
the implication of treachery in his accusation but also by
its element of truth, shouts "Liar!" Caesar is spontaneously
shocked at her denial, a reaction which would strike many
spectators as perverse, and which prompts the following
passionate altercation:

> CAESAR (*shocked*). What! Protestations! Contradictions!
> CLEOPATRA (*ashamed, but trembling with suppressed rage*).
> No. I do not deign to contradict. Let him talk. . . .
> POTHINUS. From her own lips I have heard it. You are to
> be her catspaw: you are to tear the crown from her brother's
> head and set it on her own, delivering us all into her hand—
> delivering yourself also. And then Caesar can return to
> Rome, or depart through the gate of death, which is nearer
> and surer.
> CAESAR (*calmly*). Well, my friend; and is not this very
> natural?
> POTHINUS (*astonished*). Natural! Then you do not resent
> treachery?

CAESAR. Resent! O thou foolish Egyptian, what have I to do with resentment? Do I resent the wind when it chills me, or the night when it makes me stumble in the darkness? Shall I resent youth when it turns from age, and ambition when it turns from servitude? To tell me such a story as this is but to tell me that the sun will rise to-morrow.

CLEOPATRA (*unable to contain herself*). But it is false—false. I swear it.

CAESAR. It is true, though you swore it a thousand times, and believed all you swore.

Cleopatra, "convulsed with emotion," is left alone with Ftatateeta and at once commands the death of Pothinus.

Just after Caesar rises to the heights of impassioned oratory provoked by the discovery of this murder, Shaw projects him into the totally different attitude of the vigorous conqueror "suddenly coming down to earth again" at the prospect of a battle. This surprising new mood signals the extremity of wilful vitality that Caesar reaches in the play. Once more, the dramatic moment by which Shaw highlights one of Caesar's chief qualities of greatness involves Cleopatra significantly and gains force from an ensuing murder. This time Cleopatra suffers from Caesar's indifference when his will to conquer overcomes his usual kindly sympathy. After Lucius brings him the news that reinforcements will arrive soon, Caesar shows "an elate and buoyant energy which makes Cleopatra sit up and stare." He becomes "all audacity," even "too much excited" to listen to his subordinates; and he ignores Cleopatra completely, to her childish disgust. Rufio spells out the cause for Caesar's indifference by saying, "Come: this is something like business." Caesar assents "buoyantly." In a moment of relative calm, Cleopatra bids for a note of affection from him before he departs for battle, since his last words to her were stern oratorical remonstrances. But he merely tells her, "Farewell; and be good and patient," and then goes out, "preoccupied and quite indifferent."

Humiliated, Cleopatra "stands with clenched fists, in speechless rage"; and when Rufio further irritates her, she responds with the threat that results in the death of Ftatateeta at his hands. Thus the businesslike slaughter of an enemy, later justified by Caesar, follows directly upon his unsympathetic but dynamic absorption in the business of war.

The conclusion of *Caesar and Cleopatra* fixes the impression of greatness that Shaw has communicated throughout. As a history play celebrating a great hero, *Caesar* is designed, we might say, for the purpose of inducing everyone to join the soldiers in shouting "Hail, Caesar!" at the curtain. This effect or its equivalent would not be fully attained if someone on stage dissented from the general opinion; but on the other hand, if a dissenter were transformed at the last moment, the effect would be markedly enhanced. After Caesar vindicates Rufio's slaying of Ftatateeta, Cleopatra remains the only dissenter of note in the play. Her grounds for righteous indignation eliminated, she acts "pettish and childish in her impotence" and calls Caesar "unjust and corrupt." In two successive steps, both of which magnify his heroism and virtue, Caesar changes her attitude to a favorable one, thus insuring a final effect of undiluted admiration.

The first step is the concluding example of Shaw's humanizing strategy in the play. Both aspects of Caesar's passion for humanity—his instinctive sympathy and his respect for human nature as it is—enter into the following:

> CLEOPATRA. . . . . All the world will now see how unjust and corrupt Caesar is.
>
> CAESAR (*taking her hands coaxingly*). Come: do not be angry with me. I am sorry for that poor Totateeta. (*She laughs in spite of herself.*)

Caesar's disarming slip is not contrived; he has never succeeded in pronouncing Ftatateeta's name correctly. This humanizing susceptibility to such a mistake is his "number" —his comic flaw. He continues:

> Aha! you are laughing. Does that mean reconciliation?
> CLEOPATRA (*angry with herself for laughing*). No, *no*; NO!! But it is so ridiculous to hear you call her Totateeta.
> CAESAR. What! As much a child as ever, Cleopatra! Have I not made a woman of you after all?

This question is Caesar's tactful way of stating a blunt truth: he has indeed failed to make a woman out of Cleopatra, although she has advanced as far as her age and "natural vice" would permit. To use the language of the play, he has only managed to make a "cat" out of a "kitten."

Caesar reveals implicitly that he recognizes this fact by promising Cleopatra a "beautiful present from Rome," Mark Antony, a fittingly uncomplicated male animal and his own opposite as a hero. Caesar proclaims: "Come, Cleopatra: forgive me and bid me farewell; and I will send you a man, Roman from head to heel and Roman of the noblest; not old and ripe for the knife; not lean in the arms and cold in the heart; not hiding a bald head under his conqueror's laurels; not stooped with the weight of the world on his shoulders; but brisk and fresh, strong and young, hoping in the morning, fighting in the day, and revelling in the evening. Will you take such an one in exchange for Caesar?" Cleopatra jumps at the offer to the tune of Rufio's defining comment, "You are a bad hand at a bargain, mistress, if you will swap Caesar for Antony." In effect, this remark is addressed to spectators of the time who preferred Mark Antony's type to Caesar's, and a bloodless gentlemanly hero to either. After Cleopatra, now wholly reconciled, drops a tear at Caesar's departure, most of these spectators would fall into Shaw's ideal-destroying trap by vicariously sharing the final "Hail, Caesar"—that is, by silently acknowledging that greatness by no means depends upon following English ideals, but may very well be attained when a man simply does what he naturally wants to do.

Captain Brassbound's Conversion

Shaw's next play contains a similar trap for idealists. Once again he stakes an impression of natural heroic virtue against "expiatory theories of moral responsibility, guilt, innocence, reward, punishment, and the rest." Again he recommends as "the only possible way in the end" the way without punishment, revenge, or judgment. Again the convincing image of greatness embodies the Shavio-Puritan attributes of heroic virtue and relies for its effectiveness upon the naïve feeling underlying the hero's ideas. And again the hero is a successful conqueror, even though in this case the conqueror is a woman.

These parallels between *Caesar and Cleopatra* and its successor are probably not coincidental. In composing *Captain Brassbound's Conversion,* Shaw seems to have relied more upon craftsmanship than inspiration: the actress he considered comparable in stature to Forbes-Robertson as a "classic" performer, Ellen Terry, had been clamoring for a worthwhile part, and he complied by writing the play "to please her and not as a matter of business" (*HMC*, p. 474). Moreover, Shaw began *Brassbound* soon after spending a year on *Caesar and Cleopatra,* and he finished it in two months—"with some £60 worth of journalism stolen out of the middle."[27]

It is not surprising, therefore, that the sharpshooting strategies and targets of *Captain Brassbound's Conversion* are much the same as those in *Caesar;* nor is it surprising that they are presented on a smaller scale. Here Shaw employs the broad, clear contrasts of the melodramatic mode, keeping "well within that vast tract of passion and motive which is common to the philosopher and the laborer." His main point is still the superiority of natural virtue over ideal goodness; but this time he forgoes the more subtle distinction between the "brute" and the "fool" which he had capitalized upon in *Caesar and Cleopatra.* Furthermore, instead of dealing at length with duty, honor, and the other mainstays of the gentlemanly hero, he refers to them here only occasionally, and then in distinct subordination to his central targets.

These targets can be conveniently identified by matching characters in the two plays—Britannus with Sir Howard Hallam, Cleopatra with Captain Brassbound, and Caesar with Lady Cicely Waynflete. Britannus and Sir Howard are both pessimistic idealists. Shaw's ineffectual Briton upholds justice on the grounds that "society must become like an arena full of wild beasts" without it; Sir Howard, speaking with the authority of a professional judge, warns Lady Cicely against the Moors because they have "no laws to restrain them, which means, in plain English, that they are habitual thieves and murderers." Through the character of Sir Howard, Shaw is attacking what he calls in the Notes to *Brassbound* "the pretence that our [legal] institutions represent abstract principles of justice" (p. 297). In *Caesar,* Shaw exposes this misconception by having Caesar define justice as the "right" to inflict vengeance upon an offender; in other words, laws involving punishment amount to common passions elevated into abstract principles.[28] The same blending of justice with vengeance occurs in *Brassbound,* where it is clarified with the sharp contrasts typical of melodrama. Because Sir Howard once treated Captain Brassbound's mother badly (though not illegally), Brassbound makes him a prisoner in a Moorish castle and vows: "I shall do no more than justice."

SIR HOWARD. . . . . Justice! I think you mean vengeance, disguised as justice by your passions.

BRASSBOUND. To many and many a poor wretch in the dock *you* have brought vengeance in that disguise—the vengeance of society, disguised as justice by *its* passions. Now the justice you have outraged meets you disguised as vengeance. How do you like it?

Later the tables are turned, and Sir Howard openly reveals his vengeful passion by looking at Brassbound in the "deadly way" his enemy had looked at him.

When Brassbound assumes that vengeance is a right, he is clearly manifesting Cleopatra's point of view. The similarities between the two characters extend a little beyond this: neither the captain nor the queen treats subordinates humanely. If Cleopatra were a strong English captain in her mid-thirties, she would kick her underlings as Brassbound kicks his; and if she were the chief of an escort into the dangerous land of Morocco, she would expect to shoot Moors to keep them under control, which is Brassbound's method. In *Captain Brassbound's Conversion*, however, Shaw avoids the complicating distinction between natural vice and natural virtue (which keeps Cleopatra in the feline class). Despite the captain's automatic reliance upon brute force, his "better nature"—a necessity in melodramatic villains headed for conversion—is allowed to assert itself in the quasi-romantic finale.

Lady Cicely and Caesar account for most of the parallels between the two plays. They cause the realities behind vengeance and its legal mask, justice, to be exposed; they lead the characters of second importance, Brassbound and Cleopatra, to disclose whatever is best in their natures; they demonstrate at the expense of these characters the proper way to treat enemies and subordinates; and they even make the finales of the plays quasi-romantic. The fact that Cicely wields as much influence as Caesar, except for the proportion that comes from his lofty rank, points to the personal qualities she shares with him. She exhibits the same four requisites of greatness: freedom from ideals, natural benevolence, an active intellect, and a passion for humanity. A stage direction describes her as "sympathetic, intelligent, tender and humorous," and "a woman of great vitality and humanity." Like Caesar, her vitality expresses itself in conquering (at least in a figurative sense), and her humanity prompts her to give equal consideration and sympathy to everyone she meets. Shaw visualizes her as "not merely the maternal, managing woman who likes everybody and loves nobody. She is also the adventurous, fearless woman, seeking new countries and new people to play with. That combination is not common. Have you ever noticed that the highest type of conqueror is an incorrigible explorer?"[29] This statement applies just as well (if not better) to Caesar, who announces that he is "part woman" with "nothing of man in [him] at all," and whose heralded ambition Shaw dismisses in the Notes to the play as "an instinct for exploration" (p. 207). A final link between Caesar and Cicely lies in the centrality of their roles. Nearly everything in *Caesar and Cleopatra* revolves about the hero's ideal-destroying and humanizing functions; and as Shaw remarks, all the characters in *Captain Brassbound's Conversion* are the "merest doormats" for the heroine (*Ellen Terry and Bernard Shaw*, p. 240).

The personalities and dramatic functions of Caesar and Cicely reveal important differences, of course. Whereas Shaw thought of his Caesar as an authentic restoration of an ill-represented giant of history, he obviously had no such model for Cicely. Besides being a woman of great heroic virtue, she is also Shaw's substitute for the tremulous, ladylike heroine common in the nineties: his original portrait of the great English lady. Speaking in general of such a personage, Shaw remarks: "A lady is—or in Ellen

Terry's generation was—a person trained to the utmost attainable degree in the art and habit of concealing her feelings and maintaining an imperturbable composure under the most trying circumstances" (*Ellen Terry and Bernard Shaw*, p. ix). Explaining Cicely's role itself to an actress, he insisted: "Before you can play Lady Cicely perfectly, you will have to do what the author did . . . ; that is, make a careful study of the English lady. . . . She would hardly ever show real excitement, or lose her distinction and immense self-complacency" (*Shaw on Theatre*, pp. 81–82).

The two heroic counterparts are also granted different degrees of ethical and political significance. For *Caesar and Cleopatra*, Shaw selected an episode of history which he could profitably rework to bolster his immediate purpose: the replacement of the gentlemanly hero with the naturally virtuous one. The ethical import of the play was central to him, its political import only peripheral. No doubt *Caesar* had its implications for statesmen of the nineties because of the nature of its refurbished historical episode, but Shaw did not design it to convey these implications: nearly everything in the play is meant to help project a distinctive image of heroic virtue. The same is not precisely true of *Captain Brassbound's Conversion*. For that play, Shaw similarly chose a sequence of actions which would help promote a new image of greatness, but this time he combined his main purpose with an object lesson for English imperialism. He explained the relation between this political analogy and the heroine's "heart wisdom" and "moral superiority" in a scolding letter to Ellen Terry, who at first disliked the play:

> Listen to me, woman with no religion. Send to your library for two books of travel in Africa: one Miss Kingsley's . . . and the other H. M. Stanley's. Compare the brave woman, with her commonsense and good will, with the wild-beast

man, with his elephant rifle, and his atmosphere of dread
and murder, breaking his way by mad selfish assassination
out of the difficulties created by his own cowardice. Think
of all that has been rising up under your eyes in Europe for
years past, Bismarck worship, Stanley worship, Dr Jim worship, and now at last Kitchener worship with dead enemies
dug up and mutilated. Think also on the law—the gallows,
penal servitude, hysterical clamoring for the lash, m[e]re
cowardice masquerading as "resolute government," "law
and order" and the like. Well, how have you felt about
things? Have you had any real belief in the heroism of
the filibuster? Have you had any sympathy with the pun-
ishments of the judge? Have you found in your own
life and your own small affairs no better way, no more instructive heart wisdom, no warrant for trusting to the good
side of people instead of terrorizing the bad side of them.
I—poor idiot!—thought the distinction of Ellen Terry was
that she had this heart wisdom, and managed her own little
world as Tolstoy would have our Chamberlains and Balfours
and German Emperors and Kitcheners and Lord Chief Jus-
tices and other slaves of false ideas and imaginary fears
manage Europe. I accordingly give you a play in which you
stand in the very place where Imperialism is most believed
to be necessary, on the border line where the European meets
the fanatical African, with judge on the one hand, and indomitable adventurer-filibuster on the other, said I. A-F.
pushing forward "civilization" in the shape of rifles and
pistols in the hands of Hooligans, aristocratic *mauvais sujets*
and stupid drifters.[30] I try to shew these men gaining a sense
of courage and resolution from continual contact with and
defiance of their own fears. I try to shew you fearing nobody
and managing them all as Daniel managed the lions, not by
cunning—above all, not by even a momentary appeal to
Cleopatra's stand-by, their passions—but by simple moral
superiority. It is a world-wide situation, and one totally
incomprehensible to Cleopatras of all sorts and periods. . . .
Here is a part which dominates a play because the character
it represents dominates the world. (*Ellen Terry and Bernard
Shaw*, pp. 247–48)

Clearly, Shaw worked important political implications into

Captain Brassbound's Conversion and geared his presentation of the heroine to them. A touch ironically, his lesson for imperialists is highly appropriate to a dramatization of feminine heroic virtue. To show how a nation's men should act when they dominate the world, he shows a great lady from that nation dominating everyone about her in a maternal—not manly—fashion. The political import of the play thus indirectly magnifies its ethical import.

Shaw's strategy of depicting feminine greatness in *Brassbound* culminates in one crucial and impressive scene, the trial scene in the last act. During the trial (a staple of third acts in melodrama—witness *The Devil's Disciple*), Cicely becomes perhaps the most astonishing witness in the history of melodrama. Her behavior, the outgrowth of Shaw's aim to convey a new image of the stage heroine, also remains unparalleled in the entire Shavian gallery of women. Cicely intentionally talks "nonsense" which is actually "the exact truth," and she proves by winning her case that "half a dozen such women would make an end of law in England in six months." In the process, she receives the apparently conflicting epithets "unscrupulous" and "saint," and she deserves both.

Cicely alone perceives the true motives underlying the events which have resulted in the trial. To each of the idealists, his own past and present actions are completely accounted for and justified by abstract principles of law (Sir Howard) or heroism (Brassbound). To Cicely, such principles are no more than harmfully misleading facades. We learn bit by bit that thirty years before, Howard Hallam's brother, Miles, died at a remote British protectorate with meager facilities for enforcing the law. He left a remunerative estate, a neurotic wife, and—as Sir Howard discovers too late—a son, Brassbound himself. Unfortunately for the widow and her baby, Miles put the estate in charge of a crafty agent, who proceeded to pocket all its earnings. Brassbound's mother went to England in order to enlist the legal aid of Howard, then a struggling barrister, but was driven to drink and finally to insanity by what seemed to her (and later to Brassbound) a heartless lack of desire on Howard's part to right an obvious wrong. The truth was that he could neither afford to travel a great distance nor accomplish anything effective at long range. When the maddened woman at last berated him publicly and threatened to kill him, he felt compelled to have her imprisoned, then forced her to apologize and to leave England forever. (When Brassbound learns of this further mistreatment, he is of course infuriated.) By the time Brassbound's mother died, Howard had become a titled, well-to-do Attorney General. He visited the estate, and to secure belated justice, gained control of it by tricking the agent. The rightful heir, Brassbound, now had a double grudge against his uncle. Vowing revenge in the name of duty to both his mother and himself, he became the leader of a band of outlaws and morbidly nursed the thought of vengeance. The play commences when the two men are about to meet for the first time.

Morocco, land of the fanatic Mohammedans, is the setting for Brassbound's plot to inflict poetic justice upon Sir Howard. The Captain leads the judge and Lady Cicely on an excursion which is actually a trap. At a Moorish castle, he reveals his identity to his uncle and announces that the Sheikh Sidi el Assif, who kills or enslaves Christians such as Sir Howard, will soon arrive to administer his own brand of justice. In the first conversion scene of the play, however, Cicely ingeniously belittles Brassbound's motives and convinces him that he should abandon his attempt at vengeance. When the Sheikh comes, therefore, Brassbound bargains for Sir Howard's life, a reversal that the indignant prisoner never appreciates. The Sheikh, who is attracted to Cicely, offers to take her instead. She consents with pleasure, but the Cadi, an officer of the local Sultan, backed by a letter from an American naval captain heading a search party, intervenes on behalf of the two British travellers. Brassbound, receiving an ominous look from Sir Howard after the tables are turned, poses the new dilemma to Cicely: "You persuaded me to spare him. Look at his face. Will you be able to persuade him to spare me?" Cicely must bring about a second conversion at the ensuing trial.

Her view of these events, and especially of the motives behind them, is highly independent. She deduces that the whole affair is in essence a family quarrel between strong-minded idealists. One reason she does so is largely irrelevant: she is, after all, part of Sir Howard's family, his deceased wife's sister. Primarily, however, Cicely is Shavian enough to believe that passion, not principle, is the real moving force behind significant actions, and to perceive that the justifications they give for their actions are mere rationalizations encouraged by their feelings and by false ideals. Thus she concludes that Sir Howard acted as he did toward Brassbound's mother fundamentally because he disliked her.[31] In converting Brassbound, she suggests that this might be the case, and then continues: "You know . . . that if you don't like people you think of all the reasons for not helping them, and if you like them you think of all the opposite reasons." Presumably Sir Howard thought of a clinching reason for not helping his sister-in-law when she finally insulted his integrity and threatened his life: these were clear violations of honor and of the law. At bottom, the Hallam temperament and Sir Howard's professional ideals explain his humiliating treatment of her, and later his determination to punish Brassbound. In the same vein, Cicely deduces that Brassbound is his uncle all over again: an irritable, "pigheaded" Hallam believing in "ruling people by force . . . and in revenge and punishment." The only difference is that he does not get paid for upholding these beliefs.

At the trial, Cicely reports the affair according to these distinctively Shavian interpretations. The phrase "the exact truth" reverberates through the act: it is repeated four times before the inquiry and three times during it. An exchange between Cicely and Sir Howard after she has finished testifying shows precisely what she means by the phrase in contrast to "the *whole* truth":

> LADY CICELY. . . . . Now, Howard, isn't that the exact truth, every word of it?
> SIR HOWARD. It is the truth, Cicely, and nothing but the truth. But the English law requires a witness to tell the *whole* truth.
> LADY CICELY. What nonsense! As if anybody ever knew the whole truth about anything!

Cicely never backs down from her position, even when the man she has saved implies that she has departed from the truth for his sake. Brassbound says, "a man should tell his own lies. I'm sorry you had to tell mine for me to-day." Cicely replies, "Oh, women spend half their lives telling little lies for men, and sometimes big ones. We're used to it. But mind! I don't admit that I told any to-day." In her opinion, and also in Shaw's, she has indeed told nothing but the truth.

What she actually reveals are the essential, basic causes of the affair, unobscured by conventional or "reasonable" incrustations. In the process, she also reduces other explanations to absurdity, especially if they evoke ideals. She fulfils this two-edged ideal-destroying function by deliberately adopting a naïve and flighty manner. Earlier in the play Shaw conveyed an impression of her natural virtue with a technique used frequently in *Caesar and Cleopatra:* that is, by dramatizing the "naive feeling underlying [her] ideas" in spontaneous, uncalculated moments. For exam-

ple, when Sheikh Sidi asks to have Cicely in return for
Sir Howard, the men are appalled, but she is genuinely
delighted. ("I shall be all right now that I am getting away
from the escort," she adds.) More often in the play, however, Shaw varies this technique: through most of the first
and second acts he makes Cicely sound as if she were in
fact naïve, while in the third act and at other crucial points
he has her consciously play the *naïf*.

The first of these variations, as far as dramatic effect is
concerned, serves to prepare for the second by contrast.
In Act I, for instance, the audience has already been informed that Cicely once walked across Africa with only
a dog for company, yet few spectators would be prepared
to grant her much brain power when she says in reply to
Rankin's warning against travelling in Morocco: "But I
always go everywhere. I *know* the people here won't touch
me. They have such nice faces and such pretty scenery."
Sir Howard's term for many of her stupefying comments
is "nonsense"—a mistaken estimate, but a fair translation
of the audience's immediate reaction. The culminating
instance of this type of comment and reaction occurs, significantly, just before the trial begins. Speaking to the
American naval officer, Captain Kearney, Cicely deplores
the fact that women are not permitted to accompany their
husbands on shipboard: "It's most serious, Captain. The
poor men go melancholy mad, and ram each other's ships
and do all sorts of things." Sir Howard interrupts typically: "Cicely: I beg you will not talk nonsense to Captain
Kearney. Your ideas on some subjects are really hardly
decorous." But Shaw, for the first time, has included a lis-
tener who is qualified by experience to verify the sense
of Cicely's nonsense. Thus their exchange is a minor
turning point:

> LADY CICELY (*to Kearney*). That's what English people
> are like, Captain Kearney. They won't hear of anything con-

cerning you poor sailors except Nelson and Trafalgar. *You
understand me, don't you?*
    KEARNEY (*gallantly*). I cawnsider that you have more sense
in your wedding ring finger than the British Ahdmiralty has
in its whole cawnstitootion, Lady Waynflete.

We also hear that Cicely learned such indecorous truths
from one of her uncles, the first Lord of the Admiralty.
    Cicely's intentionally staged exhibition of naïveté dur-
ing the trial is quite different from this unpremeditated
but well-grounded "nonsense." The entire trial scene takes
on its prevailing quality from the complicated impression
produced by her surface ingenuousness and the determined, almost frenetic mental activity that accompanies
it as a hidden undercurrent. For two acts Shaw has conditioned the audience to expect the flightiness that Cicely
exhibits more extravagantly than ever in this scene. But
in two quick strokes just before the trial, he proves dramatically that her intellectual faculties are in full use at
all times. The first, so striking as to be almost sufficient in
itself, unites surprise with an abrupt confirmation of the
audience's mild suspicion that Cicely may indeed work for
the welfare of her ideal-corrupted friends with her mind
as well as her womanly emotions. In order to save Brassbound, she must convince Sir Howard that he should not
give his version of the story at the trial. Accordingly, when
he sits next to her in an idle moment, "she comes to the
other end of the table, looking at Sir Howard with a troubled, sorrowfully sympathetic air, but unconsciously making her right hand stalk about the table on the tips of its
fingers in a tentative stealthy way which would put Sir
Howard on his guard if he were in a suspicious frame of
mind." This revealing action is designed to send a thrill of
enlightenment through the audience and to suggest a new
angle of vision from which to view the heroine's ensuing
actions. Shaw's second stroke reinforces the first. Cicely

asks Sir Howard if it would not be better for her to speak
in place of him at the trial, since he may be misunderstood
if he testifies against his own nephew: "The proper thing
for you to do, Howard, is to let *me* tell the exact truth.
Then you can simply say that you are bound to confirm
me. Nobody can blame you for that." He replies with an
authoritative show of suspicion: "Cicely: you are up to
some devilment." She is, of course, and the audience is now
sure of it.

Having gotten her way with Sir Howard, Cicely proceeds
to get her way at the trial. She does so by posing sometimes
as the vacuous, conventional relative worried about what
people will think of her brother-in-law, and sometimes as
the oblivious Pollyanna incapable of seeing beyond nice
faces and pretty scenery. Qute naturally, she causes confusion in the court, especially on the part of the acting judge,
Captain Kearney. But after Shaw's careful preparation,
the audience is well prepared to absorb the shock of her
peculiar rendition of the conflict between the two idealistic Hallams. She testifies as follows (I include sidelights
that illumine the effect of her words):

> I can only tell you the exact truth—
> DRINKWATER (*involuntarily*). Naow, down't do thet,
> lidy. . . .
> LADY CICELY. We had a most delightful trip in the hills;
> and Captain Brassbound's men could not have been nicer—
> I must say that for them—until we saw a tribe of Arabs—
> such nice looking men!—and then the poor˒ things were
> frightened.
> KEARNEY. The Arabs?
> LADY CICELY. No: Arabs are never frightened. The escort,
> of course: escorts are always frightened. I wanted to speak
> to the Arab chief; but Captain Brassbound cruelly shot his
> horse; and the chief shot the Count; and then—
> KEARNEY. The Count! What Count?
> LADY CICELY. Marzo. That's Marzo. . . .
> KEARNEY (*slightly overwhelmed by the unexpected pro-*

fusion of incident and character in her story). Well, what happened then?

LADY CICELY. Then the escort ran away—all escorts do— and dragged me into the castle, which you really ought to make them clean and whitewash thoroughly, Captain Kearney. Then Captain Brassbound and Sir Howard turned out to be related to one another (*sensation*); and then of course, there was a quarrel. The Hallams always quarrel.

SIR HOWARD (*rising to protest*). Cicely! Captain Kearney: this man told me— [he alludes to Brassbound's threat]

LADY CICELY (*swiftly interrupting him* [her first flash of intellectual fire]). You mustn't say what people told you: it's not evidence. (*Sir Howard chokes with indignation.*) . . .

LADY CICELY. Then Sidi came. . . . A noble creature, with such a fine face! He fell in love with me at first sight—

SIR HOWARD (*remonstrating*). Cicely!

LADY CICELY. He did: you know he did. You told me to tell the exact truth. . . . Well, that put the poor fellow into a most cruel dilemma. You see, he could claim to carry off Sir Howard, because Sir Howard is a Christian. But as I am only a woman, he had no claim on me. . . . Well, what was he to do? He wasn't in love with Sir Howard; and he *was* in love with me. So he naturally offered to swop Sir Howard for me. Don't you think that was nice of him, Captain Kearney? . . . Captain Brassbound, I must say, was nobleness itself, in spite of the quarrel between himself and Sir Howard. He refused to give up either of us, and was on the point of fighting for us when in came the Cadi with your most amusing and delightful letter, captain, and bundled us all back to Mogador after calling my poor Sidi the most dreadful names, and putting all the blame on Captain Brassbound. So here we are. . . . [She sits down.]

KEARNEY. But Sir Howard told me yesterday that Captain Brassbound threatened to sell him into slavery.

LADY CICELY (*springing up again* [her second flash of intellect]). Did Sir Howard tell you the things he said about Captain Brassbound's mother? (*Renewed sensation.*) I told you they quarreled, Captain Kearney. . . . Of course I did. Now, . . . do *you* want me—does Sir Howard want me—does *anybody* want me to go into the details of that shocking family quarrel? . . .

KEARNEY. . . . . The United States navy will have no hahnd in offering any violence to the pure instincts of womanhood. Lady Waynflete: I thahnk you for the delicacy with which you have given your evidence. (*Lady Cicely beams on him gratefully and sits down triumphant.*)

If this testimony were paraphrased "in the style of a bluebook, carefully preserving every idea"—a challenge that Shaw implies (*OTN*, III, 322)—it would be found to contain "the exact truth" according to Cicely's Shavian ideas of human motivation. By its combination of such truth and its obviously ludicrous manner, her testimony might seem to represent the first extended example in Shaw's plays of the dramatic jest in earnest. This is a technique that he carries to great lengths in his late period, when his main object is to implant ideas rather than to destroy ideals, and he is perfectly willing to have the audience respond only to the ludicrous surface of the serious event. Here, however, the very element that sets it apart from later examples, the fact that the audience learns the serious idea behind the jest, is exactly what makes Shaw's penetration through ideals in the play highly effective. The technique becomes an instrument of his immediate purpose.

Captain Brassbound's Conversion concludes with a Shavian love scene in which Lady Cicely almost consents to become Captain Brassbound's wife and commander, but is saved when he suddenly divines "the secret of command." This secret, which she has already disclosed to him, reflects back not only upon her character and behavior in the play, but also upon Shaw's fundamental dramatic point in his entire early period. Cicely states his point as follows: "Do whatever you like. That's what I always do." In other words, fulfil your will with no regard for social reticences, moral prescriptions, or ideals of any sort; be useful even at the cost of your reputation. The statement as such has little or no effect on Brassbound, who becomes preoccupied with the desire to "take service" under Cicely, but her advice begins to manifest itself in his very actions. Paradoxically, his urge to put himself in Cicely's power stimulates his will to such an extent that he gradually gains an almost mesmeric power over her. The process involves scorning all the obstructing ideals—male dominance, public opinion, love in marriage—and finding all the necessary arguments:

> LADY CICELY (*shaking her head*). I have never been in love with any real person; and I never shall. How could I manage people if I had that mad little bit of self left in me? . . .
> BRASSBOUND. Then throw away the last bit of self. Marry me.
> LADY CICELY (*vainly struggling to recall her wandering will*). Must I?
> BRASSBOUND. There is no must. You *can*.

He succeeds in overcoming her once-impregnable will, but his triumph simultaneously changes in nature. It convinces him once and for all of the fragility of ideals and of the power of his own will. He has finally found Shaw's secret of command.

Chapter 5

*Bertrand Russell on Shaw: "I think the greatest service
Shaw did was in dispelling humbug by laughter. We
all talk in a different way from that in which people talked
before Shaw, and even our emotions hardly allow
themselves such delicious exhibitions of concealed egoism
as were customary in Victorian times. No one nowadays
tells a boy: 'It hurts me more than it hurts you,'
and few people have the face to speak of 'a fate worse
than death.' It is no longer necessary to assume that
all parents love their children and all children love their
parents. We can admit to feelings of vanity, which,
though just as common formerly as they are now, were for
some reason thought to belong only to all the rest
of the world and not to oneself. There is certainly much
less insincerity in family relations and in people's
estimate of themselves than there used to be. The later
stages of the change perhaps owe most to Freud,
but the earlier stages, so far as England is concerned,
were brought about by Shaw."*[1]

Shaw's Dramatic Strategies up to *Man and Superman*

After composing ten plays whose dramatic effects are consistently geared to destroying ideals, Shaw turned to another primary aim in his next play, *Man and Superman* —that of cultivating the intellect. This shift in ethical aim, and corresponding shift in artistic method, represents a subtle but distinct change of emphasis rather than a new departure. It is a turning point, not a fresh start. Hence, a concise outline of the strategies in the ten plays before *Man and Superman* should help considerably in understanding the first major watershed in Shaw's dramatic career. The less notable differences in ethical and artistic bent that occur among the three stages of his early period, moreover, must be viewed in their true proportions if a more radical change is to stand out plainly. A systematic review of these stages should therefore stress the relative significance of the many variations, small and large, that mark Shaw's gradual development through the eighteen-nineties.

Among the variations that set the three groups of early plays apart, their dissimilarities in cumulative effect, or total impression, are most important. For example, the frustrating sense of wasted vitality conveyed by *Mrs. Warren's Profession* differs greatly from the pleasureful wish-fulfillments of its immediate successor, *Arms and the Man*.

209

In contrast, two other adjoining plays that diverge sharply in structure and content, *The Devil's Disciple* and *Caesar and Cleopatra*, differ much less in final impression: symptomatically, both conclude with overt celebrations of heroic virtue. Cumulative effects of this sort are almost impossible to describe at once precisely and briefly. Shaw's terms, "unpleasant" and "pleasant," suggest the effects of the propaganda plays and critical comedies well enough to distinguish clearly between them; and the term "celebrative," or perhaps "exhilarating," suggests the effects of the humanizations in a parallel way. More accurate and useful descriptions will arise from an account of the main causes of such effects, Shaw's ethical and artistic strategies.

For the sake of clarity, I will outline these tightly integrated strategies by artificially dividing them into four classes. Each of the early plays, we can say, has its own destructive and constructive tactics. For instance, to the extent that *Caesar and Cleopatra* is an attempt to discredit the conventional heroic embodiment of accepted ideals, the gentlemanly hero, it is also an attempt to recommend a distinctly Shavian image of natural heroism and virtue. That is, the ethical purpose of the play has a positive as well as a negative side. The play's artistic purpose can be viewed in the same fashion. *Caesar* is both a "revival" of heroic drama and an antitype of the current version of the form (much as *Arms and the Man* is both a romantic and an antiromantic comedy). It is not too implausible, then, to separate Shaw's strategies in the early plays into four categories. The following summary makes use of these semantic distinctions.

1. *Destructive ethical strategies.* The points of reference here are the targets Shaw selects for his sharpshooting: the specific ideals he seeks to destroy in each group of plays. Broadly speaking, he aims at ideals of two types:

those which pertain to the institutional structure of society
—social ideals—and those which pertain to human conduct—
moral ideals. Both represent accredited and prevalent illusions that were normally evoked without hesitation in the
popular drama of the nineties. As Shaw moves toward *Man
and Superman,* he gradually shifts his main attack from
particular illusions about society which obstruct social evolution to general illusions about humanity which impede
human evolution.

The propaganda plays, beginning this progression, attack
economic and sociological ideals, especially ones that derive
from capitalism and stand in the way of Fabian Socialism.
Shaw cares less about social defects which are remediable
by changes in law or procedure than he does about basic
attitudes toward society that work against all social improvement. Thus *Widowers' Houses* and *The Philanderer*
spread an aura of unpleasantness over pessimistic and
rationalistic attitudes, respectively, and *Mrs. Warren's Profession* attaches the stigma of prostitution to the capitalistic principles of selling oneself for a living and making
as much money as possible.

In contrast, the critical comedies attack illusions that
arise, not from established forms of social organization,
but from man's relation to society in general. These
plays feature an onslaught on moral and romantic ideals:
to Shaw, ideals that defy reality by their very nature.
Whereas *Widowers' Houses* and *The Philanderer* cast dis-
favor upon antimelioristic pessimism and rationalism, *Arms
and the Man* and *You Never Can Tell* derogate the anti-
realistic kinds. Moreover, Shaw's weapons in these comedies
are not unpleasant effects, but humane ridicule and considerate sympathy. His use of sympathy in *Candida* to
expose the illusory nature of "monogamic idealism" plainly
illustrates his changes in strategy.

The next group of plays assaults the heroic and theatrical illusions about human motivation that were propagated by the melodramatic plays of the time. Far from centering on sociological ideals—in fact, remote from any restricting social frame at all—the humanizations of heroic types of drama concern the utmost heights and depths of human conduct. In *The Man of Destiny*, a rudimentary example of this tendency, Shaw pits his own theories of heroism against the prevailing theatrical codes. In *The Devil's Disciple*, a more advanced example, he opposes the "romantic metaphysic" that dictated stereotyped motives of heroism by substituting Shavio-Puritan natural motives. *Caesar and Cleopatra* and its feminine counterpart, *Captain Brassbound's Conversion*, offer fully elaborated replacements for the approved heroic incarnations of ideals of goodness, the gentlemanly hero and the ladylike heroine.

2. *Constructive ethical strategies.* Another highly significant way of measuring Shaw's development in his early period involves examining the kinds of reality he perceives behind the ideals he attacks. Here we are dealing with a body of intricate concepts that resist rigid classification, but which Shaw confidently terms "a genuinely scientific natural history." Three phrases often used in this study sum up these major aspects of Shavian theory: Fabian Socialism, respect for reality, and natural heroism.

In the propaganda plays, Shaw postulates that the welfare state desired by Fabian socialists will gradually materialize as their concerted campaign of permeation takes its toll among existing institutions. This process, especially when adapted to the theatre, works best if its alliance with socialist meliorism goes unnoticed. Only in *Mrs. Warren's Profession*, therefore, does Shaw permit a note of meliorist aspiration to sound out, and then only for seconds. In *Widowers' Houses* the reformer is a "stage socialist" who is promptly converted, and in *The Philanderer* the Ibsenite makes the most of society as he finds it. Fabian Socialism itself is implicitly recommended in all three plays, but never mentioned.

Shaw's strategy is again largely implicit in the critical comedies. He "preaches the worth of the real" by attracting favor to heterodox behavior and by evoking sympathy for the "distinctively human" in man. The premise operating here is Shaw's conviction that individual wills, not ideals, are the sacred things in life. The common sense and sympathy of both Bluntschli in *Arms and the Man* and the heroine in *Candida* are calculated to increase the audience's respect for reality, and the breakthroughs in *You Never Can Tell*, intrigues of nature on many planes, are designed expressly as gratifying humanizations.

Quite differently, *The Man of Destiny* and the *Three Plays for Puritans* encourage admiration for man's instincts and passions, largely by presenting heroes "in whom we can recognise our own humanity." Shaw dramatizes a theory of natural heroism that credits the human will for virtue as well as courage. This theory is partially stated outright in *The Man of Destiny*; it supplies the motives for heroic virtue in *The Devil's Disciple*; and in amplified form, it underlies the impressions of greatness put forth in *Caesar and Cleopatra* and *Captain Brassbound's Conversion*.

For the sake of added precision, these aspects of "natural history" in the three groups of plays might be approached through the "genuinely scientific" basis of each. Briefly, the propaganda plays are grounded in the bluebook facts that Shaw was concerned with as a Fabian; the critical comedies reflect his independent observations of human nature; and the humanizations are founded upon his theories of natural motivation. I am exaggerating these differences, but doing so helps to clarify the fluctuations that derive from Shaw's changing ethical interests.

3. *Destructive artistic strategies.* Eric Bentley and
Martin Meisel have adequately described how the early
plays exploit and recondition contemporary modes of
drama. I have therefore slighted this subject throughout.
At any rate, of the four lines of strategy I have considered, this one clearly has the least significant bearing upon
the lasting effects of Shaw's plays. Many of the ideals he
sought to destroy are still prevalent today, though perhaps
unfashionable; but few of the actual forms of drama that
reflected these ideals are with us at all. Indeed, an act of
historical imagination is required to estimate the transitory
effects that such permeative tactics must have produced.

In brief, then, the propaganda plays represent Shaw's
exploitations of the comic, farcical, and melodramatic
problem play forms which were highly regarded in the
eighties and nineties. The critical comedies permeate three
different forms, all related to romance: romantic drama,
domestic drama, and farcical comedy. Among the humanizations of heroic types of drama, two modify quite specific
types: *The Man of Destiny,* Sardou's *Madame Sans-Gêne*
and its kin; *The Devil's Disciple,* Adelphi melodrama. The
other two humanizations, in contrast, attempt to transform
heroic drama in general: *Caesar and Cleopatra,* drama fea-
turing a great hero, and *Captain Brassbound's Conversion,*
a great heroine. Shaw's progress in this respect is marked
by a phase of close adherence to popular genres from 1895
to 1897, then a movement away from conformity and
toward the generic innovations of his middle period.

4. *Constructive artistic strategies.* Whereas critics
have treated the early plays at length as antitypes of popular genres, they have ignored them for all practical purposes as examples of distinct genres in their own right. Yet
the dynamics of a play that determine its genre are precisely those qualities of its artistry which matter most in

the long run. Dramatic effects which depend for their intensity on passing phases of theatrical appeal, literary fashion, and moral sensitivity can literally cease to exist. But effects which are built into the very fabric of a play so that they constitute its chief elements of organization are capable of maintaining their power for spectators and readers of any era. These durable qualities are the ones that give the play as a whole a chance to survive.

The organizing principles of Shaw's first three dramas are didactic. Accordingly, I have called them propaganda plays rather than comedies, tragicomedies, or the like. But their "unpleasant" dramatic effects vary: thus *Widowers' Houses* is a comic propaganda play, *The Philanderer* is a farcical one, and *Mrs. Warren's Profession* is a melodramatic one. Strictly speaking, none of the remaining early plays have didactic principles of organization. The critical comedies approximate the effects of traditional comic forms: romantic comedy (*Arms and the Man*), sentimental comedy (*Candida*), and the comedy of manners (*You Never Can Tell*). Two of the humanizations are allied with less-known traditional genres: *The Devil's Disciple* is a comic melodrama and *Captain Brassbound's Conversion* is a melodramatic comedy. Shaw calls *Caesar and Cleopatra* simply a history play, but it can be more accurately termed a modern heroic drama. Finally, *The Man of Destiny* (like Shaw's other "trifle" before *Man and Superman*, *The Admirable Bashville*) is also a heroic drama of sorts, but it hardly deserves such an exalted label.

The gist of these summaries is that early Shavian drama is permeative rather than drastically innovative. All of the first ten plays reveal a close proximity to dramatic forms that were familiar in the nineties, whether recent developments like the problem play or favored traditional genres like romantic comedy. This proximity is itself strategic:

Shaw chose to permeate established forms because of his overriding ambition to destroy ideals. To him, the popular types of drama were so intimately associated with ideals in the playgoer's mind that the essential materials for his sharpshooting strategies—spectators' assumptions that ideals would be affirmed—were available with the greatest possible artistic economy within the framework of these popular genres. Since his chief ethical purpose was to destroy accredited illusions, the artistic forms that served him best were the accredited ones of the day.

This generalization makes *Man and Superman,* with its completely innovative debate in Act III, seem more of a new departure for Shaw than it really was. He undoubtedly crossed a borderline with this play; yet in an important sense it was a borderline that he had been approaching all along. In each play and group of plays, not only in each period, Shaw's choice of artistic form derived from his immediate ethical aim. Hence, for example, when he set out to replace romantic notions of heroic motivation with his own "Puritan" notions, he adopted the framework of Adelphi melodrama and altered the motives of the heroic characters. Shaw's progress on this plane of ethical strategy, a gradual movement from illusions and realities rooted in modes of social organization to those rooted in human passion, leads straight to *Man and Superman.* In that play he crossed the borderline where human passion is linked, theoretically and dramatically, with a cosmic force. Shaw's desire to explain this force and show it in action accounts for the artistic form of *Man and Superman,* a "forensic" drama in which the action consists of a case to be argued.

None of Shaw's first ten plays are similar amalgamations of case and argument. The propaganda plays are didactic and therefore have one kind of rhetorical form; but the range of argument they contain is deliberately limited because of their peculiar permeative strategies. The Fabian idea that poverty is far from inevitable, for instance, is not even mentioned in *Widowers' Houses*. To be sure, each of the unpleasant plays represents a case and offers some of the materials for an argument about it; but the argument is left up to the spectator, who is purposely encouraged to pursue it on his own. Moreover, we cannot use the term "argument" here without blurring it considerably, since the train of thought provoked by the intellectually frustrating effects of these plays is carefully channeled toward the repudiation of an illusion. Because Shaw's main object is to destroy particular ideals, not to cultivate thought, his argument in each propaganda play is actually a didactic point, and a negative one at that.

The chief dramatic method of Shaw's early plays, then, is not that of amalgamating case and argument, but rather that of sharpshooting at ideals. There are two main varieties of this method: convicting the audience of a "meanly false judgment" and engaging it in a "conflict of unsettled ideals." The propaganda plays, with their calculated use of problem play expectations, their blameless villains and easily scandalized minor characters, exhibit the first variety conspicuously. The critical comedies, which exploit conventional expectations in general and set idealists against each other and against anti-idealists, feature the second variety. In the humanizations of heroic types of drama, finally, images of the gentlemanly hero and the ladylike heroine are the real antagonists for Shaw's exemplars of natural greatness. Again, there is a conflict of ideals, but these ideals are not directly embodied in the plays. Instead, Shaw prefers to employ techniques that he specializes in later, the argumentative speech and the jest in earnest. Thus the artistic as well as the ethical strategies of Shaw's early-period works follow a course directly to *Man and Superman*.

The "terrible art of sharpshooting at the audience"—
de-Shavianized a bit, the art of destroying ideals—is a
dramatic method that Shaw plucked out of the late Victorian Zeitgeist, developed far beyond previous dramatists,
then relegated to a secondary place in his work. His Hell
in *Man and Superman* is a perfect rest home for idealists.
Having disposed of them in this ultimate philosophic as
well as dramatic way, Shaw took up more challenging and
impressive tasks. His middle-period plays are primarily
designed not to remove obstructing illusions, but to "create
new mind." A conflict of ideas replaces the former conflict of ideals. Idealist points of view are either cancelled
out in quick order (the stage Irishman in *John Bull's
Other Island* is exposed for what he is—a Scotsman—early
in the play) or thrown into hopeless competition with per-
spectives of much greater integrity (the spokesmen for
conventional marriages in *Getting Married* never have a
chance against several freethinkers and a bishop). A large
contingent of Britannuses in the audience is no longer
necessary for the plays to exert their full effect. Again
moving with the Zeitgeist, Shaw began formulating a dramaturgy for the modern age of relativity and analysis: an
argumentative dramaturgy. Still, his apprenticeship in the
school of undercover ideal-destroying not only served him
well as an evolutionary dramatist mired in an absolutist
time, but to an immeasurable extent also made the new
age possible.

NOTES

BIBLIOGRAPHY

INDEX

Notes

1 From a letter in James' *Complete Plays*, ed. Leon Edel (Philadelphia, 1949), p. 643.
2 *Ellen Terry and Bernard Shaw: A Correspondence*, ed. Christopher St. John (New York, 1932), p. 244.
3 Recorded in Hesketh Pearson, *G.B.S.: A Full Length Portrait*, 3rd ed. (New York, 1942), p. 196. His initial "Third Manner" work, he added, was *Back to Methuselah* (composed 1918–20).
4 Pref., *Back to Methuselah* (London, 1930), p. lxxxix.
5 Meisel, *Shaw and the Nineteenth-Century Theater* (Princeton, 1963); Nicoll, *A History of Late Nineteenth Century Drama, 1850–1900*, I (Cambridge, Eng., 1946), 193–204; Bentley, "The Making of a Dramatist (1892–1903)," an often-reprinted article first published in 1963 and available, for instance, in *Modern Drama: Essays in Criticism*, ed. Travis Bogard and William I. Oliver (New York, 1965), pp. 290–312.
6 On Shaw's three periods, see also Eric Bentley, *Bernard Shaw, 1856–1950*, amended ed. (New York, 1957); and Frederick P. W. McDowell, "Another Look at Bernard Shaw," *Drama Survey*, I (1961), 34–53.
7 Postscript to Frank Harris, *Bernard Shaw* (New York, 1931), p. 428.
8 Even his aesthetic theories spring directly from his doctrine of world-betterment. In *The Sanity of Art* (1895), he maintains that the value of art lies in its "solid useful-

ness," its capacity to add a "fresh extension of sense to the heritage of the race" (*MCE*, p. 316).

9 Comments at a debate on realism in fiction; paraphrased by Stephen Winsten in *Jesting Apostle: The Life of Bernard Shaw* (London, 1956), p. 71.

10 Not 1885, the date most sources give. Shaw and all his well-known biographers and commentators except R. F. Rattray and Dan H. Laurence have mistakenly relied upon the longhand MS of *Widowers' Houses* for the seminal date of his dramatic career. The original shorthand MS, however, is dated 1884; and I suspect from Shaw's error in dating the transcribed copy that the actual date of composition was the winter of 1884–85. F. E. Loewenstein examined the shorthand MS at Ayot St. Lawrence and recorded his findings in "The Autograph Manuscripts of George Bernard Shaw," *Book Handbook*, I (1947), 89–90.

11 Report of a lecture, "Mr. Bernard Shaw on the Drama," *Times* (London), March 8, 1906, p. 10.

12 *Everybody's Political What's What?* (New York, 1944), p. 194.

13 See the section on *Emperor and Galilean* (*MCE*, pp. 49–59).

14 In the latter, see esp. pp. 232–37. Several Shaw letters of 1890–91 that were not published until 1965 (in *CL*, I) explain his stand in the *Quintessence*. Of special interest are those to William Archer, esp. pp. 257–58 and 314–19; see also pp. 266, 268–70, and 277–80.

15 But Shaw "proves" it logically in the *Quintessence* (*MCE*, pp. 19–21).

16 Before *Man and Superman*, Shaw does not use the term "Life Force" (almost surely a translation of Bergson's *élan vital*). Instead, he refers to the concept as the "world will" or "Zeitgeist." See esp. *CL*, I, 228–29, an 1889 letter.

17 *The Intelligent Woman's Guide to Socialism and Capitalism* (New York, 1928), p. 365.

18 Directly relevant to Shaw's dramatic practice after 1900 (and of some significance for its earlier phase) is his

theory that a shrewd way to implant heterodox ideas in unreceptive minds is to present them as if they were not to be taken seriously. Masked in levity, they will escape the fate of most "scandalous" ideas, immediate suppression—at worst accompanied by the suppression of the author. They may even catch on as good jokes, so that people hearing them will unwittingly help the author disperse them, like bees spreading pollen. Shaw also believes that such ideas, once lodged in normally closed minds, will gradually assert their own validity and gain acceptance: "The mask of laughter wears slowly off . . . [and] men finally see them as they really are." As Peter Keegan puts it in *John Bull's Other Island*, "Every jest is an earnest in the womb of time." Shaw calls this a general law in the evolution of ideas. Dramatists of the Ibsen school, he says (not excluding himself), have used the technique of jesting in earnest with notable effect. See the chapter Shaw added to *The Quintessence of Ibsenism* for the 1913 edition, "What Is the New Element in the Norwegian School?" (*MCE*, pp. 126–34).

19 Reprinted in *MCE*, pp. 135–46. John Gassner uses this essay profitably as a suggestive analysis of modern realistic drama in general. See his *Form and Idea in Modern Theatre* (New York, 1956), pp. 40–42, and "Shaw on Ibsen and the Drama of Ideas," in *Ideas in the Drama: Selected Papers from the English Institute*, ed. Gassner (New York, 1964), pp. 71–100.

20 For the views of these critics, see my article, "Shaw's Cross Section of Anti-Shavian Opinion," *Shaw Review*, VII (1964), 78–86.

21 Most commercially successful dramatists of the time counted on playgoers' dedication to these ideals for surefire effects of righteous indignation and sentimental, "heart-warming" affirmation.

22 See, for instance, p. 50.

23 Shaw seems to have worked out the major features of this strategy independently. Before he could have discovered Ibsen, he explained the method of his first novel, *Imma-*

turity (composed in 1879), in terms that apply almost as well to his early plays: "This design was, to write a novel scrupulously true to nature, with no incident in it to which everyday experience might not afford a parallel, and yet which should constantly provoke in [a] reader full of the emotional ethics of the conventional novel, a sense of oddity and unexpectedness. In short, not to be ironic, but to deal with those ordinary experiences which are a constant irony on sentimentalism, at which the whole work is mainly directed" (*CL*, I, 27).

24   "Mr. Bernard Shaw on the Drama," p. 10.

25   Shaw rationalizes the dramatist's use of torment in an 1895 *Saturday Review* article: "The fact is, there is nothing the public despises so much as an attempt to please it. Torment is its natural element: it is only the saint who has any capacity for happiness. . . . The artist's rule must be Cromwell's: 'Not what they want, but what is good for them.' That rule, carried out in a kindly and sociable way, is the secret to success in the long run at the theatre as elsewhere" (*OTN*, I, 94–95).

26   "The Rejected Statement" [1909], in *The Doctor's Dilemma, Getting Married, & The Shewing-up of Blanco Posnet* (London, 1932), p. 374.

27   See John Russell Taylor's *The Rise and Fall of the Well-Made Play* (New York, 1967).

28   *Dramatic Criticism: Three Lectures* (London, 1903), pp. 98–99; *Drama and Life* (London, 1907), pp. 224–25.

29   Shaw is referring specifically to his middle-period plays. The early ones do not contain the prolonged discussions of ideas that we find, for instance, in *Man and Superman, John Bull's Other Island, Getting Married,* or *Misalliance.*

30   Another was his use of levity to mask his most heterodox ideas, though this was surely more a result of temperament than connivance. See n. 18 above.

31   "A Dramatic Realist to His Critics" (July 1894), in *Shaw on Theatre,* ed. E. J. West (New York, 1958), p. 23.

32   Later on, Shaw uses such genres merely as springboards

for his own post-Ibsen forms or as immediately comprehensible reference points to put the audience on familiar ground for a while. Again, see Meisel's study.

33 In contrast, after 1900 Shaw became more like Don Juan (or Tanner in the "Revolutionist's Handbook"), who believes that for the world to evolve, the first organism which must grow is not society but the human brain. Accordingly, Shaw began what a friend referred to at the time as his "really arduous efforts to create an intellectual drama" (Beatrice Webb, *Our Partnership*, ed. Barbara Drake and Margaret I. Cole [New York, 1948], p. 311).

34 But not the one-act play in the volume, *The Man of Destiny*, which Shaw included even though he did not consider it strictly one of the *Pleasant Plays* (*CL*, I, 698). The dramatic strategies of this neo-heroic Napoleon piece align it with the *Three Plays for Puritans* more than with the critical comedies, and I have treated it accordingly. A tenuous justification on chronological grounds might be offered: Shaw began *You Never Can Tell*, his last critical comedy, a few months before he began *The Man of Destiny*. But then he also seems to have conceived *Pygmalion* (not written until 1912) before he began *Captain Brassbound's Conversion*: see *Ellen Terry and Bernard Shaw*, p. 186.

CHAPTER 2

1 Translated by Eric Bentley in *Masters of Modern Drama*, ed. Haskell M. Block and Robert G. Shedd (New York, 1962), p. 875.

2 From "The Problem Play—A Symposium," reprinted in *Shaw on Theatre*, pp. 58–66.

3 London, 1956, ed. Stephen Winsten (its first publication). Since the volume is very small and is profusely illustrated, I have not given page numbers for quotations.

4 "Mr. Bernard Shaw's Works of Fiction. Reviewed by Himself," *Novel Review*, No. 33 (February 1892), p. 240.

5 Manuscript note in Shaw's copy of Joseph McCabe's *George Bernard Shaw* (1914) as recorded in R. F. Rattray, *Bernard Shaw: A Chronicle*, rev. ed. (London, 1951), p. 39.

6 Shaw voiced this thought at the age of twenty, when he was ghostwriting musical criticisms for the *Hornet*. See *How to Become a Musical Critic*, ed. Dan H. Laurence (New York, 1961), p. 18.

7 *Sixteen Self Sketches* (London, 1949), p. 69.

8 *Music in London, 1890–94* (London, 1932), III, 163.

9 Pearson, *G.B.S.*, p. 51.

10 "The Fabian Society: What it has Done; & How it has Done it," *Fabian Tracts*, No. 41 (August 1892), p. 3.

11 The article was "Who is the Thief?" *Justice*, I, No. 9 (March 15, 1884). See *HMC*, p. 218.

12 Wicksteed, "The Jevonian Criticism of Marx: A Rejoinder," *To-Day* (April 1885), reprinted in *Bernard Shaw & Karl Marx: A Symposium, 1884–1889*, comp. Richard W. Ellis (New York, 1930). Shaw's article is reprinted in the same volume.

13 "The Fabian Society," pp. 5, 12, 16.

14 By Shaw (who edited the volume), Sidney Webb, Sydney Olivier, Annie Besant, Graham Wallas, William Clarke, and Hubert Bland (London, 1889).

15 See esp. Bland, "The Outlook," pp. 209–10, and Webb, "The Basis of Socialism: Historic," pp. 56–58 (in which he describes the "new scientific conception of the Social Organism").

16 Shaw also denounced rationalism at length in "A Crib for Home Rulers" (1888), reprinted in *The Matter with Ireland*, ed. Dan H. Laurence and David H. Greene (New York, 1962), pp. 20–23, and in 1891 *Quintessence of Ibsenism* (*MCE*, pp. 18–23).

17 The famous phrase was authored by Sidney Webb, but Shaw was the first Fabian to state the proposition.

18 Beatrice Webb, *Our Partnership*, p. 122. On the fortunes of the Fabian Society, see Shaw's triumphant preface to the Jubilee Edition of *Fabian Essays* (London, 1948); and

A. M. McBriar's *Fabian Socialism and English Politics, 1884–1918* (New York, 1962).

19 Shaw, *Letters to Granville Barker*, ed. C. B. Purdom (New York, 1957), p. 164.

20 From the 1893 Preface to *Widowers' Houses*, reprinted in *Prefaces* (London, 1934), pp. 669, 670–71. As usual, Shaw's remark is exaggerated; he began the play in 1884–85 and worked on it further in 1890 before finishing it in 1892 (see Ch. 1, n. 10; and *HMC*, p. 526).

21 Shaw speaks of *Widowers' Houses* as a "bluebook play" (*Prefaces*, p. 676). On his rent-collecting experience, see *CL*, I, 371.

22 *Prefaces*, p. 678: "The notion that the people in Widowers' Houses are abnormally vicious or odious could only prevail in a community in which Sartorius is absolutely typical in his unconscious villainy. Like my critics, he lacks conviction of sin. Now, the didactic object of my play is to bring conviction of sin."

23 Meisel states this point with precision: "In intellectual strategy the three Unpleasant Plays are essentially alike. . . . In each play, the truth to which no character penetrates is that the entire social framework is unwholesome, but remediable. In each play the characters view the social structure as if it were permanent and to be dealt with according to its permanence. Nevertheless, the implicit frame of reference for the paradoxical justifications and insoluble dilemmas of the characters is the necessity of social transformation" (*Shaw and the Nineteenth-Century Theater*, p. 132).

24 Shaw notes that the advanced socialism underlying the play "greatly confused the critics, especially those who are in the habit of accepting as Socialism that spirit of sympathy with the poor and indignant protest against suffering and injustice which, in modern literature, culminated in Victor Hugo's Les Miserables. . . . This 'stage Socialism' is represented in my play by the good-natured compunction of my hero, who conceives the horrors of the slums as merely the result of atrocious individual delin-

quency on the part of the slum landlord" (*Prefaces*, p. 669).
25   The play contains no implication that any of Charteris's philanderings has involved sex. Yet it is clear that Shaw's strategy depends for its full effect upon the current stigma attached to "clandestine sensuality." He certainly expected his pit of idealists to be at least mildly scandalized, for instance, by the opening scene: it reveals a man in rake's garb (velvet jacket, cashmere trousers, leather sandals, sprezzatura beard) embracing a lady—without a chaperone in sight. Because he assumed that an aura of licentiousness would surround what is today an altogether customary activity, *The Philanderer* is even more severely dated than its reliance on the Ibsen fad makes it.

26   The subject of the play, Shaw remarks in the Preface to *Back to Methuselah*, is "doctrinaire Free Love (pseudo-Ibsenism)" ([London, 1930], p. lxxxvii).

27   Near the end of the play, Charteris mocks Julia's love for him, and "in a paroxysm half of rage, half of tenderness, she shakes him, growling over him like a tigress over her cub."

28   Don Juan expresses Shaw's view most concisely: "Nature is a pandar, Time a wrecker, and Death a murderer. I have always preferred to stand up to those facts and build institutions on their recognition."

29   Briefly, the Fabians of the time considered the philandering relationship perhaps better than no relationship at all, but also better than marriage under contemporary laws. Under socialism, philandering would be far less preferable than marriage. Shaw leaves no doubt in the play that Julia would have demanded honorable terms in return for her lover's "joy" if (a) he would have submitted to marriage despite its faults or (b) he had not convinced her that marriage is a degrading bargain for the woman.

30   Shaw speaks of the "original foolishness" of *Widowers' Houses* in a letter to Henderson (*HMC*, p. xviii). On the revisions, see Charles H. Shattuck, "Bernard Shaw's 'Bad Quarto,' " *JEGP*, LIV (1955), 651–63.

31   In *The Author's Apology from Mrs. Warren's Profession* (New York, 1905), p. 43, Shaw acknowledges "a few relapses into staginess and caricature which betray the young playwright and the old playgoer in this early work of mine." How many more of these relapses he expurgated from the original manuscript for the 1898 printing remains an uninvestigated question. The same is true of *The Philanderer*.

32   Grein wrote in part that the play was unfit for woman's ears. "By all means let us initiate our daughters . . . into those duties and functions of life which are vital in matrimony and maternity. But there is a boundary line, and its transgression means peril—the peril of destroying ideals" (quoted in *HMC*, p. 460n).

33   *The Author's Apology*, pp. 52–53. This volume was reprinted from the Stage Society edition of the play (London, 1902) and is cited hereafter as *Apology*.

34   *Apology*, p. 43. Shaw continues: "But I protest again that the lure was not mine. The play had been in print for four years; and I have spared no pains to make known that my plays are built to induce, not voluptuous reverie but intellectual interest, not romantic rhapsody but humane concern." His denial of the "lure" in this manner has no bearing on his original use of it.

35   Great Britain. *Report from the Joint Select Committee of the House of Lords and the House of Commons on the Stage Plays (Censorship). . . . Minutes of Evidence* (Reports of the Committees, vol. VIII, London, 1909), p. 52. This is the report that Shaw refers to in his preface to *The Shewing-up of Blanco Posnet*.

36   Program note for the Strand Theatre production of 1926, printed in Raymond Mander and Joe Mitchenson, *Theatrical Companion to Shaw* (New York, 1955), p. 32.

37   Appropriately, Vivie's mother presents the identical argument with a touch of English morality. Referring to her profession, she whines: "It's far better than any other employment open to [a poor girl]. I always thought that oughtn't to be. It *can't* be right . . . that there shouldn't

be better opportunities for women. I stick to that: it's wrong. But it's so, right or wrong; and a girl must make the best of it."

38 At the time, "Miss Vavasour" was virtually a synonym for "kept woman."

39 In a letter of late 1893, Shaw says explicitly: "The mother, uncertain who the girl's father is, keeps all the old men at bay by telling each one that he is the parent" (*CL*, I, 404). Arthur H. Nethercot comes to the same conclusion solely on the basis of internal evidence in "The Vivie-Frank Relationship in *Mrs. Warren's Profession*," *Shavian*, I, No. 15 (June 1959), 7–9. In Act II, Mrs. Warren insists to Vivie that none of the men her daughter has ever met could be her father, adding, "I'm certain of that, at least."

40 See Stephen S. Stanton's introduction to *Camille and Other Plays* (New York, 1957), p. xv. Shaw seems to imply, in a letter written when the second act was "half finished and wholly planned," that he originally intended to make Mrs. Warren the central figure and her successful defense, which now follows Vivie's triumph, the *scène à faire*. "The play progresses bravely," he tells Janet Achurch; "but it has left the original lines. I have made the daughter the heroine, and the mother a most deplorable old rip (saving your presence). The great scene will be the crushing of the mother by the daughter" (*CL*, I, 404).

41 On the play as a "generic anti-type" of the highly popular courtesan play, see Meisel, *Shaw and the Nineteenth-Century Theater*, pp. 141–59.

CHAPTER 3

1 *The Green Crow* (New York, 1956), p. 204.

2 *CL*, I, 633. Shaw also says in this letter that the *Pleasant Plays* "are not 'realistic' plays. They deal with life at large, with human nature as it presents itself through all

economic & social phases. . . . These later plays are of course infinitely more pleasing, more charming, more popular than the earlier three."

3 See Shaw's ironically titled *Saturday Review* piece, "The Independent Theatre Repents," *OTN*, I, 66; and for contrast, the favorable earlier article on the Theatre, *OTN*, I, 19–24.

4 The original playbill that includes the term "domestic play" is reproduced in *HMC*, p. 435. Shaw calls *Candida* "sentimental" in *CL*, I, 466, and in an unpublished letter of July 7, 1902, to his German translator, Siegfried Trebitsch, in the Berg Collection of the New York Public Library. Neither use of the term could be construed as ironic.

5 Quoted in *HMC*, p. 538n. See also "A Warning from the Author," *Complete Plays* (London, 1937), p. vi.

6 From his 1897 *Saturday Review* article, "Meredith on Comedy," a revealing discussion of the *Essay on Comedy* (*OTN*, III, 87). Shaw opposes Meredith on the evolutionist grounds that the audience's sense of proper conduct must not be appealed to but altered.

7 In his acute analysis of modern "tragi-comedy," "Tolstoy: Tragedian or Comedian?" in *Pen Portraits and Reviews* (London, 1932), p. 263.

8 His distinction occurs in *HMC*, p. 740; see pp. 102–3 of the present study. The term "critical comedy" is used here in Shaw's sense, not that of Bonamy Dobrée in *Restoration Comedy*.

9 Passages given in Irving McKee, "Bernard Shaw's Beginnings on the London Stage," *PMLA*, LXXIV (1959), 472, 478.

10 Shaw quotes from them in "A Dramatic Realist to His Critics" (July 1894), in *Shaw on Theatre*, pp. 25–32.

11 *Music in London*, I, 226; *London Music in 1888–89* (London, 1932), p. 271.

12 "My Memories of Oscar Wilde," in Frank Harris, *Oscar Wilde* (New York, 1960), p. 349.

13 Pearson, *G.B.S.*, p. 170n.

14 See, for example, *OTN*, I, 263–64; II, 21–28, 77, 126; and *Pen Portraits and Reviews*, pp. 260–61 (an 1898 statement).

15 "The Religion of the Pianoforte," *Fortnightly Review*, LXI (1894), 262, 264.

16 The standard edition of 1930 reads: "What a man! Is he a man?" Presumably Shaw decided to allow Sergius a comic inch of backsliding.

17 Shaw stressed the fact that "deep feeling" underlies the "gay badinage" of the play (*HMC*, p. 734). In 1896 he informed Ellen Terry: "When I used to read the play before it was produced, people used not to laugh at it as they laughed in the theatre. On my honor it was a serious play—a play to cry over if you could only have helped laughing" (*CL*, I, 660). He explained the complete sincerity of Raina's role to at least two actresses: Alma Murray (*CL*, I, 422) and Lillah McCarthy (McCarthy, *Myself and My Friends* [New York, 1933], pp. 92–94). Similarly, Shaw noted that Sergius must express his caricaturable ideals with unquestioned conviction (*CL*, I, 442). These admonishments comply with Shaw's general concept of realistic drama as "the exhibition and discussion of the character and conduct of stage figures who are made to appear real by the art of the playwright and the performers" (*MCE*, p. 138).

18 *Letters from George Bernard Shaw to Miss Alma Murray* (n.p., 1927), Letter XV (unpaged). In 1920, Shaw called the play "a simple theatrical projection effected by a bag of the oldest stage tricks" (*Shaw on Theatre*, p. 132).

19 Sergius's potentialities become especially apparent when he states Shaw's idea of true courage: "Oh, (*fervently*) give me the man who will defy to the death any power on earth or in heaven that sets itself up against his own will and conscience: he alone is the brave man."

20 See *Pen Portraits and Reviews*, p. 143. Shaw's attack on pessimism and its characteristic attitude, cynicism, reflects his temperamental aversion to writers such as Shakespeare (in a few plays, notably *King Lear*), Schopenhauer, and

the naturalistic dramatists. In his eyes, these writers gained a clear perception of reality but failed to discard their romantic ideals, which made reality ugly in contrast. He defined pessimism in 1902 as an "illusion founded on the common practice of comparing the *status quo*, not with the socially practicable alternatives to it, but with an individual's ideal" (quoted in Rattray, *Bernard Shaw*, p. 152). Two important letters on *Arms and the Man*, just published in 1965 (*CL*, I, 427–29), stress the antipessimistic content of the play.

21 Pearson, *G.B.S.*, p. 168.

22 From a 1944 retort to an erring critic, reprinted in Mander and Mitchenson, *Theatrical Companion to Shaw*, p. 43.

23 Shaw describes Morell as "Helmer getting fair play" (*CL*, I, 612).

24 2nd ed. (London, 1960), p. 150. Even in 1905 Conservatives exploited this widespread idealism as a defense against progressive movements. See William S. Adams, *Edwardian Heritage: A Study in British History, 1901–1906* (London, 1949), Ch. 5.

25 In the first act, Burgess says to Morell: "Times 'as changed mor'n I could a believed. Five yorr (year) ago, no sensible man would a thought o' takin' up with your ideas. . . . But to-day, if henyone was to offer to bet me a thousan' poun' that you'll end by bein' a bishop yourself, I shouldn't venture to take the bet." Coming from a bourgeois (Burgess), this comment is authoritative.

26 "Why I Am a Social-Democrat," *The Why I Ams* (three articles by political radicals; London, 1894), pp. 3–6. The advent of Social-Democracy, Shaw says, will by no means bring the millenium; to Fabians, Social-Democracy is not the religion that it is to other groups. Shaw's best description of the "secular apocalypse" in Marxian theory appears in *The Intelligent Woman's Guide to Socialism and Capitalism*, p. 441.

27 See, for example, Arthur H. Nethercot, *Men and Supermen: The Shavian Portrait Gallery*, 2nd ed. (New York, 1966), pp. 12, 247, 274.

28 See *Florence Farr, Bernard Shaw, W. B. Yeats: Letters,*
    ed. Clifford Bax (New York, 1942), p. 31. In *The Au-
    thor's Apology from Mrs. Warren's Profession* (p. 58),
    Shaw takes issue with critics who consider it natural for
    clergymen to be saintly: "All this is not only not natural,
    but not dramatic. A man's profession only enters into the
    drama of his life when it comes into conflict with his
    nature."

29 From a note added by Shaw to the text of Maisie Ward's
    Gilbert Keith Chesterton (New York, 1943), p. 231n.

30 Explaining the presence of naive "Candidamaniacs" in
    audiences before 1904, Shaw informed James Huneker
    that one part of the play "stirs the ordinary emotions to
    a very high degree, all the more because the language of
    the poet, to those who have not the clew to it, is myste-
    rious and bewildering and therefore worshipful" (letter
    excerpted in Huneker, "The Quintessence of Shaw,"
    reprinted from his *Iconoclasts* in *George Bernard Shaw:
    A Critical Survey,* ed. Louis Kronenberger [Cleveland,
    1953], pp. 18–19). As for recent critics, Bentley (who
    may be simply overstating) remarks that "Shaw invariably
    puts the truth in Eugene's mouth" (*The Playwright as
    Thinker,* amended ed. [New York, 1955], p. 133).

31 He also shows a touch of Platonic or Shelleyan poetic
    madness: "Marchbanks" is twice dramatically juxtaposed
    with "mad as a March hare."

32 Note printed in John S. Collis, *Shaw* (New York, 1925),
    p. 117. The preface to the *Pleasant Plays,* however,
    speaks of Eugene's "incoherent, mischievous, and even
    ridiculous, unpracticalness" (p. ix).

33 In 1896 Ellen Terry told Shaw that her daughter, Edith,
    said she would never marry because "she would not stay
    anywhere where she was not entirely happy." Shaw's reply
    throws light on the situation in which he places March-
    banks, particularly when Candida's status as a mother is
    kept in mind. He wrote: "Tell Edy that the two things
    that worthless people sacrifice everything for are happi-
    ness and freedom, and that their punishment is that they

get both, only to find that they have no capacity for the happiness and no use for the freedom. You have a ready example to point this piece of maternal wisdom. You are not in the least free: you are tied neck, wrists & ankles to your profession and your domestic arrangements, and your happiness has been picked up in casual scraps on your way to your work. Edy on the contrary is quite free & has nothing to do but be happy. Yet who would choose her life instead of yours? Tell her to go and seek activity, struggle, bonds, responsibilities, terrors—in a word, life" (*CL*, I, 693).

34 The words I have omitted blur this picture but should be noted: "I am the man, Morell: I am the man." Morell is also "the man."

35 Nethercot's essay first appeared in *PMLA* in 1949; it is revised and expanded on pp. 7–17 of *Men and Supermen*. I will cite page numbers in the text.

36 See Ch. 3, n. 30.

37 Lexy rejects her denunciations, and she retorts: "You don't believe me? . . . You think I'm jealous." We learn later, of course, that she is afflicted with "Prossy's complaint."

38 Eric Bentley is another prominent critic who, in my opinion, has misread the play. See *The Playwright as Thinker*, p. 134; and "The Making of a Dramatist (1892–1903)," in *Modern Drama: Essays in Criticism*, ed. Bogard and Oliver, pp. 304–7. Stephen S. Stanton may simply have relied upon Nethercot in "Shaw's Debt to Scribe," *PMLA*, LXXVI (1961), 580; and E. J. West certainly did in his edition of Shaw's *Advice to a Young Critic and Other Letters* (New York, 1955), pp. 17, 18, and 52.

39 Huneker, "The Quintessence of Shaw," in *George Bernard Shaw*, ed. Kronenberger, p. 18.

40 Winsten, *Salt and His Circle* (London, 1951), pp. 103–4.

41 *HMC*, p. 543. G. K. Chesterton, in his erratic book on Shaw, comes closer than any other critic to an approximation of Shaw's idea of Candida, and his statement is illuminating. *Candida*, he says, "is something much better than

Shaw. The writer touches certain realities commonly outside his scope; especially the reality of the normal wife's
attitude to the normal husband, an attitude which is not
romantic but which is yet quite quixotic; which is in-
sanely unselfish and yet quite cynically clear-sighted. It
involves human sacrifice without in the least involving
idolatry" (*George Bernard Shaw*, enl. ed. [London, 1961],
p. 118).

42   Prompted by Candida, Eugene grasps this in symbolic
terms. At the beginning of Act II, inspired by Morell's
heroics in leaving him alone with Candida, he envisions
the poker in her hand as a sword of honor that bars his
way to the gate of Heaven. But Candida induces him to
discard his heroics, and he proceeds to imagine that the
sword is really a flaming, revolving one which keeps him
away from the gate of Hell, not of Heaven. During this
transformation, Candida becomes "an angel" to him and
makes him realize that he is in Heaven already. Since
Heaven for him is a state of happiness "where want is
unknown," and since violating the flaming sword would
cast him out, he understands that the homage of prayer
is the only part of himself that he can give to her without
ruining his own happiness. The flaming sword, of course,
is also symbolically the warning against enjoying the fruit
of the Tree of Knowledge. The implication, which carries no dramatic force (and is not meant to), is that
Candida will cease to be an angel for Eugene if his illusion is corrupted by knowledge of her real domestic
nature. Obviously this occurs in the finale.

43   Shaw foreshadowed this particular image of Candida in
a music review three or four months before writing the
play. See *Music in London*, III, 226.

44   Nethercot, *Men and Supermen*, p. 12; Bentley, *The Playwright as Thinker*, p. 134; and Stanton, "Shaw's Debt to
Scribe," p. 580.

45   *The Doctor's Dilemma, Getting Married & The Shewing-up of Blanco Posnet* (London, 1932), p. 230.

46   *The Playwright as Thinker*, p. 135. See also his *Bernard*

Shaw, p. 137: "Morell is at the end crushed and speechless."

47 Letter printed in Richard Burton's Bernard Shaw (New York, 1916), p. 231.

48 Quoted by George A. Riding, "The Candida Secret," Spectator, CLXXXV (1950), 506, partly reprinted in HMC, p. 545. Other statements by Shaw on "the secret in the poet's heart" appear in Huneker, "The Quintessence of Shaw," in George Bernard Shaw, ed. Kronenberger, pp. 18–19; in Shaw, Sixteen Self Sketches, p. 101; and in Patrick Hogan and J. O. Baylen, "G. Bernard Shaw and W. T. Stead: An Unexplored Relationship," Studies in English Literature: 1500–1900, I (1961), 137–38.

49 "Tears of happiness" seems to have been the standard response to the play for many years. See HMC, pp. 477, 543.

50 Nethercot says bafflingly: "Of course the tantalizing 'secret' is embedded only in the final stage direction and would therefore not challenge the spectator for solution" (Men and Supermen, p. 7).

51 Shaw said that the hero of the play was "nobody else but Richard Mansfield himself," and that the heroine was "simply a delineation of Ellen Terry" (HMC, pp. 471, 445).

52 Pearson, G.B.S., p. 173.

53 The letters were probably lost or discarded in America, where Ellen Terry was touring at the time. The editor of the Terry correspondence does not indicate that Shaw's reply is missing, but the letter of November 1, 1895, clearly alludes to a later one. Note "I am interested in the bicycling"; Ellen's letter of March 10 does not mention it. Also, the "magnificent article . . . on Church-going (of all subjects!), for a new quarterly" which Shaw had just finished when Ellen's letter arrived is "On Going to Church," not published until January, 1896 (Savoy, No. 1, pp. 13–28). See Ellen Terry and Bernard Shaw, p. 15.

54 CL, I, 565. Madame Sans-Gêne was Victorien Sardou's Napoleon play, a highly popular Scribean product. Shaw

later reviewed the opening and called Sardou's hero "nothing but the jealous husband of a thousand fashionable dramas, talking Buonapartiana" (*OTN*, III, 110).

55 This questionable chapter in the history of the Lyceum is approached from a balanced critical view in St. John Ervine's *Bernard Shaw* (New York, 1956), pp. 288–92. Shaw's view emerges day by day in his letters to Golding Bright and Ellen Terry.

56 *CL*, I, 718. In October 1896, Shaw referred to it as "the dullest filth"; in March 1897, as "that wretched comedy"; in September, as "the dullest trash" (*CL*, I, 678, 735, 799).

57 Shaw states in a letter of September 22, 1896: "The decision of the Haymarket management to produce a romantic play of the [Prisoner of] Zenda type seems to indicate that they have reconsidered any notion they may have had of a new departure in drama" (*CL*, I, 663). In a letter to Pearson, he refers to *You Never Can Tell* as one of his "potboilers written for immediate production" (*G.B.S.*, p. 379). Still, Shaw was by no means sure that he could strike Haymarket pay dirt. When the prospective comanager, Cyril Maude, was evidently planning its initial runs for the season beginning in September 1896, he asked Shaw to submit a play for consideration. Henderson states without qualification: "Shaw, knowing the requirements of the Haymarket Theatre, complied by writing *You Never Can Tell*" (*HMC*, p. 432). But the 1896 letter quoted above continues: "There is one person who will not be surprised if 'You Never Can Tell' is produced elsewhere; and that person is the author." Maude accepted the play, started rehearsals with Shaw assisting in April 1897, then agreed two or three weeks later that the production was impracticable. See Shaw's anonymous chapter in Maude's *Haymarket Theatre* (London, 1903), pp. 211–17, reprinted in *Shaw on Theatre*, pp. 84–89; and his letter in *CL*, I, 753.

58 Pref., *Pleasant Plays*, p. x. Shaw's range of humanizing intentions in the play can be glimpsed from a unique angle in his review of the play that replaced it at the Haymarket Theatre after he had called a halt to rehearsals.

Quite obviously, Shaw visualized Cyril Maude and his associates reading the review with his own play clearly in mind, and he took the rare opportunity to instruct them all the more forcefully by encouraging them to compare the two. See *OTN*, III, 158–63.

59 Meisel, *Shaw and the Nineteenth-Century Theater*, pp. 255–56.

60 His musical voice "soothes the savage beast." Meisel gives examples of musical notation translated into intelligible stage directions in William's part (ibid., pp. 58–59).

61 Bohun startles nearly everyone by turning out to be the son of William the waiter. ("It is only the accident of birth," William explains.) But Bohun is not entirely a contrasting figure; his function is simply a step beyond that of his mellifluous father, who creates the atmosphere that makes sensible discussion possible.

62 Shaw said in 1904 that *You Never Can Tell* "has always seemed merely a farce written round a waiter. It ought to be a very serious comedy, dancing gaily to a happy ending round the grim-earnest of Mrs. Clandon's marriage and her XIX century George-Eliotism" (*Letters to Granville Barker*, p. 45).

63 Some readers of the play may consider Bohun a rationalist like Mrs. Clandon. Shaw notes that he is "physically and spiritually, a coarsened man: in cunning and logic, a ruthlessly sharpened one." Bohun is not a rationalist, however: he is a highly intelligent pragmatist who tramples over sentimentalities in his quest for facts, contradictions, and the realities they entail. He says himself that his business is to get people what they really want; and in accord with his Nature-supporting role as personified intellect, he uses reason to this end.

CHAPTER 4

1 *English Literature in the Sixteenth Century*, Oxford History of English Literature, III (Oxford, 1954), p. 187.

2 In Shaw's propaganda plays he puts the blame for the

evils he depicts on the existing structure of society, not on individuals. Then, in the critical comedies, he handles the ridiculous characters by improving some (Sergius, Marchbanks), by exposing the attractive depths in others (Morell, Mrs. Clandon), and by shielding all of them from derision and contempt.

3 Martin Meisel contends that Shaw's play was "deliberately remedial" (*Shaw and the Nineteenth-Century Theater*, p. 356). It was started in July 1895, almost immediately after Shaw had seen the Sardou version of Napoleon.

4 Letter in George W. Bishop, *My Betters* (London, 1957), pp. 122–24.

5 Shaw called Forbes-Robertson a classical actor because he could "present a dramatic hero as a man whose passions are those which have produced the philosophy, the poetry, the art, and the statecraft of the world, and not merely those which have produced its weddings, coroners' inquests, and executions" (*OTN*, III, 201).

6 The latter was Shaw's original subtitle for it (*HMC*, p. 562n); but Meisel treats it convincingly as adventure melodrama, "a sub-genre presenting the perils of Europeans in a barbarous, heathen clime" (*Shaw and the Nineteenth-Century Theater*, p. 206).

7 *Pen Portraits and Reviews*, p. 86; Pref., *Man and Superman*, p. ix; Notes to *Caesar*, in *Three Plays for Puritans*, p. 206.

8 Brassbound asks her what he should do now that he has lost his purpose in life (revenge). She replies: "It's quite simple. Do whatever you like. That's what I always do." Shaw discusses her as "the great lady" in a 1900 letter to Janet Achurch (*Shaw on Theatre*, pp. 80–83).

9 Letter of May 4 in *CL*, I, 754; see also *CL*, I, 583, 698, 736, and 771. Two other factors doubtless played an important part in his decision. First, he was elected a member of the St. Pancras Vestry (later County Council) just before May 4; in the letter quoted in the text, he goes so far as to state that "there is better work to be done in the Vestry than in the theatre." (Note that he says theatre,

not drama.) Second, the expected performances of both *The Man of Destiny* and *You Never Can Tell* fell through within a few days of Shaw's decision.

10 The prefaces and stage directions are only part of the story. Inspired by William Morris, Shaw also pioneered in bookmaking and printing. See Joseph R. Dunlap, "The Typographical Shaw: GBS and the Revival of Printing," *Bull. of the N.Y.P.L.*, LXIV (1960), 534–47. On January 5, 1898, Shaw wrote Ellen Terry: "The book of plays still creeps through the press. Oh those proofs, those proofs! Imagine going through a play again and again, scanning the commas, and sticking in words to make the printing look decent—to get the rivers of white out of it!" (*Ellen Terry and Bernard Shaw*, p. 208).

11 On December 15, 1898, Shaw told Golding Bright that *Caesar and Cleopatra* "is now finished, except for the final revision and the arrangement of the stage business. . . . I shall take no trouble to get the play performed, as I shall be busy enough with its successor, which, with 'The Devil's Disciple' and C. & C., will form my next volume of plays" (*Advice to a Young Critic*, pp. 102–3).

12 Shaw in Archibald Henderson, *Table-Talk of G.B.S.* (London, 1925), p. 56.

13 "Socialism at the International Congress," *Cosmopolis*, September 1896, quoted in *Selected Passages from the Works of Bernard Shaw*, comp. Charlotte F. Shaw (London, 1912), p. 210. One of the Maxims for Revolutionists in *Man and Superman* repeats this thought with no reference to Wagner's hero.

14 The line was originally "Amen, and God damn the King!" —nothing like the amended foreshadowing of Creative Evolution, but perhaps more appropriate to the character of Dick and to the general tone of the play. I suspect that Shaw gave up hope that any actor would speak the original line properly; in the typescript he explained: "The actor must take care that this does not sound like a vulgar expletive. It is the solemn imprecation of a dying man, and should be uttered with conviction and dignity." See

McKee, "Bernard Shaw's Beginnings on the London Stage," p. 479.

15 Meisel, *Shaw and the Nineteenth-Century Theater*, pp. 195–204.

16 Later on he explains that "Burgoyne pleads all through for softening and easing the trial by reciprocal politeness and consideration between all the parties, and for ignoring the villainy of his gallows, the unworthiness of his cause, and the murderousness of his profession" (*CL*, I, 734–35).

17 Shaw warned Mrs. Mansfield that "it is extremely difficult to hold up the horror of the court-martial scene against Burgoyne & the rest" (*CL*, I, 830). He was more specific in a letter to Ellen Terry: "The woman's part is not so difficult where she has anything to say; but the listening to the court martial—the holding on to the horror through all the laughing—that will be the difficulty" (*CL*, I, 733).

18 He does not begin following his real nature consistently until his revelation of it in Act II. Before, his unpleasantly brittle and sardonic manner is broken by sharply contrasting moments of extreme sympathy, which occur only when he is unprovoked by shows of "virtue."

19 These features are pointed out by Meisel in *Shaw and the Nineteenth-Century Theater*, p. 349.

20 Shaw, "*Caesar and Cleopatra*," *New Statesman*, I (1913), 112. In this rejoinder to Desmond MacCarthy, Shaw comments significantly on the union of unscrupulous wilfulness and extreme kindness in Caesar: "If there is a point in the play on which I pride myself more than another, it is the way in which I have shown how this readiness to kill tigers, and blackguards, and obstructive idealogues . . . is part of the same character that abhors waste and murder, and is, in the most accurate sense of the word, a kind character."

21 *HMC*, p. 556. Shaw elaborates upon this return to human nature in an article of April 30, 1898: "Mr. Shaw's Future. A Conversation," *Academy*, LIII (1898), 476. The article is attributed to C[larence] R[ook], but Shaw ap-

parently followed his usual practice of composing such "interviews" himself. This one is probably "the Julius Caesar article" that he refers to in a letter of January 29, 1898, to Ellen Terry (*Ellen Terry and Bernard Shaw*, p. 213).

22 "The Heroic Actors," *Play Pictorial*, No. 62 (October 1907), reprinted in Mander and Mitchenson, *Theatrical Companion to Shaw*, p. 63.

23 The constructive aspects of the Notes, though subordinated to the destructive ones, include the outlines of a complete Shavian philosophy, Shaw says in an unpublished letter of September 18, 1903, to Siegfried Trebitsch, his German translator. The letter is in the Berg Collection of the New York Public Library.

24 "Without passion no man can be good or bad: he can at most be harmless or mischievous; and in either case he is the genuine fool of Scripture" (from *Christian Commonwealth*, July 20, 1910; quoted in *Selected Passages*, comp. Charlotte F. Shaw, p. 214).

25 Nevertheless, the entire scene (the second part of the third act), like the opening prologue and the first scene of the third act, contains nothing indispensable to the total effect of the play. All three can be omitted in performance or reading without appreciable damage to the dramatic structure. In 1912 Shaw replaced the opening scene with a speech delivered by the god Ra, and as early as mid-1899 he implied that he had planned the third act as a removable segment of a play that would normally stay off the boards if it were not cut. He wrote Ellen Terry on June 1, 1899: "With a line or two altered, and the third act struck bodily out (because it makes the play too long), . . . the public would take it with rapture" (*Ellen Terry and Bernard Shaw*, p. 238). See also "The Heroic Actors," in Mander and Mitchenson, *Theatrical Companion to Shaw*, p. 64; and a Shaw letter in William A. Page, *Behind the Curtains of the Broadway Beauty Trust* (New York, 1927), p. 217.

26 "She is an animal—a bad lot" (*Ellen Terry and Bernard*

Shaw, p. 238). Defending his portrayal of her to Gilbert Murray, Shaw states: "I am not quite convinced that I have overdone Cleopatra's ferocity" ("Six Letters from Bernard Shaw to Gilbert Murray," *Drama*, No. 42 [Autumn 1956], p. 24).

27   *Ellen Terry and Bernard Shaw*, p. 240. Shaw began the play on May 3, 1899, and completed it on July 7 (ibid., p. 239; *HMC*, p. 474).

28   In *The Sanity of Art*, Shaw asserts: "Passion is the steam in the engine of all religious and moral systems. In so far as it is malevolent, the religio[n]s are malevolent too, and insist on human sacrifices, on hell, wrath, and vengeance" (*MCE*, pp. 303–4).

29   Verbal comment recorded in Bishop, *My Betters*, p. 127.

30   The Hooligan cockney Drinkwater tells Rankin that Captain Brassbound's business is smuggling under the guise of escorting tourists: "All we daz is hescort, tourist *hor* commercial. Cook's hexcursions to the Hatlas Mahntns: thet's hall it is. Waw, it's spreadin civlawzytion." Thus Brassbound is a "filibuster"—an irregular adventurer—spreading civilization by smuggling guns with the aid of Hooligans (Drinkwater), aristocrats (Redbrook, Johnson), and stupid drifters (Marzo).

31   "The gulf of dislike is impassable," Shaw says through the Devil in *Man and Superman*.

CHAPTER 5

1   "George Bernard Shaw," *Virginia Quarterly Review*, XXVII (1951), 2–3.

Selected
Bibliography

WORKS BY SHAW

Advice to a Young Critic and Other Letters, ed. E. J. West. New York, 1955.

The Author's Apology from Mrs. Warren's Profession. New York, 1905.

Bernard Shaw & Karl Marx: A Symposium, 1884–1889, comp. Richard W. Ellis. New York, 1930.

Bernard Shaw and Mrs. Patrick Campbell: Their Correspondence, ed. Alan Dent. London, 1952.

"Caesar and Cleopatra," *New Statesman*, I (1913), 112–13.

"Civilization and the Soldier," *Humane Review*, No. 4 (1901), pp. 298–315.

Collected Letters, 1874–1897, ed. Dan H. Laurence. New York, 1965.

Collected Plays, Standard Constable Ed. 16 vols. London, 1930–50.

Ellen Terry and Bernard Shaw: A Correspondence, ed. Christopher St. John. New York, 1932.

Everybody's Political What's What? New York, 1944.

Fabian Essays, ed. Shaw. Jubilee Ed. London, 1948.

Fabian Essays in Socialism, ed. Shaw. London, 1889.

"The Fabian Society: What it has Done; & How it has Done it," *Fabian Tracts*, No. 41 (August 1892).

Florence Farr, Bernard Shaw, W. B. Yeats: Letters, ed. Clifford Bax. New York, 1942.

"Ibsen," *Clarion*, June 1, 1906. (Unpaged photoprint.)

The Intelligent Woman's Guide to Socialism and Capitalism. New York, 1928.

Letter to *Times* (London), June 23, 1910, p. 12.

Letters from George Bernard Shaw to Miss Alma Murray. N.p., 1927.

Letters to Granville Barker, ed. C. B. Purdom. New York, 1957.

Letters (unpublished), Berg Collection, New York Public Library.

Letters (unpublished), Bernard F. Burgunder Collection of Shaviana, Cornell University Library.

London Music in 1888–89. London, 1932.

Major Critical Essays. London, 1932.

The Matter with Ireland, ed. Dan H. Laurence and David H. Greene. New York, 1962.

"Mr. Bernard Shaw on the Drama," *Times* (London), March 8, 1906, p. 10.

"Mr. Bernard Shaw's Works of Fiction. Reviewed by Himself," *Novel Review,* No. 33 (February 1892), pp. 236–42.

"Mr. Shaw's Future. A Conversation," *Academy,* LIII (1898), 476. (Attributed to C. R. [Clarence Rook] but almost certainly written by Shaw.)

More Letters from George Bernard Shaw to Miss Alma Murray (Mrs. Alfred Forman). Edinburgh, 1932.

Music in London, 1890–94. 3 vols. London, 1932.

My Dear Dorothea, ed. Stephen Winsten. London, 1956.

"My Memories of Oscar Wilde," in *Oscar Wilde,* by Frank Harris, pp. 345–61. New York, 1960.

Our Theatres in the Nineties. 3 vols. London, 1932.

Pen Portraits and Reviews. London, 1932.

"*Un Petit Drame:* Bernard Shaw's First and Hitherto Unpublished Play," ed. Stanley Weintraub, tr. Norman Denny, *Esquire,* LII (December 1959), 172–74.

Platform and Pulpit, ed. Dan H. Laurence. New York, 1961.

Plays: Pleasant and Unpleasant. 2 vols. Chicago, 1898.

Plays Pleasant and Unpleasant. 2 vols. London, 1898.

"Postscript: After Twentyfive Years," in *Back to Methuselah,* pp. 246–61. World's Classics. New York, 1947.

"Preface," in *Three Plays by Brieux*, pp. vii–liv. 2nd ed. New York, 1911.

Prefaces. London, 1934.

"The Religion of the Pianoforte," *Fortnightly Review*, LXI (1894), 255–66.

The Religious Speeches of Bernard Shaw, ed. Warren S. Smith. University Park, Pa., 1964.

Selected Passages from the Works of Bernard Shaw, comp. Charlotte F. Shaw. London, 1912.

Shaw on Theatre, ed. E. J. West. New York, 1958.

"Six Letters from Bernard Shaw to Gilbert Murray," *Drama*, No. 42 (Autumn 1956), pp. 24–28.

Sixteen Self Sketches. London, 1949.

"Some Unpublished Letters of George Bernard Shaw," ed. Julian Park, *University of Buffalo Studies*, XVI (1939), 115–30.

Three Plays for Puritans. Chicago, 1900.

Three Plays for Puritans. London, 1900.

An Unsocial Socialist. New York, 1906.

"A Warning from the Author," in *Complete Plays*, pp. v–vi. London, 1937.

"Why I Am a Social-Democrat," in *The Why I Ams*, pp. 3–6. London, 1894.

Widowers' Houses. London, 1893.

WORKS VALUABLE CHIEFLY FOR MATERIAL BY SHAW

Belmont, Eleanor Robson. *The Fabric of Memory.* New York, 1957.

Bishop, George W. *My Betters.* London, 1957.

Burton, Richard. *Bernard Shaw: The Man and the Mask.* New York, 1916.

Collis, John S. *Shaw.* New York, 1925.

Cornwallis-West, George. *Edwardian Hey-Days.* New York, 1931.

Ervine, St. John. *Bernard Shaw: His Life, Work and Friends.* New York, 1956.

Gollin, Richard M. "Beerbohm, Wilde, Shaw, and 'The Good-Natured Critic,'" *Bulletin of the New York Public Library*, LXVIII (1964), 83–99.

Great Britain. *Report from the Joint Select Committee of the House of Lords and the House of Commons on the Stage Plays (Censorship).* . . . *Minutes of Evidence.* Reports of the Committees, VIII. London, 1909.

Grein, Alice A. [Michael Orme, pseud.]. *J. T. Grein: The Story of a Pioneer, 1862–1935.* London, 1936.

Harris, Frank. *Bernard Shaw.* New York, 1931.

Henderson, Archibald. *Bernard Shaw: Playboy and Prophet.* New York, 1932.

——. *George Bernard Shaw: His Life and Works.* Cincinnati, 1911.

——. *George Bernard Shaw: Man of the Century.* New York, 1956.

——. "George Bernard Shaw Self-Revealed," *Fortnightly Review*, CXXV (1926), 433–42, 610–18. (Imaginary conversation based on Shaw's answers to a questionnaire.)

——. *Table-Talk of G.B.S.* London, 1925.

Hogan, Patrick, and J. O. Baylen. "G. Bernard Shaw and W. T. Stead: An Unexplored Relationship," *Studies in English Literature: 1500–1900*, I (1961), 123–47.

Hood, Samuel S., ed. *Archibald Henderson: The New Chrichton.* New York, 1949.

Hyndman, Rosalind T. *The Last Years of H. M. Hyndman.* London, 1923.

Joad, C. E. M., ed. *Shaw and Society.* New York, 1953.

Jones, Doris A. *Taking the Curtain Call: The Life and Letters of Henry Arthur Jones.* New York, 1930.

Langner, Lawrence. *G.B.S. and the Lunatic.* New York, 1963.

"Letters of English Authors from the Collection of Robert H. Taylor," *Princeton University Library Chronicle*, XXI (1960), 200–236.

Loraine, Winifred. *Head Wind: The Story of Robert Loraine.* New York, 1939.

McCarthy, Lillah. *Myself and My Friends.* New York, 1933.

Mander, Raymond, and Joe Mitchenson. *Theatrical Companion to Shaw.* New York, 1955.

Page, William A. *Behind the Curtains of the Broadway Beauty Trust*. New York, 1927.

Pearson, Hesketh. *G.B.S.: A Full Length Portrait*. 3rd ed. New York, 1942.

_____. *G.B.S.: A Postscript*. New York, 1950.

Rattray, R. F. *Bernard Shaw: A Chronicle*. Rev. ed. London, 1951.

Richards, Grant. *Author Hunting*. New York, 1934.

Rouche, Jacques. "Portraits: G. Bernard Shaw," *Revue d'Histoire du Théâtre*, X (1958), 300–303.

Stuckey, Laurence. "Man and Superman," *Drama*, XVI (1926), 205–206. (Shaw speech to Shakespeare Club.)

Times (London), November 10, 1911, p. 4. (Report of Shaw lecture to the *Times* Book Club.)

Tolstoy, Leo. *Tolstoy on Shakespeare*, ed. V. Tchertkoff. New York, 1906. (Shaw letter.)

Ward, Maisie. *Gilbert Keith Chesterton*. New York, 1943.

Wilstach, Paul. *Richard Mansfield: The Man and the Actor*. New York, 1908.

Winsten, Stephen. *Jesting Apostle: The Life of Bernard Shaw*. London, 1956.

_____. *Salt and His Circle*. London, 1951.

BACKGROUND WORKS
AND STUDIES OF SHAW

Abrams, Meyer H. *The Mirror and the Lamp*. New York, 1958.

Adams, Elsie B. "Bernard Shaw's Pre-Raphaelite Drama," *PMLA*, LXXXI (1966), 428–38.

Adams, Robert M. *Strains of Discord: Studies in Literary Openness*. Ithaca, 1958.

Adams, William S. *Edwardian Heritage: A Study in British History, 1901–1906*. London, 1949.

Adler, Jacob H. "Ibsen, Shaw, and *Candida*," *JEGP*, LIX (1960), 50–58.

Albert, Sidney P. "Bernard Shaw: The Artist as Philosopher,"

Journal of Aesthetics and Art Criticism, XIV (1956), 419–38.

Austin, Don. "Dramatic Structure in *Caesar and Cleopatra,*" *California Shavian,* III (September–October 1962), unpaged.

Barzun, Jacques. *Darwin, Marx, Wagner: Critique of a Heritage.* 2nd ed. New York, 1958.

———. *The Energies of Art: Studies of Authors Classic and Modern.* New York, 1956.

Bentley, Eric. *Bernard Shaw, 1856–1950.* Amended ed. New York, 1957.

———. "The Making of a Dramatist (1892–1903)," in *Modern Drama: Essays in Criticism,* ed. Travis Bogard and William I. Oliver, pp. 290–312. New York, 1965.

———. *The Playwright as Thinker: A Study of Drama in Modern Times.* Amended ed. Cleveland, 1955.

Berst, Charles A. "Propaganda and Art in *Mrs Warren's Profession,*" *ELH,* XXXIII (1966), 390–404.

———. "Romance and Reality in *Arms and the Man,*" *Modern Language Quarterly,* XXVII (1966), 197–211.

Brecht, Bertolt. *Brecht on Theatre: The Development of an Aesthetic,* ed. and tr. John Willett. New York, 1964.

Brustein, Robert. *The Theatre of Revolt: An Approach to the Modern Drama.* Boston, 1964.

Bullough, Geoffrey. "Literary Relations of Shaw's Mrs. Warren," *Philological Quarterly,* XLI (1962), 339–58.

Burke, Kenneth. *Counter-Statement.* 2nd ed. Chicago, 1957.

———. *The Philosophy of Literary Form.* Rev. and abr. ed. New York, 1957.

Carpenter, Charles A. "The Quintessence of Shaw's Ethical Position," in *Modern Drama: A Norton Critical Edition,* ed. Anthony Caputi, pp. 402–8. New York, 1966.

———. "Shaw's Collected Letters," *Modern Drama,* IX (1966), 190–94.

———. "Shaw's Cross Section of Anti-Shavian Opinion," *Shaw Review,* VII (1964), 78–86.

Chesterton, Gilbert K. *George Bernard Shaw.* Enl. ed. London, 1961.

Couchman, Gordon W. "Comic Catharsis in *Caesar and Cleo-*

patra," Shaw Review, III, 1 (1960), 11–14.

———. "Here Was a Caesar: Shaw's Comedy Today," *PMLA,* LXXII (1957), 272–85.

———. "Shaw, *Caesar,* and the Critics," *Speech Monographs,* XXIII (1956), 262–71.

Coxe, Louis O. *"You Never Can Tell:* G. B. Shaw Reviewed," *Western Humanities Review,* IX (1955), 313–25.

Crane, Ronald S., ed. *Critics and Criticism.* Chicago, 1952.

Dickson, Ronald J. "The Diabolonian Character in Shaw," *University of Kansas City Review,* XXVI (1959), 145–51.

Dietrich, Richard F. "Shaw and the Passionate Mind," *Shaw Review,* IV, 2 (1961), 2–11.

Dunlap, Joseph R. "The Typographical Shaw: GBS and the Revival of Printing," *Bulletin of the New York Public Library,* LXIV (1960), 534–47.

Ellehauge, Martin. *The Position of Bernard Shaw in European Drama and Philosophy.* Copenhagen, 1931.

Elliott, Robert C. "Shaw's Captain Bluntschli: A Latter-Day Falstaff," *MLN,* LXVII (1952), 461-64.

Ellmann, Richard, ed. *Edwardians and Late Victorians.* English Institute Essays, 1959. New York, 1960.

Fergusson, Francis. *The Idea of a Theater: A Study of Ten Plays.* Princeton, 1949.

Fremantle, Anne. *This Little Band of Prophets: The British Fabians.* New York, 1960.

Frye, Northrop. *Anatomy of Criticism.* Princeton, 1957.

Gassner, John. *Form and Idea in Modern Theatre.* New York, 1956. (Reprinted with additions in 1966 as *Directions in Modern Theatre and Drama.*)

———, ed. *Ideas in the Drama: Selected Papers from the English Institute.* New York, 1964.

Geduld, Harry M. "Shaw's Philosophy and Cosmology," *California Shavian,* I (May 1960), unpaged.

Gerould, Daniel C. "George Bernard Shaw's Criticism of Ibsen," *Comparative Literature,* XV (1963), 130–45.

Hamon, Augustin. *The Twentieth Century Molière: Bernard Shaw,* tr. Eden and Cedar Paul. London, 1916.

Holberg, Stanley M. "The Economic Rogue in the Plays of

Bernard Shaw," *University of Buffalo Studies*. XXI (1953), 29–119.

Holt, Charles L. " 'Candida': The Music of Ideas," *Shaw Review*, IX (1966), 2–14.

Irvine, William. *The Universe of G.B.S.* New York, 1949.

Jackson, Holbrook. *Bernard Shaw*. London, 1907.

Jones, A. R. "George Bernard Shaw," in *Contemporary Theatre*, pp. 57–75. Stratford-upon-Avon Studies, No. 4. New York, 1962.

Kaufmann, R. J., ed. *G. B. Shaw: A Collection of Critical Essays*. Englewood Cliffs, N. J., 1965.

Kaye, Julian B. *Bernard Shaw and the Nineteenth Century Tradition*. Norman, Okla., 1958.

King, Carlyle. "G.B.S. on Literature: The Author as Critic," *Queen's Quarterly*, LXVI (1959), 135–45.

King, Walter N. "The Rhetoric of *Candida*," *Modern Drama*, II (1959), 71–83.

Kronenberger, Louis, ed. *George Bernard Shaw: A Critical Survey*. Cleveland, 1953.

———. *The Thread of Laughter: Chapters on English Stage Comedy from Jonson to Maugham*. New York, 1952.

Krutch, Joseph Wood. *"Modernism" in Modern Drama: A Definition and an Estimate*. Ithaca, 1953.

Lamm, Martin. *Modern Drama*, tr. Karin Elliott. Oxford, 1952.

Laurence, Dan H. "Genesis of a Dramatic Critic," *Modern Drama*, II (1959), 178–83.

Lauter, Paul. " 'Candida' and 'Pygmalion': Shaw's Subversion of Stereotypes," *Shaw Review*, III, 3 (1960), 14–19.

Leary, Daniel J. "The Moral Dialectic in *Caesar and Cleopatra*," *Shaw Review*, V (1962), 42–53.

Lewis, Allan. *The Contemporary Theatre: The Significant Playwrights of Our Time*. New York, 1962.

Loewenstein, F. E. "The Autograph Manuscripts of George Bernard Shaw," *Book Handbook*, I (1947), 85–92.

McBriar, A. M. *Fabian Socialism and English Politics, 1884–1918*. New York, 1962.

MacCarthy, Desmond. *The Court Theatre, 1904–1907*. London, 1907.

———. *Shaw*. London, 1951.

McDowell, Frederick P. W. "Another Look at Bernard Shaw," *Drama Survey*, I (1961), 34–53.

McKee, Irving. "Bernard Shaw's Beginnings on the London Stage," *PMLA*, LXXIV (1959), 470–81.

Mayer, David. "The Case for Harlequin: A Footnote on Shaw's Dramatic Method," *Modern Drama*, III (1960), 52–59.

Mayne, Fred. *The Wit and Satire of Bernard Shaw*. New York, 1967.

Meisel, Martin. *Shaw and the Nineteenth-Century Theater*. Princeton, 1963.

Mills, John A. "The Comic in Words: Shaw's Cockneys," *Drama Survey*, V (1966), 137–50.

———. "Language and Laughter in Shavian Comedy," *Quarterly Journal of Speech*, LI (1965), 433–41.

———. "Shaw's Linguistic Satire," *Shaw Review*, VIII (1965), 2–11.

Nethercot, Arthur H. "Bernard Shaw, Ladies and Gentlemen," *Modern Drama*, II (1959), 84–98.

———. *Men and Supermen: The Shavian Portrait Gallery*. 2nd ed. New York, 1966.

———. "The Vivie-Frank Relationship in *Mrs. Warren's Profession*," *Shavian*, I, No. 15 (1959), 7–9.

Nicoll, Allardyce. *A History of Late Nineteenth Century Drama, 1850–1900*. Vol. I. Cambridge, Eng., 1946.

O'Donnell, Norbert F. "The Conflict of Wills in Shaw's Tragicomedy," *Modern Drama*, IV (1962), 413–25.

———. "Ibsen and Shaw: The Tragic and the Tragi-Comic," *Theatre Annual*, XV (1957–58), 15–27.

———. "Shaw, Bunyan, and Puritanism," *PMLA*, LXXII (1957), 520–33.

Oppel, Horst. "George Bernard Shaw: *Mrs. Warren's Profession*," in *Das moderne englische Drama: Interpretationen*, ed. Oppel, pp. 11–27. Berlin, 1963.

Park, Bruce R. "A Mote in the Critic's Eye: Bernard Shaw and Comedy," *Texas Studies in English*, XXXVII (1958), 195–210.

Perrine, Laurence. "Shaw's *Arms and the Man*," *Explicator*, XV (1957), item 54.

Pettet, Edwin B. "Shaw's Socialist Life Force," *Educational Theatre Journal*, III (1951), 109–14.

Quinn, Michael. "Form and Intention: A Negative View of *Arms and the Man*," *Critical Quarterly*, V (1963), 148–54.

Reinert, Otto. "Old History and New: Anachronism in *Caesar and Cleopatra*," *Modern Drama*, III (1960), 37–41.

Roppen, Georg. *Evolution and Poetic Belief*. Oslo Studies in English, No. 5. Oslo, 1956.

Roy, Emil. "World-View in Shaw," *Drama Survey*, IV (1965), 209–19.

Sharp, William. "*Getting Married*: New Dramaturgy in Comedy," *Educational Theatre Journal*, XI (1959), 103–9.

Shattuck, Charles H. "Bernard Shaw's 'Bad Quarto,'" *JEGP*, LIV (1955), 651–63.

Smith, J. Percy. *The Unrepentant Pilgrim: A Study of the Development of Bernard Shaw*. Boston, 1965.

Spenker, Lenyth. "The Dramatic Criteria of George Bernard Shaw," *Speech Monographs*, XVII (1950), 24–36.

Stanton, Stephen S., ed. *A Casebook on Candida*. New York, 1962.

———. "Introduction," in *Camille and Other Plays*, ed. Stanton, pp. vii–xxxix. New York, 1957.

———. "Shaw's Debt to Scribe," *PMLA*, LXXVI (1961), 575–85.

Stewart, J. I. M. *Eight Modern Writers*. Oxford History of English Literature, XII. Oxford, 1963.

Stigler, George J. "Bernard Shaw, Sidney Webb, and the Theory of Fabian Socialism," *Proceedings of the American Philosophical Society*, CIII (1959), 469–75.

Sypher, Wylie, ed. *Comedy*. New York, 1956.

Thompson, Alan R. *The Dry Mock: A Study of Irony in Drama*. Berkeley, 1948.

Walkley, Arthur Bingham. *Drama and Life*. London, 1907.

———. *Dramatic Criticism: Three Lectures*. London, 1903.

———. "Leaving Aristotle Out," *Times* (London), June 20, 1910, p. 12.

Watson, Barbara B. *A Shavian Guide to the Intelligent Woman.* London, 1964.

Webb, Beatrice. *Diaries, 1924–1932,* ed. Margaret I. Cole. London, 1956.

———. *Our Partnership,* ed. Barbara Drake and Margaret I. Cole. New York, 1948.

Weintraub, Stanley. "Shaw's Mommsenite Caesar," in *Anglo-German and American-German Crosscurrents,* ed. Philip A. Shelley and Arthur O. Lewis, II, 257–72. University of North Carolina Studies in Comparative Literature, No. 31. Chapel Hill, 1962.

West, Alick. *George Bernard Shaw: "A Good Man Fallen Among Fabians."* New York, 1950.

West, E. J. " 'Arma Virumque' Shaw Did Not Sing," *Colorado Quarterly,* I (1953), 267–80.

Whitman, Robert F. "The Dialectic Structure in Shaw's Plays," in *Shaw Seminar Papers—65,* ed. Norman Rosenblood, pp. 65–84. Toronto, 1966.

Williams, Raymond. *Drama from Ibsen to Eliot.* London, 1952.

Wilson, Edmund. *The Triple Thinkers.* Rev. ed. New York, 1948.

Young, G. M. *Victorian England: Portrait of an Age.* 2nd ed. London, 1960.

Index